# This Book
# Belongs To

## Kay Frysinger

# Fading Voices and Haunting Memories

# Fading Voices and Haunting Memories

From the World War II Era

## Gloria Miller

**VANTAGE PRESS**
New York

Cover design by Susan Thomas

FIRST EDITION

Published by Vantage Press, Inc.
516 West 34th Street, New York, New York 10001

Manufactured in the United States of America
ISBN: 0-533-14497-3

Library of Congress Catalog Card No.: 2002096168

0 9 8 7 6 5 4 3 2 1

To those who served in World War II

# Table of Contents

# Foreword

Gloria Miller understood her life would be changed forever on December 7, 1941. She was still a teenager, full of youthful hopes and romantic dreams. Reality hit. Gloria married Art. She worked for the government. He went off to war. Not an uncommon story on the surface.

In this book, Gloria Miller weaves her personal experiences betwixt the accounts of people with whom she has been personally connected. These were ordinary people who accepted extraordinary challenges, people who faced their fears and rose to occasions beyond their control. In most cases, these Americans had remained silent for half a century, perhaps early proponents of "moving on." One man's wife insisted he would never talk with Gloria *even if she was a friend*. He did. They all did. Gloria Miller had a special gift for withdrawing heartfelt, often painful memories from these survivors.

When Gloria announced to her friends that she was writing a non-fiction book, I was not doubtful nor cynical. It seemed like such a "Gloria" thing to do. The goal *would* be accomplished! I first met Gloria Miller in 1969 when I was a young teacher beginning my first job. I knew she had completed her college education later than most traditional college students, but it never occurred to me that the war might have been responsible. (We early Baby Boomers had our own war to worry about and were embarrassingly naïve about the struggles of the previous generation.) I knew Gloria had raised three children and had worked in her husband's business. I soon realized what a powerhouse of energy she was: Always the first to try new educational innovations, working on an advanced degree, becoming a curriculum coordinator, conducting an extensive genealogy study of both her family and Art's family, taking on the role of a school administrator. Gloria Miller's inner drive frightened people many years her junior. Retirement did not bring rest, but an opportunity to try something different. The book became her life! And Gloria made her book come to life.

Tears often came to Gloria Miller's eyes as she spoke of her last interview. As all good writers do, she became personally connected to every story. This personal involvement will be important for young readers who know only the facts of the war, but have never felt its humanity. For the first time, these Americans will understand the real sacrifices made to ensure the survival of future generations.

—Linda Thompson

# Acknowledgments

I would be remiss if I did not thank the following people for helping me with my writing endeavor, *Fading Voices and Haunting Memories: From the World War II Era*.

Firstly, I want to thank the people who graciously consented to share their personal stories in *Fading Voices and Haunting Memories*: Liesl Sondheimer, Kenneth Walter (deceased), Frederick Mills, Mr. X, Commander John Searles, Ret., Doyt Hanthorn, Robert Polter, Ross Clum, Harold Barrick (deceased), John McNett, Arthur Miller, Nolan Core, Betty Early (widow of Willis Early), and Duane Edgington.

Secondly, I want to thank Kathleen Brinkmeir and Pauline Ingmire (deceased) for their editing help and their helpful and frank comments about the content.

Thirdly, I want to thank Betty Grouver for her help in preparing the manuscript and her meticulous attention to important details.

Finally, I want to thank my family, especially my husband, Art, for his understanding and encouragement as the project progressed from the beginning to the end. And, of course, many thanks to our children, Marsha, Muriah, and Mark, as they maintained an encouraging and positive image of what I was attempting to accomplish.

# Fading Voices and Haunting Memories

# Prologue

This book, *Fading Voices and Haunting Memories: From the World War II Era,* is a collection of articles and personal stories, told by people who lived during the World War II years. The stories reveal ordinary people, who demonstrated undaunted courage and unwavering perseverance as they responded to the demands that World War II placed upon them. The characters in the book tell their own stories in their own words, and in so doing, they reveal what life was like during the World War II years. The personal anecdotes expose the innermost thoughts and feelings of normal, regular, everyday Americans who worked and fought to help regain peace in the world.

We must always remember that WAR IS HELL ON EARTH! War occurs when evil men seek to enslave and kill innocent men, women and children. And the painful dichotomy is that when war breaks out, principled and peaceful men must pick up THEIR OWN guns in order to stop the slaughter.

The generation that came of age in the World War II years was thrust into this violent period of history, and many minds have been indelibly imprinted with the haunting memories of the cruelty, death and destruction that they witnessed. Out of this period in America's history have come numerous stories that reveal the fine caliber of the American people that fought valiantly to liberate the oppressed people that were under the jackboot of the German, Italian and Japanese tyrants and their military forces. The people who lived during the World War II years are now aging and soon their voices will be silenced and the world will lose the opportunity to hear their amazing stories.

Prior to the World War II years, the United States had been in the demoralizing depths of the Great Depression, when Franklin Delano Roosevelt became president on March 4th, 1933. The American people had been experiencing extremely austere times, and many farmers had lost their farms, city workers had lost both their jobs and their homes, one in every four workers was unemployed, and hungry people stood in long bread lines to get food for their families. There had been a run on the banks and many people had lost all their money.

1

Immediately after taking office, President Roosevelt created programs, funded by the government, that would help provide jobs for the unemployed. The various reforms and self-help activities he implemented became known as the New Deal. Slowly but steadily the people were able to get jobs and climb out of the poverty that once held them captive. The people credited Roosevelt with their improving economy and they re-elected him to a second term for 1937–1941.

The American people were well aware that World War II had already started in Europe, and that the Japanese were becoming increasingly aggressive in the Pacific, and they broke precedent and elected Roosevelt to a third term in office for 1941–1945. He won thirty-eight of the forty-eight states, indicating that the American voters obviously felt this was not the time to change presidential leadership. Although there already existed a considerable number of people with strong isolationist views in the United States, Roosevelt thought it to be politically expedient to his own career to keep America out of the war.

During this time, Winston Churchill and Roosevelt became close friends and acted as confidantes for each other. Churchill often begged Roosevelt for aid in England's fight against Germany. Roosevelt told him that the United States would increase the amount of military and other critical supplies being sent to England, but no American men would be sent to fight in England's war. Roosevelt knew that the young people that were coming of age at that time had been raised in the throes of the Great Depression, and the last thing they wanted to do was to go to war and fight for another country.

The Japanese surprise attack on Pearl Harbor on December 7th, 1941 shocked the American people into the harsh realities of being at war. The violent and perilous years of World War II had begun for America, and the war was on an accelerated movement toward total involvement on land, sea and air.

This book includes the story of a Jewish family's escape from Nazi Germany and certain death and it brings to mind the persecution of the Jews in Germany. A coppersmith who worked on the docks at Pearl Harbor relates his story of saving injured sailors on that fateful day of the Japanese attack. The seldom-told story of the German occupation of the English Channel Islands indicates how close Hitler came to invading England. The veterans' stories included in the book are examples of American soldiers, just ordinary "guys," many of whom were farm boys, who served and fought in remote and distant parts of the world.

2

The American home front played a very important part in bringing a successful conclusion to the war. Immediately after the Pearl Harbor attack, rationing of many important items was put into effect. The American home front willingly put the needs of the American troops first, and they worked long hours to quickly turn out ships, planes, tanks, munitions, food, clothing, and anything else the military needed. Without the necessary equipment the outcome of the war could have been disastrous for the United States.

Interwoven throughout the book is the story of the author and her marriage to a soldier and the experiences and mishaps she had in going with him on his stateside assignments. When he was deployed overseas, she returned to Lima, Ohio and worked in the office for the United States Corps of Engineers, which had a defense contract for power shovels and cranes to be built by the Lima Locomotive Works.

Descriptions of armed encounters are briefly mentioned in the book and are included to give the readers a sense of time, place, and the chronology of the battles. World War II took place on six continents and geographic information is included to assist in the understanding of the magnitude of the areas on which the armed conflicts were fought. Specifics of the battles are left to dedicated WWII historians.

There was something very unique that happened in America after the attack on Pearl Harbor. The sneak attack incensed the American people and served as a unifying force that brought them to collectively support the war effort. The commitment that the American people felt was unfathomable and the enemies of the United States did not realize what they had unleashed against themselves.

None of the people whose stories appear in *Fading Voices and Haunting Memories* felt regret for living at this traumatic time in America's history. Actually they felt a sense of pride in what they had accomplished for their country. Most of all, they are extremely cognizant that World War II cut a monumental swathe through their generation and they do not want the sacrifices those people made to ever be forgotten.

# Part One
# Prelude to War

# Adolf Hitler Ascends to Power

Who was the man called Adolf Hitler? Who was the tyrant that started World War II? How could this man convince people to follow him and create such havoc in the world? What evil consumed him and made him have such little regard for human life? Let's take a brief look at his past for possible answers to these questions.

Alois Schicklgruber was a civil service worker and in 1876 had changed his last name to Hitler. He was fifty years old when his son, Adolf, was born. Adolf's mother was a simple peasant girl and his father's third wife. Alois planned for Adolf to be in civil service, but Adolf wanted to be an artist, though he did not apply himself to his studies and eventually dropped out of school.

After Adolf's father died his mother pampered him, and he became undisciplined and lazy. Twice Adolf attempted to enter the Academy of Fine Arts, but could not get accepted because he lacked a high school diploma, and his work did not indicate that he possessed artistic talent. After his mother's death he was consumed by feelings of insecurity. Although he lacked education and was poor, he had developed a sense of superiority and he looked at the people around him and treated them as if they were inferiors.

Adolf moved to Vienna and it was there that he saw many successful Jews and he blamed them for his own failures. He was distrustful of everyone and believed that life was a struggle. He believed that authority, not democracy, was the way to save the world. He understood that democracy was government by discussion, and he absolutely refused to discuss because he wanted to command. He was quarrelsome and would not listen to the views of others, and would shout and become hysterical with those who would not agree with him. He believed that having the unquestioning support of the masses was the only way to achieve power. In 1913, he moved to Munich and his hatred of the Jews and the Hapsburg rulers of Austria increased.

Adolf had no friends and his life was unsettled until World War I. His life had been a failure in school but he did well in the Bavarian Army in World War I. He was an excellent soldier and spent most of four years at the front in France. He earned several medals for bravery, including the Iron Cross.

Germany was the first to begin using chlorine gas in April 1915 against the Allied armies. The statistics show that 30 out of 100 American soldiers were either killed or wounded by the poisonous clouds of chlorine gas. Before the war was over all the armies on all the fronts began using poison gas. Hitler survived a poison gas attack just before the Armistice was signed.

At the end of WWI Hitler returned to Germany, which had just suffered a devastating defeat and the German people were very disillusioned. Conditions in Germany were very poor, the country had just lost land and valuable resources, and the people were being heavily taxed. Hitler attended a meeting of the German Workers Party and he liked the fact that it was a small group and that he could soon become a leading figure of the party. He began making speeches and miraculously, several thousand people would come to listen to him.

Hitler left the army in 1920 and in 1923 he attempted to seize the Bavarian government in Munich. The coup d'etat failed and many of his followers were killed. Hitler and his assistant, Rudolf Hess, were imprisoned and while in prison, Hitler dictated most of his book *Mein Kampf* (My Struggle). The book explained his political ideas and his plans of how to strengthen Germany, which included the defeat of France, dominance of central Europe and the seizure of the rich agricultural areas and industrial sections of Russia. The rest of the world did not take Hitler's schemes seriously, but to the defeated and demoralized German people, he offered hope and they began to follow him in increasing numbers.

Hitler used the psychology of multitudes of people gathered together, watching animated parades of men in uniform, and listening to stirring patriotic music to set the atmosphere for him to tell the German people to follow him and he would give them a happy, secure and prosperous future. It seemed that Hitler had a hypnotic effect upon the people when he spoke, which explains his meteoric rise to leadership in Germany. He was clever, he had a plan, and he told the German people what they wanted to hear.

On January 30, 1933 Hitler was appointed chancellor of Germany, and he quickly put restrictions on organized labor, he outlawed rival political parties, he arrested political opponents and had them sent to concentration camps, and he began rebuilding Germany's military strength. One of the first things he did was to bring the National Socialist German Workers Party into a more powerful position which was a part of his ultimate plan. The Party became known by the name "Nazis."

Hitler systematically began a plan to remove all Jews from participation in German society. He had written in *Mein Kampf*, "Today I believe that I am acting in accordance with the will of the Almighty Creator, by defending myself against the Jew, I am fighting for the work of the Lord."

In June 1934 Hitler systematically looked for all his opponents in the Nazi Party and had them executed. In 1935 he passed the Nuremberg Laws, which stripped the Jews of their citizenship, and forbade them to have sexual relations with subjects of German or kindred blood. He considered several methods of expelling the Jews from the Third Reich, such as transporting them to other countries, but eventually he ordered the SS units, the Einsatzgruppen, to create a plan. The Einsatzgruppen plan was to build six death camps, and Jews were to be loaded into boxcars, taken to death camps, gassed, and then cremated. Approximately six million Jews and one million Gypsies were put to death in these camps. Never have such heinous, depraved acts of inhuman treatment against a group of people occurred on such an astronomical scale. There is no doubt that Hitler and his Nazis wanted to annihilate the entire Jewish population.

When the first news of Hitler's extermination policy reached the United States and England, it was too repulsive and reprehensible to be believed, but in 1942 the reports were verified. Although Great Britain and the United States formally accused Germany of genocide, the Allies never came to an agreement of how they could stop the killings. Therefore, the boxcars loaded with Jews kept rolling into the death camps and the killings continued.

# Jewish Family Escapes Nazi Germany, As Told by Liesl Sondheimer

*(Liesl Sondheimer is a highly respected and admired Jewish lady in the Lima/Allen County community. She has given many lectures on her experiences and life in Germany under Nazi rule. A two-hour documentary entitled* A Simple Matter of God and Country *premiered in Lima in March 2001 and received an Emmy Award in the Midwest Region in the spring of 2002. The documentary relates how Liesl and her husband escaped Nazi Germany and arrived in the United States in 1938. The following is the story in her own words of her struggle to save her family and get to the United States, as told on January 24, 2001 to the author of* Fading Voices.*)*

My name is Liesl (Elizabeth) Bing Sondheimer. I was born in Nuremberg, Germany in 1907 to upper middle-class parents. My grandfather was co-owner of the Lowenbrau Brewing Company and was considered wealthy. My father made a lot of money selling hops to the brewery industry, but he was much more involved in his hobbies, especially archeology and would take me with him to digs. He taught me a lot about that. He was also fascinated with geology and botany. My father was a real philosopher—he was an agnostic, and he did not believe in organized religion. He kept a fossil on his desk to remind him of the "smallness of the human condition."

My mother was a musician and a singer. I had a brother who was two years younger than I. My grandfather on my mother's side, the one who owned the Lowenbrau business, built a beautiful large home. My grandparents lived on the first floor and my great-grandmother lived in an apartment of her own, also on the first floor. We lived on the second floor in a spacious apartment. We had a wonderful family life. Our home was destroyed by the bombings in World War II.

When I was six years old my peaceful life came to an end when World War I broke out and I did not see my father for four years. My father was drafted into the German army, became an officer, and received the Medal of Honor—the Iron Cross. My husband, who was

10

much older than I, also fought in World War I, became an officer and received the Medal of Honor, the Iron Cross. I now have both their medals.

I went to school in Nuremberg and studied to be a social worker. I was in school and my mother had a good friend that I was visiting and he told me I should go and visit this man who was a physician and tell him that he was angry with him because he had not written. This was like a bet. So I went to Stuttgart to see this man, but I couldn't find him in the phone book, so I went to the police. And they said he had just settled there as a physician, and they told me how to find his office. He hadn't had any patients yet, and I told him I didn't want to disappoint him, but I was there because of a bet I had, and then I told him about the bet. He laughed and wrote it down as if I had been a patient and I left. He then ran after me and asked me if I would like to have dinner that night with him. And that is how I met my husband.

A year later, on March 14, 1928, Martin Sondheimer and I were married and we moved to Stuttgart. Martin had originally studied to be a psychiatrist under Sigmund Freud in Vienna, but he decided that was not an exact science and he later chose to be an internist, specializing in heart disorders. Martin and I had two daughters, Hannah and Marian.

Then Hitler came to power and, of course, everything changed. Eventually, in 1935, Hitler decreed the Nuremberg Laws, which deprived Jews of property rights and legal protection. Jewish doctors could not treat non-Jewish patients. Jews could only buy groceries in Jewish grocery stores. The children had to go to Jewish schools. We were not allowed to have cleaning help. Eventually, we all had to wear the Star of David on an armband so everybody knew who we were. The Nazis confiscated our house. It was a nice house, but they took it and we had to move to a small apartment.

After the Nuremberg Laws were passed, if a Nazi wanted to shoot a Jew he could. We were outside the law. Nobody can imagine what it was like to be outside the law. We lived in fear from morning till night.

In 1936, a friend of my husband who was also a physician decided to leave Germany and emigrate to the United States as he had relatives in Hot Springs, Arkansas. He asked my husband and me to accompany him on this trip to see if we wanted to settle there. He was a general practitioner and had a wife and a little baby. When we came to Hot Springs I was absolutely shocked at how the Negroes were treated!

11

They had their own drinking fountains! They could not walk on the sidewalks! They were treated like we were, only they were not killed! We didn't see any place else in the United States—just Arkansas, and I said I couldn't live there. I thought it was just as bad as Germany, so we went back to Germany. That was a terrible mistake.

Between 1936 and 1938, horrible things happened to us. Hannah, our older daughter, was in an evangelical school, which was around the corner from where we lived. She was the only Jewish child in the school and they were not allowed to keep a Jewish child there. This is what I always try to stress when I give my talks—there were unbelievably courageous people—and you wondered where they got their courage to stand up against all odds and risk their life. There was a teacher in this school that said, "I'm not going to let this child out of my school—I'll keep this child in my school regardless of what anybody says." And she saved my daughter from having a difficult life. This daughter's life was more normal.

Our other daughter had to start school in a Jewish school and she was not protected by anybody. We don't know what all happened to her. She was beaten, she was spit upon, and was treated badly. She was discriminated against and went through terrible experiences. We could not protect her. Therefore, her life was difficult and it still is. There was nothing we could do to protect her.

Other things happened to us. My husband had been the physician to the mayor of Stuttgart before these laws came out. When the mayor got sick, he could have cared less about these laws. The mayor was the chief Nazi of the city and when he got sick, he sent his chauffeur to get my husband to come to his house and take care of him. I would sit up at night and worry and wonder if he would return safely.

We lived in a tiny apartment in a ghetto where only Jews lived. One day the children were playing with their doll carriages in front of our house and a Nazi came with two very wild German shepherd dogs. They turned over the doll carriages and the children began to cry. This annoyed the Nazi—I was standing in the doorway—and he took out his revolver and was going to shoot the children. What kept him from doing it, I'll never know, but at that moment he called off his dogs and walked on.

Another thing that happened was that I spoke English very well as I had learned it in school, nobody else in our family spoke it, so my husband decided to take English lessons in case we were able to emigrate. A man who taught him was from London, England, and he called me one day and said he knew I spoke English very well and that he was doing some translations. He said, "I'm not able, my German isn't good enough and I wonder if you would help me. Of course I will pay you." As it turned out, he was a spy for England. In Stuttgart there were fifty factories making munitions—strange enough this was unknown to the United States. When I came to America I tried to tell the government officials they were making munitions, and they are planning on a war. But the Americans didn't believe it. There were Porsche and Mercedes plants, but they were making munitions not cars.

The man from England was trying to figure out what they were doing. I just knew he was a spy trying to get the information, but of course I felt I needed to do what I could to help England. I knew why he wanted the information—I hoped, with God's will, I would get out of Germany before they discovered what I was doing. He wanted to know how much money he could pay me. I knew that I could not accept his money because the Nazis had confiscated all of our own money. If I suddenly had some money, I could be in serious trouble.

I asked the English spy if he could take my mother's, my grandmother's and my jewelry to England for me. He promised he would and he did. And I got our jewelry back as promised. About four weeks after we came to the United States I heard that he had been caught as an English spy and was hanged. Those were dangerous times and often we came close to losing our lives. My parents and my grandmother—their lives were always in danger as they were still living in Nuremberg.

The United States had a quota and only so many people were allowed to come to the U.S. There were two consulates, one in Stuttgart and one in Hamburg. We knew what was happening at the consulate in Stuttgart because we lived there. The clerk at the American consulate was a crook. At this time, when you wanted to emigrate you had to have an affidavit and get a number. We got an affidavit because a cousin of my father lived in New York and he gave us the affidavit. We got a number, which was high, and I knew that if we would have kept this number, we would not have survived. So I asked the clerk what it would take to give us a lower number, and he told me he wanted a Persian rug. We had no money but we did have a Persian rug. In the darkness of night, we brought this rug to him and he gave us a lower number. And eventually we got out.

But that is not where this story ends. I always told my children and grandchildren that it was the wrong thing to do and it filled me with guilt for the rest of my life. I wondered what happened to the people who got our number? When questioned further by a grand-daughter-in-law, I said, "When faced with losing your life you would do anything." You are forever filled with this guilt. I never thought I would find out who got our number—but I did. That was a terrible experience.

Many years later, my husband had already died, and the city of Stuttgart had invited ninety people to come back. The mayor of the city was the son of the former Field Marshall Irwin Rommel who was a successful field marshal for Hitler, but then he turned against Hitler and was involved in a plot to kill him. But of course, this never happened. Hitler found out who was in on this plot, and they were all hanged, but because Rommel was such a successful field marshal Hitler gave him the privilege of taking poison instead of being hanged. Rommel's son, who was then seventeen years old, had never forgotten that he had promised his father that he would always stand up for what is right.

The city of Stuttgart paid for everything, bus fare so we could see the country, our flight and our lodging. We could bring our children on this trip, so Hannah and her husband joined me. Marian said she could not, would not go back. She had too many terrible memories. She could not go back. So we went. It was a very bittersweet experience.

One evening we were all sitting around the table and we were talking about how we got out and some said they got out because of the famous Raoul Wallenberg, a Swedish count, who had helped thousands of Jews escape until he was arrested by the Russians in January 1945. Many were telling their stories. One person said he and a friend were in a concentration camp and there was a cigarette butt on the ground and his friend bent down to pick it up and he was shot to death. Everybody was telling how he or she had survived. And I was telling how we survived—how we got out. And this woman about my age asked, "And what number did they give you?" And when I told her, she cried, "You got my mother's and my sister's numbers!"

Then I asked her, "What happened to your mother and sister who got our numbers?"

She angrily replied, "Of course, they perished in a concentration camp!"

Going back in time to 1938, a few days before we were to emigrate from Germany and travel to America, I went to Nuremberg to say goodbye to my parents and grandmother and the beautiful churches which I absolutely loved and then to see my synagogue. I found my synagogue in flames! People were standing around in a circle watching the synagogue burn. The Nazis were having a great time laughing, singing and throwing sacred objects into the fire—prayer books, the Torah which contains the five books of Moses, the Old Testament, silver objects, sacred things—they threw them into the fire. And I was standing there—this was before we had to wear the star on our sleeve, so they didn't know who I was, or that I was a Jew—I just stood there with the other people, in a circle looking at the fire. The people were all looking pretty grave, but the Nazis were having a good time.

The man who made my documentary has to document everything I said because everything has to be 100 percent true, so he wrote to the German archives and they sent him a picture of everyone standing around this fire. So it was documented. I never knew that anyone had taken a picture and I could not recognize myself in the picture. There was so much confusion on this terrible night in Nuremberg.

On the 9th of November 1938, just four weeks after we left Germany, the infamous "Crystal Night" (Kristallnacht) happened. It was a "pogrom," when people of a particular race or religion are hunted down and killed, wounded or taken prisoner. This night was called "crystal night" because of the crystals that were broken in the Jewish homes and the glass in the Jewish storefronts. The Nazis killed many Jewish men, women and children that night. Many were taken into custody. We were fortunate to have left Germany before this terrible night. My parents and my grandmother were still in Nuremberg. The teachers from the school that Hannah had attended came and got them and hid them from the Nazis. Who knows if Martin, our two daughters and I would have survived the pogrom that horrifying night in Nuremberg.

These were dreadful times. We came so close, but by some little incident, by luck, or something, we were saved at the last minute. It always looked like we would all perish. We promised each other that we would always stay together, my husband, our two children, and myself, and we would not be separated. We would either go together or die together.

When we left Germany, we went first to Holland. We just couldn't wait to get on that train to Holland. Holland was safe—it had not yet been taken over by the Nazis. The Nazis came at the border to the train to look into our luggage. We were not allowed to take money with us. Each of us was allowed to take $10. How would you like to come to a foreign country with just $40? We had taken a lot of things with us—ridiculous things like soap, toilet paper—things that we thought we wouldn't be able to buy. Things to help us for the next couple days in this great country. And we had all these suitcases. The girls were each clutching a doll and they had little suitcases that had doll clothes in them that my mother had made for their dolls. The Nazi did not look in our big suitcases, but he told us to open the little suitcases. He wanted to look in the little suitcases the girls had. He opened them up and threw the doll clothes all over the floor. The girls started crying. He said to me, "When you go to America tell them we are good people. You see, I didn't open all your suitcases—I just opened the girls' little suitcases." He then said, "Heil Hitler!" and disappeared. We got across the border.

From Holland we went to England, where my husband had a brother who had escaped to England before we left. Then we took the ship, *The New Amsterdam* to the United States and we disembarked in New York City.

The American customs people were no better than the German Nazi customs people. They were suspicious and they didn't believe anything we were saying. We had to open all our suitcases we had brought. It was October 1st, 1938. We had no money. They were looking for something.

My uncle loaned us enough money to begin our first year, to be paid back later. My brother had come to get us and the children were sitting on the suitcases crying. We were looking for a place to stay. He had been in the United States for a couple years. He had had an affidavit from Charles Lindbergh, but we won't get into that right now. This is a whole different story. Anyhow, we rented an apartment on the fifth floor without an elevator, no bathroom facilities, little heat, furnished, and with mice in the piano. It was all we could afford. Not long after we had moved into this horrid place, the American customs people came—of course, I didn't know they were coming and the children were in a tub in the living room taking a bath. There was this knock at the door and they announced they were the American customs people. When they saw the poverty that we were living in they decided that we had not smuggled as they had thought.

Not very long after that someone found out that my husband was a physician. They had a young boy whose parents had been killed in a concentration camp and there were some wealthy relatives that could take him in, but they were not ready yet. They were looking for someone to take in this boy and they were looking for someone who could care for this boy who had asthma. My husband could care for the boy. They came to this horrid place and asked us to take him in, but we said we didn't have enough room but we would take him in. They said they did not like this place where we lived. The boy was nine. They said they would furnish us with an apartment if we took the boy. We were immediately moved to a decent apartment in the suburbs, and there was a decent school nearby.

We still had no money. We were so poor. One day I broke a bottle of vinegar that cost seven cents—and I cried. I could not replace it. If the children at school went to the zoo and the kids needed to take some money—our girls could not go. We were terribly, terribly poor.

My husband had to take an English language exam to practice medicine and it took a long time to pass. He had to pass the American Board of Medicine. He had to study and it took 1½ years, but he finally passed. There were no openings in New York and we discovered that most of the states required a two-year internship for doctors before they could practice medicine. We had to pay back the money we had borrowed. We found out that the state of Ohio did not have that law about the two-year internship, so we decided to go to Ohio. He had to pass the medical exam at Ohio State University. Then we traveled from town to town. We felt that we had to live in a middle-sized town, where it was possible to make a living quickly. Everybody said they were over crowded and we would have to go on to another town.

We came to Lima and my husband started a practice here. My mother, father and grandmother came to Lima and stayed here until they died. I had cousins and aunts that died in concentration camps. My husband's sister was a nurse in Theresienstadt ghetto, actually a concentration camp, at Terezin, Czechoslovakia. She had been forced to sleep with many German officers coming to the camp. She committed suicide after liberation day. It is hard to understand that this happened in Germany because the German people were well educated. We had great poets, philosophers, musicians, and scientists. Education did not prevent this catastrophe.

The Nazis murdered one million children. What they did was absolute evil—100 percent evil.

People in concentration camps questioned, "Where is God?" Many lost their faith. Some did not. How could people degenerate to such a degree? If you resisted you would be killed. Fifteen million people died because of Hitler. It is hard to understand—Hitler had charisma and people followed him. Now, we have Nazis in this country, too. They are against Jews and blacks. We have terrorists here, too. I worry what will happen. When I talk with young people, students, I tell them to be well informed and to stand up against evil.

# Gloria Becomes Aware of Events in Europe

The engineer started the train with a little jerk and then the train began to move slowly and smoothly away from the Lima station. My father winced at the engineer's jerky start and then he smiled and waved goodbye to me. I had the sense of being quite grown-up and returned his wave, then settled back in my seat. I was nearly fifteen years old and I knew that Dad always had qualms about me going to Detroit to spend a week with my mother and stepfather. Actually, Dad had been given sole custody of me by the court when he and my mother divorced when I was just two and a half years old, and he was not required to give in to Mother's requests for these yearly visits. Dad knew that my life at home was not very pleasant, and since I did well in school, he likened my Detroit visits to a reward. He worked for the Baltimore and Ohio Railroad and could get free passes for me to ride on the train, therefore my train trips were no strain on the family budget.

I had learned from my previous visits to Detroit that the lifestyle of my mother and her husband, Jimmy, was quite different than anything I would experience at home on the farm. Knowing that Dad might not approve of some of the things I saw at my mother's house I just kept everything to myself for fear he would not permit me to go there anymore. Obviously Mother and Jimmy's home life reflected a more prosperous style of living, but there wasn't anything inappropriate going on, just a lot of entertaining, with a few alcoholic beverages being served along with examples of Mother's excellent food creations and very enthusiastic playing of pinochle and poker.

Jimmy had built a successful insurance business and he and Mother often entertained his clients and friends in their home. Also, when I visited with my mother, all her family members, who lived in Detroit, would come to see me. There would be aunts, uncles and cousins there that I hardly knew. They were all very friendly toward me and always asked a lot of questions about how well I did in school and how I liked living where I did. But, I really think that my visit was an excuse for a family get-together. Their visits also included lots of card playing, mostly poker, a little drinking, and lots of storytelling. They were a happy bunch of people, they laughed a lot, and loved to talk about the days when they were poor young kids living in Virginia. It appeared that my Uncle Mike was the mischievous one, both past and present, who got in the most trouble. I enjoyed watching this group of almost strangers/relatives, but, I also felt as if I was under scrutiny by these people and that they were secretly wondering what kind of a job my father was doing in raising me. Deep within my heart my feelings of loyalty and love were strongest for my father back on the farm in Ohio, but as I was getting to know my mother and Jimmy better, I was beginning to appreciate them more and I enjoyed my expanding number of family members.

On my previous visit in 1938, I had asked Jimmy to tell me where he had come from. He had what I considered a distinguished English accent and I was curious about where he had lived and what his boyhood was like. Never having met a "foreigner" before, I was intrigued by what he told me and he seemed genuinely pleased that I cared enough to ask. I sat on a footstool at his feet and he began to tell me about his past.

"I had a great childhood. I was born on the Island of Alderney, in the English Channel, which is approximately ten miles from the coast of France. My father is English and my mother was French. I learned to speak both English and French, although, I have forgotten a lot of the French language. I have a brother and a sister, both younger than I. My mother's name was Sophia and she died in 1928. My father's name is James John Cleal. My name is James Reginald and my brother's name is Reginald James, and my brother's son is named James Reginald (and he is called 'little Jim')—I guess my family was stuck on those two names. My sister's name is Lillian and she and her husband, Charles Cooley, own a general store on the island. My mother was from a very large family and from her side of the family I have three uncles that are approximately the same age as I. One uncle works in India and one works in Africa, and one is a judge in England. These three uncles and I keep in touch with letters. I wish I could see them more often."

At this point Jimmy reached in the drawer of the end table by his chair and pulled out some pictures of these people and he was proud to show off his family. Jimmy then continued to tell about his life. "The lifestyle on Alderney is relaxed and friendly. Most of the houses are made of stone and most of the people have a small greenhouse and

20

well-tended vegetable and flower gardens. Fishing is good off the rocky shores of the island, the English Channel waters are quite cold, and lobster traps set in those cold waters yield an abundance of lobsters for those people who make the effort to trap them. My family is very fond of lobster and they always have traps set. The island is noted for the excellent herds of dairy cows and the rich dairy products produced there. The bakery does something very nice for the islanders. On Sunday mornings when the people walk to church they can drop off a casserole or pot roast pan and put it in the ovens at the bakery. When church is over the people stop at the bakery and pick up their fully-cooked Sunday dinners.

"I played the cornet in the Salvation Army Band on the island. You see, my family is very much involved with the Salvation Army. You probably don't know this, but a Methodist minister who worked in the slums of London started the Salvation Army. The Salvation Army is a very important part of life there on the island.

"Schooling on the island ends for most of the young people at eighth grade. If a person wants further schooling they need to go to the more expensive schools on the mainland. My formal schooling ended at eighth grade. My father was a barber and he taught me that trade, but I also worked at the local gas company. It didn't take me long to figure out that the opportunities for advancement were limited if I stayed on the island and I began to dream of going to America.

"I saved my money and in 1912, when I was twenty-two years old, I booked passage on the *Titanic* and was ready to leave the island in search of a more lucrative job in America. Several days before I was to sail, my boss at the Alderney Gas Company asked me to see if I could sell my ticket for my trip to America. He wanted me to stay for several more months and train my replacement. I found a woman on the island that wanted my ticket and I sold it to her."

At this moment Jimmy's voice broke, and when he regained his composure, he continued. "When I read the headlines of the paper on April 15th, 1912, that the *Titanic*, this unsinkable and beautiful passenger ship, had hit an iceberg and sunk—I couldn't believe it! I would have been on that ship! It was fate. Most of the men went down with the ship. I surely would have not survived. It was fate—it must not have been my time to die. I often think about the lady that bought my ticket. I heard that she had taken her young son with her on the trip and that when the call came for the women and children to go to a certain place on the ship they did as directed. She took a football her son had brought with him and tied it around his neck to provide buoyancy in case he fell into the water. I was told that he did fall into the ocean, but was picked up by people in one of the lifeboats. I don't know what happened to his mother. I see this awful scene in my mind, over and over." At this point, Jimmy's voice again broke and it took him awhile to regain his composure.

I then asked, "When did you finally get to America?"

Jimmy answered, "I arrived in America in 1914. I'm not certain why, but I came to Detroit and found a job working in the Briggs factory. I began selling insurance at night and my insurance business was doing very well, and I decided to quit the factory work. Your mother's brother, Mike, worked at that factory, and he introduced me to her."

At that moment Mother walked into the living room and picking up on our conversation she said, "Yes, I know, it was meant to be that we should meet—but it is also meant to be that Mike is coming over tonight. And Jimmy, you need to go out and buy some beer for them to drink!"

I left for home the next day and did not talk about my visit in Detroit unless I was asked specific questions. When Dad picked me up at the train depot he asked, "How was your trip?"

I simply answered, "It was great. Mother gave me some of her old clothes and she bought a new dress for me for school." That was the end of me talking about any specifics about my time spent in Detroit with Mother and Jimmy. I knew better than to talk to Dad about Jimmy because Dad held a great resentment toward him.

A year later, in 1939, I was on the train to Detroit again. I was all excited about this trip because I would soon be a freshman in high school and Mother said she would alter several of her dresses to fit me and maybe even buy me one new dress. My mother was a beautiful woman and she had beautiful and stylish clothes and I couldn't wait to see what she had in mind to give me.

During this visit to Detroit, Mother took me to work with her one day. She was a telephone operator in the Recorders Court Building. She had made arrangements for me to sit in several of the courtrooms and watch the people that had been summoned to appear before the judges. I found it fascinating to hear the people tell the judges their stupid reasons for having committed their crimes. I found it to be very interesting and the day passed quickly.

The next day Mother and I rode on the bus, through the tunnel, to Windsor, Canada, where she purchased six pieces of china to add to her every-day set of English china. We then found a little tearoom and had tea and crumpets before catching the bus back to Detroit. I thought the tea and crumpets sounded very "English" and that appealed to me very much. My visit also included two evenings of visiting with friends and relatives. There was also a trip to the horse races at Hazel Park where I had an Uncle Joe Bommarito who worked as a bartender. My Uncle Joe was Italian and was married to my Aunt Mabel, Mother's older sister. I also overheard that he always had "inside" information about things at the track, and I naively wondered what this meant because it was always said with a wink of the eye.

And then suddenly it was the night before I was to leave. We had eaten dinner and the dishes were finished. Mother was doing the final sewing on a dress that she was altering for me. Jimmy was reading the newspaper. I walked into the living room and sat down.

Jimmy put down his newspaper and looked at me with a serious look on his face and asked, "Gloryann, what do you know about Hitler?"

I told him, "I only know that he is a German dictator who is making a lot of trouble for the countries in Europe." A very simplistic answer, to be sure, but current events were seldom discussed at my father's house.

At this point Jimmy explained to me what the Nazi party stood for and what was happening in Europe. He said, "If Hitler continues to take over more European countries, the Channel Islands might be on Hitler's way if he tries to go into England. I am very concerned about the safety of my family in Alderney. Not only Alderney could be in for trouble, but also all the other Channel Islands. They are all close to the coast of France, but Alderney is the closest."

Not until my August 1939 visit in Detroit was I aware of the gravity of the situation in Europe. But it took on new meaning to me now because of Jimmy's family there. However, I was certain that the war in Europe could not affect me in any way. After all, I lived on a farm in Ohio, in the middle of the United States. How would I ever be affected? It was the end of August 1939 and I would be starting my first year in high school when I returned home. Doing well in school was uppermost in my mind.

# Situation at Dunkirk
## Foreshadows Coming Conflicts

After Jimmy's talk with me I had a better understanding of how Adolf Hitler had risen to power and had rebuilt Germany's armed strength. Obviously there was a dangerous situation developing in Eastern Europe. The newspapers indicated there was a great possibility that Hitler intended to take control of all the Eastern European countries. Great Britain had become alarmed by the ruthless takeover of Austria and Czechoslovakia, and Great Britain joined with France in saying they would support Poland if Germany attacked them.

On September 1, 1939, Germany attacked Poland. On Sunday, September 3, at 11:00 A.M., the British government announced that a "state of war" existed between Britain and Germany. At 5:00 P.M. France joined with Great Britain. King George VI of the Greater British Empire spoke to his people: *"For the second time in the lives of most of us, we are at war . . ."*

The news reports were indicating that Germany was fighting battles in Poland, Belgium, and France. There were battles at sea and shipping was interrupted and ships were being sunk. I didn't understand everything and it all sounded very complicated to me.

It was now May 1940, school was out and my summer school vacation had started, when there was a special newscast over the radio—"The Belgians, French, and British Troops Retreat to Sea!" I had been so busy finishing my freshman year in high school and studying for final exams, I had not paid any attention to the news. Dad was sitting by the radio and the announcer was saying that the Belgians had lost their battle with the advancing German army. The Belgian soldiers, the remainder of three French armies, and a British Expeditionary Force had been driven back to the beaches of Dunkirk. They were trapped and would surely be taken prisoners or would be killed. Eventually the news media was able to reveal the remarkable events that took place in this seemingly hopeless situation.

It was May 24th to the 26th, 1940, and the German Panzers had been chasing the Belgian, French, and British soldiers to the beaches of Dunkirk, when suddenly the German soldiers received orders from Hitler to cease firing. That two day halt gave the English Royal Navy a chance to organize an "armada" of sorts, made up of yachts, barges, lifeboats, motor boats, destroyers, gunboats, anything capable of making the trip to Dunkirk and back. The Germans had mined the English Channel, therefore sailing in these waters had become very dangerous. From the ports on the south coast of England came brave Englishmen in little boats willing to make the risky trip to Dunkirk to save the lives of their trapped countrymen.

The brave civilian rescuers were not prepared for what they saw on the beaches at Dunkirk. There were dead bodies that had been lying there for several days rotting in the sun. Wounded men were trying to help their comrades who were also wounded. The stench was over-whelming. Many men were standing in the cold Channel waters up to their necks, hoping a boat would come to get them in time. The men were lined up in rows. They were orderly, no pushing, no shoving—displaying the typical English stoic behavior.

Each rescuer took as many men as his boat would hold and quickly sailed back to England. Upon reaching England he would unload and return to Dunkirk to pick up more living soldiers. The dead soldiers had to be left on the beach.

On May 26 to June 4, the small boats and big ships dared to sail the dangerous waters of the Channel to Dunkirk and make the return trip to England. Meanwhile, the French attempted to fight off the enemy giving a few more hours to pick up the remaining living soldiers from the battle-scarred Dunkirk. Overhead there were German planes dropping bombs and strafing the vessels on the Channel waters. English fighter pilots did their best to discourage the German intruders.

In nine days, approximately 338,226 men were removed from Dunkirk and brought across the Channel. Of this total, 225,000 were British and the rest were French and Belgian. Six British and three French destroyers were sunk, nineteen British destroyers damaged, eight ferry ships were sunk, 235 of approximately 848 of the Allied ships and miscellaneous small craft were lost. The Royal Air Force suffered heavy losses trying to fight off the German Luftwaffe, which tried to stop the evacuation.

There was no way the English could proclaim a victory at Dunkirk, but it was a miracle that so many men were rescued.

As my father and I sat by the radio listening to the news, it was the first time I heard my father say, "It's a damn shame, it's a damn shame that the world has come to this!" He was visibly upset as the details of Dunkirk came over the radio. Dad hated anything "English" because of his dislike for the man my mother had married. His prejudice ran deep within his soul, but now his overriding concern for mankind took over and he openly cried for the men at Dunkirk.

On June 4th, the flames of Dunkirk burning could be seen from the Dover Cliffs. On this day, Winston Churchill made his famous speech to rally the people for the worst, which was still to come. His speech was delivered to the House of Commons and within a few hours Churchill's speech was broadcast to the homes of the English people:

"This struggle was protracted and fierce . . . The enemy was hurled back by retreating British and French troops . . . The Royal Air Force engaged the main strength of the German Air Force, and the Navy, using nearly 1,000 ships of all kinds, carried over 335,000 men, French and British, out of the jaws of death and shame, to their native land. We must be very careful not to assign to this deliverance the attributes of a victory. Wars are not won by evacuations. But there was a victory inside this deliverance, which should be noted. It was gained by the Air Force."

" . . . I will pay my tribute to these young airmen. The great French Army was very largely, for the time being, cast back . . . The Knights of the Round Table, the Crusaders, all fall back into the past . . . these young men, going forth every morn to guard their native land and all that we stand for, holding in their hands these instruments of colossal and shattering power, of whom it may be said that: 'Every morn brought forth a noble chance. And every chance brought forth a noble knight,' deserve our gratitude, as do all the brave men who, in so many ways and on so many occasions, are ready, and continue to be ready, to give life and all for their native land."

"I have, myself, full confidence that if all do their duty . . . we shall prove ourselves once again able to defend our Island home, to ride out the storm of war, and to outlive the menace of tyranny, if necessary for years, if necessary alone. . . . that is what we are going to try to do. That is the resolve of His Majesty's Government—every man of them. That is the will of Parliament and the nation. The British Empire and the French Republic, linked together in their cause . . . will defend to the death their native soil, aiding each other like good comrades to the utmost of their strength. Even though large tracts of Europe have fallen or may fall into the grip of the Gestapo . . . we shall not flag or fail, we shall go on to the end, we shall fight in France, we shall fight on the seas and oceans, we shall fight with growing confidence and growing strength in the air, we shall defend our Island, we shall fight on the beaches, we shall fight on the landing-grounds, we shall fight in the fields and in the streets, we shall fight in the hills; we shall never surrender, and even if this Island . . . were subjugated and starving, then our Empire beyond the seas, armed and guarded by the British Fleet, would carry on the struggle, until in God's good time, the New World, with all its power and might, steps forth to the rescue and the liberation of the Old."

These inspiring and well-chosen words were heard around the world, and Britains everywhere were stirred by Churchill's oratory, by the ornate language, by his use of language reflecting Shakespeare, the King James Bible, and Britain's historical past. Churchill was the 'man of the hour,' and he was probably the only person who could speak in such an eloquent manner to the English people and offer them hope and resolve, when in their hearts they knew that at that moment it appeared Hitler and his war machine could not be stopped.

Across the ocean, the United States was stirred and sympathetic when they heard of the happenings at Dunkirk. Churchill again requested help from his friend Roosevelt, and again he was told that America would increase the amount of supplies sent to Britain but would not send men to fight. Roosevelt reminded Churchill about the dangers the American ships were facing from the German submarine wolf packs in the Atlantic Ocean.

# German Troops Invade Channel Islands

I wondered that with all that activity in the English Channel and the Germans now poised on the opposite edge of the Channel, just how safe were the people who lived on the British-owned Channel Islands. Guernsey, Alderney's closest neighbor, was the first of the Channel Islands to fall under the jackboot of the German Nazis, as later told to me by Jimmy.

"It was in the evening of Friday, the 28th of June, 1940, when the farmers of Guernsey formed long queues of trucks, horse-drawn carts and vans along the White Rock Quay, patiently waiting to unload their cargoes of 'chips.' That was what they called the twelve-pound baskets of tomatoes, and this year's crop was exceptionally nice. The tomatoes would be placed in the holds of waiting British freighters. It was a beautiful early-summer evening and the farmers, although they were British, chatted in the local French *patois*, the same French language my mother used. There was no talk of war that evening as the men enjoyed the summer sun and a chance to visit with their friends while they waited for their turn to unload their tomatoes that were destined for the British market.

"Suddenly, at five minutes to seven, six planes appeared in the sky. Three of the planes roared high into the sky and flew across the island from east to west. The other three planes lost altitude and came roaring toward the waiting farmers. One farmer recognized the insignia and yelled a warning, 'Jerries!' By then they could all see the swastika and iron cross quite plainly. It was too late and the crowd panicked as the machine guns began to strafe the farmers. Desperately the farmers tried to find a safe place to hide from the barrage of machine gun bullets. Safe places were hard to find. A few jumped into the sea. In a matter of moments the planes were gone but behind them they left forty-four innocent dead and dying civilians. And that was the beginning of the Germans arriving in the Channel Islands."

Jimmy continued, obviously upset when thinking about his homeland.

"The German occupation of Alderney differed somewhat from that of her neighboring island, Guernsey. Guernsey is larger, being approximately a thirty-square-mile area with a population of approximately 47,000, as compared to Alderney's six-square-mile area and a population of less than 1500. When word was received in the Channel Islands that the British would send ships to evacuate any people who wished to leave, the people of Alderney held a mass meeting at Les Butes and nearly all of the population on Alderney decided to leave the island.

"The Alderney people were told that they could only take a small suitcase and an overcoat or a blanket with them. Many of the people decided to bury somewhere on their property a portion of their treasured belongings such as jewelry, silver and china in hopes that it would still be there 'when' they returned. The painful decisions on what to take and what to leave behind had to be made quickly. Although it was nearly July and the weather was warm, they all decided to dress in layers, which would save more room in their small suitcases for other things.

"At the Les Butes meeting they were requested to have each home owner fill out a card with the address of the house, the owner's name and list all the family members living in the house, plus list the contents of the house. These cards were collected and placed on file for future reference when the island would someday be free of German occupation. The British began their evacuation of Alderney on Sunday, June 23rd, and took the Alderney people to Weymouth, England. In just five days, a total of 22,656 British citizens were evacuated from the Channel Islands.

"The German troops arrived on June 30th on Guernsey and Jersey and arrived on Alderney on July 2nd. Later the Germans decided to move the few people that had opted to stay behind on Alderney over to the island of Guernsey."

Jimmy said, "It took awhile before my family could let me know where they were and what had happened. My sister described their departure and said that as they were leaving the island on the ship, she looked back and saw that the prized Alderney dairy cattle had been turned loose and were wandering down the streets of Alderney. My family said they felt like frightened and disheartened expatriates as they left Alderney and had to face the uncertainty of where they were going and when they could, if ever, return to their beloved island. (Little did they know it would be almost five years before they would be able to return to their homes.) My elderly father, my brother Reg, and Reg's wife Jessie with their two children, my sister Lillian and her husband, Charlie, were together and were a comfort for each other. They assured me in their letters that they were certain they would survive and that their indomitable English spirit would get them through these tragic days.

"They were moved several times and for some unknown reason were in London during part of the time of the blitz. The nightly races for the bomb shelters were too much for my elderly and ailing father and he died during their stay in London. He was temporarily buried somewhere nearby.

"The Germans were trying to break the will of the English people by targeting places like hospitals, churches, museums, business districts, apartment buildings. Their objective was to cause the most disruption and anguish as they possibly could. But the Germans grossly underestimated the enduring stamina and fortitude of the English people. They also never counted on the accuracy of the English radar and their anti-aircraft guns.

"Nevertheless, my uprooted family was put under a tremendous strain, especially while living in London. At some point during those critical days of the war, they were moved to Scotland where housing was made available for them. In return, they were all expected to help in the war effort in some way. Although mail service was slow, my brother and sister were able to get an occasional letter off to me and they kept me informed as to my family's well being."

# Skirmishes and Differing Opinions

In the meantime there were an alarming number of American merchant ships being sunk by the German submarine wolf packs. These costly skirmishes became a cause of great concern for President Roosevelt. As Roosevelt increased the amount of aid being shipped to England, he found it very difficult to maintain a public posture of neutrality to Congress and his political foes. Also, at this time, Winston Churchill began begging for the fifty American destroyers that were mothballed, but the United States was slow to respond on this matter. However, gradually America was getting involved in Great Britain's war.

President Roosevelt was serving his second term as president of the United States, and he knew that the large campaign contributions made by Joseph Patrick Kennedy were mostly responsible for his election. Kennedy and Roosevelt, although they both belonged to the Democratic Party, held opposing views as to whether the United States should help England during World War II. As Hitler's armies conquered one European country after another, voices within the U.S. began to be heard on the subject of isolationism as the approach that the U.S. should take toward Great Britain. Two very popular people who publicly advocated isolationism were Joseph Patrick Kennedy and Charles Augustus Lindbergh.

Joseph Kennedy, one of the wealthiest men in the United States, had been appointed as ambassador to Great Britain, from 1937 to 1940. Ambassador Kennedy and his large glamorous family were busy in London's social scene and were constantly in London's society news. In private and in public Joseph Kennedy made his views about appeasement known. At a party in London the ambassador met Charles Lindbergh and they became close friends. Both of these charismatic men were strong advocates of isolationism and tried to influence decisions coming out of the White House.

Page Huidekoper was a twenty-year old New Yorker and was Joseph Kennedy's secretary in London. She is quoted as having heard Joseph Kennedy say: "If you think I'm a hundred percent isolationist, well, if there's such a thing as a thousand percent isolationist, I'm that."

A file of Kennedy's remarks labeled "Kennediana" was carefully assembled by the British Foreign Office and leaked to the press and to visiting American politicians. Defeatist remarks, such as, "Britain was the past, Germany the future," and, "America will have to learn to live with Hitler," were not what the English people wanted to hear from the American ambassador. However, some people in the United States felt that if Germany won the war quickly, Joseph Kennedy should be the next U.S. president because he would be the best man to work with Hitler.

In April 1940, President Roosevelt sent diplomat Sumner Welles to England to get a second opinion of the situation in England. The reports that came back made Britain's chances look bleak. About this same time CBS's Berlin correspondent, William Shirer, was permitted to go to the front and advance with the German Panzer columns. He would then broadcast back to the American people about the invincibility of the Nazi war machine. His American listeners began to wonder if there was any point in sending aid to a country about to be overrun by the Nazis. (Quotes from, *England—1940,* by Robert Jackson.)

The great American hero, Charles Lindbergh, nicknamed "Lone Eagle," was equally negative in his public comments about England's chances in World War II. Lindbergh was an admirer of Hitler and the German military. Lindbergh went before Congress in 1941, and testified against the Lend Lease Act, and stated he would rather have a negotiated peace. Later that year he resigned his commission in the United States Army Air Corps Reserve after President Roosevelt had criticized him for his attitude.

(NOTE: Regardless of Lindbergh's isolationist views, after the United States entered the war, he made valuable contributions to the war effort. Lindbergh served as a consultant and technical advisor to manufacturers of military aircraft. In 1944 he was sent to the Pacific to study the operation of P-38 twin-engine fighter planes. He flew about fifty missions and was given credit for extending the range of the P-38 by 500 miles. After the war he received many awards for his contributions to aviation. He was a man of strong convictions and exceptional talents and his contributions to America's war effort were of far greater impact than those short-lived ideals he had about Hitler and the Nazi war machine.)

# Part Two
# Germany's Aggression Spreads

# England in 1940–1941

Winston Churchill was having a difficult time trying to keep his cabinet focused on the idea that England should fight Germany and not acquiesce to Hitler's promises and threats. There were a few members of the Cabinet that were pressuring Churchill to seek some sort of mediation agreement with Hitler to keep England safe from a German invasion. Churchill's response was, "Nations which went down fighting rose again, but those which surrendered tamely were finished."

Churchill continued to aggressively request more American assistance, but Roosevelt remained reluctant to openly support sending additional supplies to England because it would become a political issue for him. More and more Americans were advocating an isolationist policy. Joe Kennedy was sending his own children back to America because he feared an invasion and was telling people that the Germans would be in London in a few weeks.

The Waldorf-Astoria hotel in New York City was the place where many parties were held to celebrate German victories in Europe. Gerhart Westrick, a leading Nazi business lawyer, who had been sent to America to make discreet contacts with top business executives, hosted the parties. Westrick was an executive with the International Telephone and Telegraph Corporation. He was a businessman, a Nazi, and was in America to urge executives from such companies as Ford, General Motors, and several oil companies to retain their business ties in Europe. Attendance at these parties did not indicate that the executives were pro-Nazi, they were mostly businessmen checking about the safety of their company's European investments. They were being told that the war was about over.

London was showing evidence of preparations for war. Gas masks were being issued to the people. Soldiers were sandbagging buildings, barrage balloons were tethered along the coastlines, trenches were being dug in various places, barbed wire was being strung in strategic locations, and blackouts were ordered at night. Valuable pieces of art had been removed from the British Museum and stored at a secret location. In other areas, factories had been camouflaged, signs were removed from railway stations, and antitank obstacles were being constructed. Yes, England was preparing for a German invasion.

After Churchill learned that France was asking Germany for an armistice, he made another rallying call to the British stating that he anticipated there would soon be an air battle over England and he assured the British people that they had the courage to withstand the anticipated bombing:

"I do not at all underrate the severity of the ordeal that lies before us, but I believe our countrymen will show themselves capable of standing up to it, like the brave men of Barcelona."

" . . . What General Weygand called the 'Battle of France' is over. I expect that the battle of Britain is about to begin. Upon this battle depends the survival of Christian civilization. Upon it depends our own British life and the long continuity of our institutions and our Empire. The whole fury and might of the enemy must very soon be turned upon us. Hitler knows that he will have to break us in this island or lose the war. If we stand up to him, all Europe may be free, and the life of the whole world may move forward into broad sunlit uplands; but if we fail, then, the whole world, including the United States, and all that we have known or cared for, will sink into the abyss of a new dark age made more sinister and perhaps more prolonged, by the lights of perverted science. **Let us therefore brace ourselves to our duties and so bear ourselves that if the British Empire and the Commonwealth last for a thousand years, men will still say, this was their finest hour.**"

Churchill is regarded as a very colorful figure in history, and one who possessed persuasive oratorical skills. He wore tall hats, bow ties, smoked cigars, and gave two-fingered salutes. He began work each morning while still in bed. Upon arising he would begin dictating to his secretaries while wearing his bathrobe and sometimes forgetting to put in his dentures. Marian Holmes, a secretary on Churchill's staff, stated that she never saw her boss drunk. She said he drank with food. Alcohol was his fuel, but none of his staff, his ministers, or his generals, ever saw him lose control. However, Ambassador Kennedy suggested otherwise to the people in Washington.

Britain had developed a very sophisticated system of detecting, and direction-plotting of aircraft which used secret Radio Direction Finding (RDF) stations (radar) that were located along the eastern and southern coasts. British aircraft were fitted with equipment that would "blip" a certain way to distinguish if aircraft were friend or foe. The Fighter Command was divided into groups, and each group was divided into sectors. RAF squadrons were assigned to a sector. At command headquarters, the Women's Auxiliary Air Force, WAAF, would plot the movements of planes on a huge map table, and then would calculate the course the fighter pilots would need to take to intercept the incoming enemy planes. The squadrons of fighter planes would be dispatched according to the information received. Germany did not have this technology.

Hitler's plan was to destroy Britain's air force and navy in 1940, and then place a blockade of U-boats around England, and he would then follow up with a merciless bombing strategy that would break the spirits of the starving English. At this point, Hitler believed the English would request an end to the war. If they did not request an end to the war, then in 1941, Germany would invade England.

Churchill realized that keeping England's navy and air force strong had to be top priorities. Consideration had to be made about the French Navy, if France was going to be taken over by Germany. Churchill knew that if Germany conquered France, then Germany would increase its naval power by the acquisition of the French navy. Churchill gave the French Admiral Marcel Gensoul at Mers-el-Kebir, at the military port of Oran in French North Africa the following choices: (1) join the British, (2) sail to a neutral port, (3) scuttle, or (4) be attacked by the British warships.

When it was known that the French would not comply with any of the British terms, Churchill, who no longer trusted the French, ordered, "Settle this matter quickly!" In ten minutes, the English Royal Navy began its takeover of the French navy. Unfortunately, 1,250 French navy men were killed. Within a week, most of the French navy had been put out of action or seized. Sir John Dill issued a memorable quote, "I never had seen anything comparable: the two nations who were fighting for civilization had turned and rent each other while the barbarians sat back and laughed."

With considerable trepidation because he had acted quickly on the matter of the French navy without getting Parliament's support beforehand, Churchill appeared before Parliament and explained the motivations for the destruction of the French Navy. He said, *"The action we have already taken should be, in itself, sufficient to dispose, once and for all, of the lies and rumors which have been so industriously spread by German propaganda and Fifth Column activities, that we have the slightest intention of entering into negotiations in any form and through any channel with the German and Italian governments. We shall, on the contrary, prosecute the war with the utmost vigor by all means that are open to us, until the righteous purposes for which we entered upon it have been fulfilled."*

Churchill sat down and with tears running down his face, he acknowledged the cheers from all sides of the House. He had not been certain how Parliament would react to his very bold decision regarding the French navy.

In the United States there was a decided turn in favor of assisting England because there was now a feeling that under Churchill's leadership, England was going to fight, where before there was the feeling that the English might capitulate the same way that France did.

Hitler made a speech to the Reichstag on July 16th, 1940, which he called his Final Appeal to Reason and he stated that "A great empire will be destroyed, an empire which it was never my intention to destroy or even harm . . . I consider myself in a position to make this appeal since I am not the vanquished begging for favors, but the victor speaking in the name of reason."

The response to Hitler, from an announcer on the BBC radio was, "Let me tell you what we here in Britain think of this appeal of yours to what you are pleased to call 'our reason and common sense'. Herr Fuhrer and Reichskanzler, we hurl it right back at you, right in your evil-smelling teeth." When the German high command heard the brash response from the BBC announcer, they thought the British were crazy, because they all felt certain that the war was almost over and that very soon England would be defeated.

The Royal Air Force fighter pilots were a lively group of young men, dedicated to their jobs and each other. Almost every day, they were sent out on hazardous missions to meet the enemy, and they realistically knew that each day could be their last, so when they had a chance to party—they did. There were certain pubs they liked to frequent, and they liked to drink and they needed to let off steam. Their jobs were dangerous and they missed some of their friends that had been lost over the channel waters. The pilots had developed several good-luck superstitions, such as carrying a present with them from someone they loved. Another superstition was to take a leak against the tail wheel of the plane before taking off. The pilots said, "To be honest, you needed a pee before going into combat—you just did."

The number of fighter-pilot sorties began increasing because the number of convoys had increased. There were sometimes too many ships to try to protect all at once. It was decided that a smaller number of ships per convoy could receive heavier protection from the English fighter planes that were available. Also, many convoys were now trying to get through the English Channel during the night hours. But the German bombers with German fighter escort planes were constantly harassing the English convoys both day and night, in the English Channel.

Several well-known American correspondents wanted to see first-hand what was happening in England. They soon discovered that at Dover, at Shakespeare Cliff, they could watch convoys being bombed, and Spitfires and Hurricanes attempting to duke it out with the German bombers and Messerschmitt 109s and 110 fighters. Art Menken was filming the action for American newsreels, and Ed Murrow and Eric Sevareid were there to broadcast for CBS. Back home, America was about to receive first-hand reports of the valiant efforts being expended by the British against terrific odds.

Hitler's General Hermann Goring, in charge of the German air force, had designated August 13, 1940, as Eagle Day. The English pilots did not know this, but this date would mark the beginning of a concentrated effort of the Luftwaffe to destroy the Royal Air Force, their pilots, the airfields, and the radar installations. Goring estimated that they could knock out the Royal Air Force in four days, and that the invasion could begin in a month.

England's Air Vice Marshal Hugh Dowding had observed the mistakes that Hitler had made on his invasions of other countries and made his preparations accordingly. Eagle Day did not go as well as Goring had planned. Dowding had dispersed his planes and equipment in such a way that the German bombers did not do the damage they expected. The German losses were far greater in men and planes than the British.

Churchill was pleased with the way the Royal Air Force had performed and in August he visited the command center and watched the Women's Auxiliary Air Force (WAAF) push wave after wave of German bombers across the plotting table and the fighter squadrons engage the enemy. The Prime Minister imagined in his own mind the courage it took on the part of these airmen. Also, he was extremely impressed by the intensity and skill of the WAAF plotters. After viewing the work at the command center and thinking of his outnumbered pilots challenging the invaders, he made a statement that would soon be heard around the world: "*Never in the field of human conflict has so much been owed, by so many, to so few.*"

It took a little political maneuvering, between May and August 1940, but Roosevelt and the Prime Minister of Canada were able to come to an agreement that would provide for the fifty old United States destroyers to be sent to England.

Although Churchill had repeatedly asked for these destroyers, he was slightly upset that Canada had entered into secret negotiations behind his back to accomplish what he was unable to do. The fact that there was practically no resistance from Congress and the public against Roosevelt sending the old destroyers to England seemed to indicate that the people in the United States were becoming more and more sympathetic toward England's struggle with Germany.

In August 1941 Churchill and Roosevelt met on a cruiser off the coast of Newfoundland. They discussed their concerns over the June 1941 German invasion of the Soviet Union and Hitler's apparent objective to destroy the Russian armies. Roosevelt had offered lend-lease materials to Russia, but they were slow in reaching the Russian areas that were in the greatest need. Prior Soviet pacts with Germany and the Soviet's war against Finland created attitudes of distrust in Great Britain and the United States that were anticommunist, but when the choice was between helping the communists or the Nazis, the communists were chosen.

The Atlantic Charter was created at the meeting of Churchill and Roosevelt on that ship in the North Atlantic, and it proclaimed to the world the areas of agreement between these two political figures. It was not a treaty and, therefore, did not need ratification by their governmental bodies. The following points of agreement were:

- to respect the right of every nation to choose its own form of government
- not to seek gains, territorial or otherwise
- to guarantee freedom of the seas
- to conduct peaceful world trade

The German U-boats were becoming a constant menace in the Atlantic Ocean in 1941. America's merchant ships carrying lend-lease materials to Great Britain would often fall prey to the prowling submarines. In retaliation and in assistance to the British navy, the American naval ships began tracking the U-boats and radioing their locations to the British. In September a German submarine fired two torpedoes at the American destroyer *Greer*, whereupon Roosevelt used this incident to issue a "shoot-on-sight" policy. (Roosevelt did not mention that the *Greer* had been following the U-boat for two hours.) After an attack on the *Kearny* and the sinking of the *Reuben James*, Roosevelt was able to persuade Congress to remove all restrictions on American shipping.

It was now apparent that America was in an undeclared war at sea and was not maintaining a neutral posture with a "shoot-on-sight" policy in effect. In spite of Roosevelt's critics, his wishes prevailed. Hitler protested but he had invaded Russia and did not wish to challenge the United States at this time. Great Britain felt buoyed by the increased assistance coming from their friend in the west.

# Dover Receives First German Shelling

Dover, England, is located where the English Channel narrows to only twenty-one miles wide, and due to its location Dover has been involved in many of England's previous conflicts, dating back to the time of the Roman conquests. When the people of Dover heard Winston Churchill's words about Germany's plan for the subjugation of England, they were alerted and began to get prepared for possible future involvement in WWII.

Dover Strait connects the North Sea and the English Channel and is very shallow at that point, with an average depth of less than one hundred feet. It separates England and France at their closest location. On a clear day, the people of Dover could stand on their famous cliffs and watch the German positions on the opposite shore making preparations for the planned invasion of England. The Invasion of Britain did not happen, but the Battle of Britain did happen, and Dover received the first German shelling in August 1940.

Just two months after the evacuation of Dunkirk, the Germans began a steady and ever-increasing shelling of Dover. More bombs were dropped on Dover per square mile than any other British location. The farmers in the surrounding fields were often strafed and needed to seek shelter immediately. But the continual danger and destruction did not deter the stalwart people of Dover. They would just quickly clean up the debris and rubbish and then go about their daily business. They also had to deal with many salvos of six- or eight-inch shells and then later they had thousands of incendiaries that were dropped on them. Sometimes the shelling could last as long as five hours at a time. The Germans went from daytime shelling to nighttime, and then they started shelling Dover at any time. The resolve of the Doverites held firm throughout this traumatic period of their history.

There was no warning sound when a shell was coming in, only when it exploded. The Germans were at Cap Gris Nez and it took about one minute for a shell to reach Dover from the French coast. The people at Dover knew that if they saw the flash, they had one minute to take cover.

42

There were other reminders in Dover about the war, such as limited access into the town by a pass only. Many pieces of war machinery were hidden in strategic locations on the beaches, the cliffs, and out in the countryside. There was a sign notifying people that part of the sea front was mined. Dover owned a large range finder that calculated the height and range of German planes for the operators to relay this information to the people operating the antiaircraft guns. Dover had a huge cannon that fired a 380-pound shell that guarded the coast but did not get into a lobbing contest with Jerry across the channel.

Many businesses and shops were actually pillboxes that were totally camouflaged. The people of Dover had many secret devices of war cleverly hidden in different locations. Dover had, in reality, built a fortress, but managed to maintain the look of an English town.

There were barrage balloons on steel cables guarding the coastline around Dover, and the Germans made a game of shooting the balloons down, but the people of Dover were not easily discouraged and would quickly replace the deflated balloons. The steel cables were an effective determent to the German dive-bombers.

The people of Dover continued on with their daily duties, with a matter-of-fact attitude, even though many of their business buildings, homes and churches had been bombed. They were living with danger each day, and they also lived with death because many of their family and friends had been injured or killed by the relentless German shelling and bombing.

Many convoys carrying important cargoes to England needed to pass through the narrow Strait of Dover, which connects the English Channel and the North Sea. The Royal Air Force pilots were kept busy trying to protect the convoys from the Luftwaffe. Foreign war correspondents would come to Dover because they could stand on the cliffs and watch the English and the German pilots duke it out, while the convoys tried desperately to maneuver safely through the narrow passageway. The pilots were in life-and-death struggles in the air over the Strait of Dover, and the war correspondents wrote many electrifying stories based on what they saw there.

Dover had an excellent decontamination center and there were many gas masks evident throughout the town, because there were great concerns about the possibility of the Germans using poison gas on the Dover people. They were well aware that poison gas could be delivered in one minute by a shell and three minutes by a plane.

There were twelve cave shelters in Dover's white cliffs that could hold most of Dover's population during the air raids. The cliffs are in solid chalk and there is 180 feet of chalk for protection overhead against extremely heavy bomb attacks. The caves were well equipped with stores of food, water, heat, light, and medical facilities. The people could be sustained for an indefinite period of time in the caves. The British always worried about an invasion, and the Dover people were no exception, and they felt fortunate to have the caves available. When the war of nerves was about to get to a family, they were free to go to the safe haven of the caves, where there was always a marshal on duty. Old and young alike could go to the caves for a much-needed respite from the war.

The people of Dover took their responsibilities seriously, and all the people who were able helped with civil defense, cleaned away the bomb rubble, or acted as air-raid patrol wardens. Meanwhile, the people raised their children, went to church, attended the cinemas and the pubs. The normal population of Dover is about 36,000, but during the worst of the blitz it was reduced to about 15,000. The farmers continued to till the surrounding fields despite the frequent strafing by the Jerries.

Dover was definitely scarred by the bombings and the shellings, but the citizens had the remarkable attitudes of perseverance and determination to carry on as nearly to normal as possible. They mourned quietly for those who had been killed by the escalating war. They were very cognizant of their rich heritage and links to important battles of history. They knew that their geographic location could place them where a considerable amount of action would take place. They were ready, and if not, there were always the caves.

# Germany Invades Russia—Barbarossa

Hitler had a hidden agenda when he entered into the Nazi-Soviet Pact of 1939. Secretly he did this because he could not get the British to capitulate, he did not want to have a two-front war, and he thought that the United States and the Soviet Union were getting ready to offer aid to Great Britain. Secretly he assured himself that he could invade the Soviet Union whenever he decided to do so. Since the British were still standing strong and he could not force them to capitulate, he foolishly made the decision to invade the Soviet Union in the spring of 1941. He named the ill-fated operation Barbarossa, after a medieval German emperor, and he boldly figured he could secure for himself a part of his territorial objectives that he had set forth in *Mein Kampf.*

Hitler wanted to seize the regions in the Soviet Union that contained resources that Germany desperately needed. He thought he could take these rich lands easily from the Soviets, but he had not reckoned with the problems of fighting over such large expanses of land.

Basically, Stalin and Hitler did not trust each other, and they were both treacherous men with hidden agendas. The Soviet war with Finland had been a disaster for Russia, and Stalin did not want to get into a war with Germany, so he agreed to send supplies to Germany.

Hitler's plans for Barbarossa were hindered and delayed by his ill-fated friend, Mussolini, who had invaded Greece and who was involved in a humiliating defeat by the Greek armies. Hitler had to divert forces to help his inept friend.

Stalin had begun shipping supplies to the German military, as per their agreement, and was thinking that would make a friend of Hitler and prevent any sort of German invasion into his country. Stalin had ignored his intelligence information and maintained these delusions until the day the German armies launched an invasion of the Soviet Union. Stalin had been completely duped.

The German offensive was a three-pronged invasion along a front of two thousand miles, with three million men. With lightning speed, the Panzer units moved too far ahead of their own infantry, and the Germans became stymied in December. At this point the Soviets came back with strong counterattacks and the German offensive was slowed to a halt in the winter of 1941–1942. In America, FDR assessed this situation, and knew he did not want the Germans to get the rich resources of the Soviet Union, so he ordered lend-lease assistance to be sent to the Soviet Union, much to the consternation of the members of Congress and his political friends.

The Germans were particularly brutal in their treatment of the people in their occupied regions, and the Soviet people suffered greatly during this time of conflict. The Soviet people were fighting tenaciously to defend their homeland, and they were not fighting for political or economic reasons. Hitler was fighting to take over rich Russian regions, which had industrial capabilities and a multitude of important resources for Germany's consumption. Russia's leading port was located at Leningrad, which also appealed to the greedy German dictator.

In October 1941 the Germans laid siege to the beautiful cultural city of Leningrad and the siege lasted for 900 days. It did not end until January 1944. The German armies tried to get the Russians to surrender by starving them and submitting them to heavy artillery shelling and bombardment. The Russians fought back as best they could, considering their supply routes were almost completely cut off. Only minimal amounts of food and supplies arrived in the winter months of 1941–1942 and their people were dying in their homes, in the streets and at work at an alarming rate. One million people died in Leningrad, 600,000 from starvation and the rest from the bombing and artillery attacks.

The Russian workers began moving their machinery to the center of the country, hopefully out of the reach of the Germans. They had to constantly battle the extremely cold conditions, insufficient supplies of food and medicine, and very poorly constructed housing facilities. The Russian workers knew they were fighting to save their country and, amazingly, they persevered. Despite these deplorable conditions under which they had to work, they began to turn out tanks, guns, and munitions for their armies fighting on the fronts in the early months of 1942.

Hitler was not yet ready to give up on capturing more Russian land. He had begun to plan more offensives against the Russians, in opposition to the advice of his generals. Hitler hated Stalin and he was obsessed with the idea of capturing the industrial city of Stalingrad, which the Germans had already turned into a heap of rubble. It became a place of fierce fighting from block to block and building to building. Strategic moves by the Soviets trapped 200,000 German troops there.

The German soldiers had been sent into battle without warm clothing and winterized equipment, and they were cold and desperate. They hid in cellars and any place they could find shelter, and they were under constant shellfire. They had to resort to eating their packhorses because their food was running out. Operations were performed under crude conditions, medicines were becoming unavailable, and the intense cold made their survival questionable. Many German soldiers were succumbing to madness and suicide, and many more had become psychologically unfit to continue fighting.

Thousands of Germans died from starvation and the cold. Thirty thousand wounded Germans escaped by airlift and thirty thousand more were made prisoners of war. Usually the men placed in Soviet prison camps did not live long enough to be released. Hitler never took the blame for any of his mistakes or defeats in his military planning. In December 1941 he replaced his generals, and made himself the supreme commander of the Russian campaign. He began to direct the operations on the eastern front. He refused to permit the German troops to withdraw and establish winter positions, and his irrational decisions resulted in his troops suffering and dying in astronomical numbers in Stalingrad.

After the defeat at Stalingrad, Hitler could have salvaged his overextended forces by exercising military logic with strategic retreats and counterattacks where needed and could have concentrated his forces on what would have been a narrower front. Instead, he decided to attack the Soviets at Kursk. The Soviets heard of his plans and prepared to do battle with the onslaught. Both sides threw everything they could into the battle. The Germans had one million troops, 2,700 tanks, 1,800 aircraft and 10,000 pieces of artillery. The Soviets had 1.3 million men, 3,300 tanks, and 20,000 pieces of artillery waiting to meet the Germans.

Hitler launched his offensive against Kursk on July 5th, 1943 and it ended on July 12th. The Germans met a well-prepared and equipped Russian army and savage fighting ensued. The largest tank battle of WWII took place in the battle of Kursk. The Germans executed a fighting withdrawal, leaving behind enormous amounts of their equipment and approximately 70,000 dead officers and men.

At this time, Hitler heard about the Allies invading Sicily and he decided to transfer a Panzer corps to help defend Mussolini's Italy. In the back of his mind he anticipated an Anglo-American invasion and he felt that after he defeated the Allies he would go back and fight the Soviet Union with his entire military force.

The Soviets kept chasing the retreating German armies during the first months of 1944. In March 1944 Hitler issued a directive which named approximately thirty cities which he considered to be fortified places and he ordered them to be defended down to the last man. The troops were warned that if they did not obey the directive they would be executed. The only withdrawal that could be made was with Hitler's permission, and this order resulted in many German troops being sacrificed because they had been stationed in a hopeless situation.

The Soviets launched a series of offensive actions on June 22, 1944 that surpassed any of the other Russian campaigns. Six million Russian and German soldiers were involved. The Soviets struck in the north and south, and launched an especially large offensive on the central front. Within one week the German lines were broken, 130,000 German soldiers were killed and 66,000 were taken prisoner. (Statistics of the number of Russians killed are seldom available.) At one point the Soviet forces had advanced to just 400 miles from Berlin.

In the meantime, the Anglo-American forces had landed on the beaches of Normandy and were moving across France. On July 20th, there was an unsuccessful assassination attempt on Hitler's life by a few of his own officers, and Hitler ordered a purge of his higher echelons. Italy had left the war, and Hitler's allies were also trying to find ways to get out. Allied bombing was wreaking havoc on German transportation, oil facilities, and important industrial cities. The outcome of the war was becoming evident—but the Germans fought on.

The Russian army invaded German-controlled Poland in 1944. All of Poland had been under German domination and control since Germany had invaded Russia in 1941. Many Poles had been persecuted and killed by the Nazis, and many Poles had been deported to forced labor concentration camps. When the Russians arrived, the Polish underground helped them drive the Germans out of Poland.

As Roosevelt and Churchill observed the Russians moving into Poland they became very concerned about what Stalin's precise motivations might be. Stories of mass killings by the Soviets were at first denied and later admitted. Hitler continued to make irrational military decisions, which resulted in the deaths of thousands upon thousands of his troops. It appeared that the only two leaders who could trust each other were Roosevelt and Churchill.

# Part Three
# Japanese Aggression in the Pacific Theater

# Japanese Attack Pearl Harbor—
# December 7th, 1941

It was 1941, I was a junior in high school and I was engrossed in my studies and my high school friends. I felt sympathy for the people who were uprooted by the war, but when you are sixteen and far removed from the fighting you don't constantly dwell on it. I would hear from Mother and Jimmy that his people were safe, and for that I was very grateful. If I had a date and would go to a movie and I would see scenes in the newsreels of some of the battles both on land and at sea, I would think about how frightened the soldiers and sailors must be. It just didn't seem like a real world where those battles were taking place. I would think about how Ohio was such a nice safe place to live and I was thankful that our young men would not have to go fight. During this time I must have been totally self-absorbed because the most important things to me were keeping up with my school work, playing the flute in the school band and orchestra, getting a part in the school play, and going places with friends—all those activities that teenagers desire.

It was Sunday, December 7th, 1941, and my father was sitting by the radio with this look of disbelief on his face. He called to Lucille, my stepmother, and me to come and listen to the news. The radio announcer was saying that Pearl Harbor had been attacked! The chilling details of the destruction and the mounting number of deaths and missing Americans kept coming on the radio. Lucille left the room because the news disturbed her. However, I sat down close to Dad and together we listened to the radio announcer give details of how several hundred Japanese planes came without warning and how they practically destroyed America's Pacific Fleet and killed a lot of people in about an hour's time. (I'm ashamed to say I did not know where Pearl Harbor was on the map.)

Dad turned to me during this broadcast with a sad look on his face and said, "Gloryann, the world has changed today and your life will never be the same because we are in for a lot of trouble. You will see many of the young men you know go to war."

Dad sat in his chair, shaking his head, and saying over and over: "My God! Oh, my God! Why did this have to happen? Why? What did we ever do to the Japanese to deserve this!"

When I went to bed that night I felt sick, my stomach was upset, I was restless, and when I finally went to sleep I had troubling dreams.

The next day at school was a day of "slow motion." The teachers tried to teach but ended up talking about the attack on Pearl Harbor with their classes. There was no animation, no smiles that day. Everyone seemed to be trying to comprehend what this meant to us and to our country. Those of us in high school had heard about World War I—but that was supposed to have been the "war to end all wars." We knew about Hitler and what he was doing in Europe, but that was far away. We could not remember discussions involving Japanese animosity toward our country. Why would Japan want to attack us? What had we done to provoke the Japanese? One thing was now for certain, our idyllic existence in rural Ohio was shaken. We knew instinctively that our lives had been changed on December 7, 1941.

Again Dad and I sat close to the radio and listened as President Roosevelt addressed our nation on December 8th.

"Yesterday, December 7, 1941—a date which will live in infamy—the United States of America was suddenly and deliberately attacked by naval and air forces of the empire of Japan. The United States was at peace with that nation and at the solicitation of Japan was still in conversation with its government and its emperor, looking toward the maintenance of peace in the Pacific. We will gain the inevitable triumph, so help us God . . . Americans will remember the character of the onslaught against us . . . This form of treachery shall never endanger us again . . . The American people in their righteous might will win through to absolute victory."

When President Roosevelt went before Congress, he did not request a declaration of war, instead he asked for recognition that "a state of war has been thrust upon the United States." Congress passed the resolution with one dissenting vote. Germany and Italy then declared war on the United States on December 11th. The U.S. Congress responded by declaring war on those countries. Within just a few short days, the United States was now at war on two very large fronts—the Atlantic Ocean and the Pacific Ocean.

Cities along our east and west coastlines were put on alert and blackouts were ordered and radios were silenced. If the Americans thought we were being overly cautious they changed their minds in a hurry when enemy planes flew over San Francisco Bay on the night of December 8th. The Japanese wasted no time in the Pacific and immediately attacked the Philippines and also sent a landing party in to British-owned Malaya. The war seemed to be on a fast track.

The United States had had a peacetime draft that became law on September 16, 1940. After the Pearl Harbor attack, Congress and the War Department changed what became the military draft to extend the terms of enlistment or induction to six months after hostilities end. Young men were flocking to recruitment centers to enlist and to eventually go fight for their country. This didn't mean they weren't afraid—it just meant they knew their country needed them.

Times of war mold the thinking of young people and this was to become a generation of people dedicated to protecting the peace in their own country and ultimately restoring peace in the world. On December 8th, as I again sat with my father in front of the radio listening to the news, I, too, felt the sobering thoughts, *our country is at war and some horrible things are going to happen before it is all over.* Instinctively the young people of my generation knew that they were going to be called upon to face many challenges. I hoped I that I could do what would be expected of me. I felt like such a weakling.

Details of the Japanese attack on Pearl Harbor indicate there had been warnings that were ignored, there were blips on the radar that showed a group of planes headed toward Pearl, but the warnings had been dismissed as a probable American flight exercise. The first attack came before 8:00 A.M. when the Japanese Rising Sun insignias on the planes were spotted and the warning alarm was sounded. **"Enemy air raid at Pearl Harbor! This is not a drill!"** But it was too late and what followed was a disaster for the American Pacific Fleet. There was basically no opposition as the first wave of Japanese planes flew over.

When the second wave of planes arrived approximately thirty minutes after the first wave departed, the Americans were better prepared to fight them off. The damage from the two waves of enemy planes included six battleships that were either sunk or about to go under, two more battleships badly damaged, three cruisers and three destroyers also hit. The army and the navy received heavy losses in aircraft and nearly 3,000 men were killed and 1,000 were wounded. Of the three

53

hundred fifty Japanese planes that took part in the raid, only nine were lost in the first attack and twenty were lost in the second attack.

America, instead of becoming paralyzed and demoralized by these events, became united in a commitment to defeat these enemies at all costs. The enemies had grossly underestimated what our large nation could do with our stores of natural resources, industrial capacity, large population, and our technological superiority. By this sad turn of events, Winston Churchill finally got his wish of America coming to fight beside the battle-weary English.

The remaining days of December 1941 became a nightmare, as the following events took place:

December 8—President Roosevelt told the American people that a "state of war has been thrust upon us."

December 8—The Japanese bombed Clark Airfield in the Philippines.

December 8—Enemy planes flew over San Francisco Bay in the evening.

December 9—China declared war on Germany, Italy, and Japan.

December 10—Guam surrendered to the Japanese.

December 11—Germany and Italy declared war on the United States.

December 22—Japanese troops landed on Luzon.

December 23—American Troops on Wake Island surrendered to the Japanese.

December 25—British troops surrendered to Japanese at Hong Kong.

There was not much to celebrate on December 31st on New Year's Eve in the way of military victories. Everyone sensed that the coming months, and possibly years, were going to be difficult, but they had no idea how difficult and how long it would take. The motivational force that kept the American people moving forward, even when the events were the most foreboding, was the people's belief that the evil and aggression being forced upon innocent people needed to be eliminated from the world. They felt the cause was just and right. The Americans had accepted this challenge of Herculean proportions, knowing full well that the costs would be astronomical in both lives and money.

# Kenneth Walter, Coppersmith, Saves Injured Sailors

(Kenneth Walter was at Pearl Harbor on December 7, 1941. The following is his account of what happened on this day, in his own words.)

I was a twenty-eight-year-old civilian working in the Navy yards at Pearl Harbor. I was a coppersmith by trade and did a lot of sheet work there. I had a "White Pass" which meant I could go anyplace on the shipyards. I was earning $1.65 an hour, which was good pay at that time. I was living in Honolulu on Castle Street. I had been working on the *Oglala*, a minelayer, the day before and had left my tools at work. I had burnt my eyes with a welder and had an appointment to go to the Navy Hospital and have them take a look at my eyes. It was Sunday, December 7th, 1941.

I was dressed in my best suit because I intended to go to church after seeing the Navy doctors. I was in my car approaching the yards when I heard, "This is not a drill! This is an attack! Get to Hickam Field!"

I heard the planes coming, and I pulled to the side of the road and dove out the passenger door into a ditch. Some of the planes going over were strafing and my car ended up with approximately ninety bullet holes in it. Fortunately, I did not get hit.

An army truck came along and had me get onto the bed of the truck and we got to the gate a little after 8:00. More Japanese planes came in about then, they were coming in really low and we could see the faces of the Japanese pilots, they were almost eye level. We were so close we could see the Japanese pilots make their bombing/torpedo run. We could see the bombs and torpedoes go to their targets. I can still see their leering faces.

I forgot about going to the Navy Hospital, I forgot about having my good suit on and going to church. Being close to Number One Dry Dock, my big Irish friend, Kelly, and I helped fight fires around the *Pennsylvania,* the *Cassin,* and the *Downes.* After the fires were out we

55

went to find something to eat. We went to a little place and got a Spam sandwich and coffee.

While we were eating, a Navy doctor came in and asked for volunteers. At first he didn't say for what. Kelly and I agreed. Then the doctor told us for what. We were to go out in a boat and pick up survivors. As we looked at the burning oil and dense smoke, I wondered what was behind all that dense smoke. The doctor said he could order some sailors that were standing there to go, but he could not order Kelly and me because we were civilians. The doctor told us, "Whatever you do now would be to help mankind." The doctor said a prayer over us volunteers that were ready to put ourselves in danger to help save as many men as we could. The doctor cautioned us that most of these sailors were burned and that they should be picked up under their arms so as not to tear off the skin.

On the docks we saw young sailors, just kids, sixteen and seventeen years old, being carried on stretchers and placed on trucks. Blood was running out the back of the trucks. It was a terrible scene.

When Kelly and I got in the boat with the three sailors, I noticed we were in a wooden boat, with a gasoline engine, and were headed toward the heavy smoke and fire. We picked many live, burnt, and dead men out of the water and made many trips to the docks to unload. As I helped, I had some of these young kids die in my arms. I was praying for all of them, the ones alive and the ones dead. It was Hell!

I was just a little guy and I was getting tired. I came across this big fellow, probably 300 pounds and he was sort of down in a hole. I didn't think I could lift him. The guy was hurt bad, he needed my help. I said a prayer and started to lift the man. Just then I felt a hand on my shoulder and I felt strength go through my body and I lifted the man into the boat. I'm convinced the hand on my shoulder was my "angel," helping me do what I was supposed to do in this situation.

When I picked up one young man who was badly burned, he kept pointing at his chest. I figured out that he was wearing a cross under his dog tags. He put his fingers on the cross, smiled and said, "Tell my mother I love her." Within a couple minutes he passed on.

I worked until 10:00 at night then went back to the restaurant and ate another Spam sandwich and drank a cup of coffee. Martial Law had been declared. I worked all night, looking for men to pull out of the water, and I also worked at putting out fires on ships. The next morning, Monday, Kelly and I were asked to go back on some of the ships to

56

see how many trapped men we could find. We worked all day getting men out.

We would hear some tapping coming from behind the armor-plated walls. I had a blowtorch and would cut a hole through the metal and then Kelly and some volunteers would help get the men out. There were still some fires to be put out and I helped some more on that. All in all I worked for fifty-four hours. It was chaotic. I know I helped save some lives. I pulled many men out of the water. I believe that God touched me and gave me the strength to do what I did. I was tireless. The day lasted into the night. Fifty-four hours later, it was Tuesday, and I went home.

Some things you never forget. I had dreams—these were disturbing times—I would see planes with red Rising Sun circles on the wings coming at me.

This interview was taken on August 21, 2000. Mr. Kenneth Walter died on September 6, 2000. Cause of death was congestive heart failure.

# Events After Pearl Harbor Attack—1942

After Japan had attacked Pearl Harbor, their military leaders agreed that they should not just sit back and wait for the United States and its Allies to recover, but the Japanese military leaders were split on what to do next. Some of their leaders wanted to invade Hawaii, others wanted to take control of Australia, and there were also those who wanted to move into the Indian Ocean and link up with Germany. The Japanese were concerned that there could be a possible invasion of Serbia if the Russians won in their battle with Germany, and they needed to have resources and men ready, in case that should happen.

The British were unable to contribute much in the way of supplies and men to help the Allies in the Pacific Theater, as they had been stretched to their limits. China was in a similar situation and was just barely able to survive. It was an accepted fact that the United States would be providing the major amount of supplies and men, therefore, the Allies all agreed that the United States should take the leadership role of the Allied forces in the Pacific.

However, within the United States there was rivalry among the military leaders, and it was settled by giving Douglas MacArthur command of the Southwest Pacific, consisting of Australia, the Philippines, the Solomon Islands, and the Dutch East Indies. Admiral Chester W. Nimitz was given command of the rest of the Pacific Ocean Theater. MacArthur's arrogance and ego would sometimes get in the way of the cooperation needed between the two commanders. Nimitz had a more cooperative personality and can be credited with what conformity and concurrence existed between the two areas of command in the Pacific.

Australia had been sending troops to help the British in the Middle East, and had lost part of its army at Singapore. They began receiving troops and supplies from the United States. However, they would not have been able to withstand an invasion by the Japanese. At first, Australia was not aware that the Japanese had made the decision not to invade them, but would instead begin seizing bases to provide themselves with harbors and air fields from which they could strike at Australia and render them unable to fight back.

Previously on December 8th, 1941, when the Japanese bombed the air base at Clark Field on Luzon, all the U.S. bombers and all but a few of the fighter planes were destroyed. On December 22nd, General MacArthur deployed his troops before they were capable of stopping the invading Japanese. MacArthur was then forced to order his men to retreat into the jungles of Bataan and try to fight a delaying action. There had been no storing of supplies, medicine and food in Bataan, resulting in the American and Philippine troops becoming weak from hunger and disease.

America's War Department was not able to send the needed assistance to the beleaguered troops in Bataan, and the chiefs of staff realized that the Philippines were about to become a casualty of the war. President Roosevelt made the decision to send MacArthur to Australia because he feared that MacArthur would be captured. Lieutenant General Jonathan M. "Skinny" Wainwright assumed command in the Philippines.

By now the Japanese were using the southern tip of Bataan to launch bombing, artillery and amphibious assaults on Corregidor. On May 6th, the lack of food, water and ammunition made it impossible for the troops to continue fighting. Wainwright sent the following message to Washington: "With profound regret and with continued pride in my gallant troops, I go to meet the Japanese commander."

The infamous Bataan Death March followed the surrender, in which 1,875 American prisoners, who were suffering from malnutrition and jungle diseases, were forced to march for sixty miles. At least 600 died. Men who could not keep up the pace established for the march, or who accepted food and water from civilians, were hacked or bayoneted to death. (The details of the barbaric treatment that occurred against these men were not revealed until three prisoners escaped in the summer of 1943. The story was released to the American public in early 1944.) The battle in the Philippines resulted in 12,000 Americans being surrendered. It is also estimated that 10,000 Filipinos died at this time.

To go back in time to February 1942, the news coming out of the Pacific theater was bleak, and the morale of the American people was at a low point. The shock of the Pearl Harbor attack still hung heavy on the hearts and minds of the American people. President Roosevelt and his naval and air advisors devised a plan to bomb Japan, using army bombers taking off the carrier, the *Hornet*, to get deep into Japan's waters, then they would fly from there, drop their bombs on Japan, and fly to safety in China. Lt. Colonel James H. Doolittle, a famous peacetime aviator, was selected to lead the raid. Specially chosen aviators and crews trained for one month. They would be flying modified B-25 bombers off carrier-length runways.

On April 18th, the carrier *Hornet* joined the *Enterprise* task force and they headed for Japan. The sighting of Japanese picket boats caused the B-25s to take off earlier than planned. They dropped their bombs and headed for China. The extra distance exhausted the fuel supplies on some of the planes and one plane came down in Russia, fourteen made it to China, and one crew of eight came down in Japanese territory where three of the men were shot for war crimes.

Roosevelt's plan did give a psychological lift to the American people. He told the people that the raid had originated from Shangri-La, referring to the popular novel *Lost Horizon,* and a fictional Himalayan retreat. Actually, the daring operation, with all its planning and risks, only inflicted minor damage. However, the emperor's residence was among the places that were damaged, and this greatly humiliated the Japanese military leaders.

The first five months of the war with Japan made the American people begin to think that the Japanese military forces were invincible. The United States had experienced huge losses at Guam, Wake Island, The Philippines, Bataan and Corregidor. Doolittle's raid helped somewhat, but it could not completely erase the effect of the daily newspaper headlines and radio news commentators' reports of battles taking place all over the world. During this period of time, the British were doing no better than we Americans, as they lost Hong Kong, British Borneo and Singapore, where their troops surrendered after just several weeks of fighting. Winston Churchill was appalled and he said, " . . . it was the worst disaster and largest capitulation of British history."

The situation in the Pacific was about to change when the cryptographers, working at Pearl Harbor, broke the Japanese naval code. They gathered information that the Japanese planned to attack Port Moresby, in New Guinea. With the advance warning, the carrier *Lexington* and a task force proceeded to the Coral Sea. A naval battle ensued, with both sides receiving heavy damage. The Battle of the Coral Sea was the first time the United States successfully thwarted a Japanese offensive. The *Lexington* was lost in this battle, which was a significant loss.

Midway Island, which is actually made up of two small islands, is approximately 1,100 miles northwest of Pearl Harbor. The Americans wanted to maintain possession of this island, and the Japanese also wanted it. The Japanese wanted to get revenge for the Doolittle raid and they planned a very complicated and involved battle, using almost the entire Japanese navy. The Japanese planned a diversionary attack on the Aleutian Islands in the North Pacific to draw American naval strength away from their intended target.

American cryptographers were again helpful because they decoded information about the Japanese plans to invade Midway. Midway began receiving needed reinforcements and the marines stationed there were able to reinforce and improve their defenses against air attacks and amphibious landings. The Japanese thought they were going to launch a surprise attack, instead they were actually heading into an ambush.

The men at Midway still had to face heavy odds. Due to lack of fuel, the U.S. had to send its battleships back to the West Coast, and the *Yorktown* had been damaged before and could not operate at full efficiency, plus its crews were inexperienced. The Japanese's situation was hindered because they did not have radar and several of their battleships and two carriers could not participate.

On June 4th, the incoming attack wave was spotted. American torpedo planes and four medium bombers were headed for the Japanese strike force. American antiaircraft fire took out sixty-five Japanese aircraft. The Japanese decided that they needed to strike a second attack at Midway's airfield. They mounted the second wave before the first wave returned. They began removing torpedoes and bombs from the reserve aircraft, but before they were finished, the American planes began their attacks on their strike force. The Japanese suffered severe losses as the torpedo squadrons from the *Hornet*, the *Enterprise*, and the *Yorktown* struck.

Japan lost four carriers, more than 250 aircraft, and many experienced crews and pilots. The Japanese leaders tried to keep the news of this crushing defeat a secret. The Japanese lost control of the sea at this battle, but the importance of this battle was not realized until later.

Plans were approved by the Joint Chiefs of Staff to begin offensive operations in the South Pacific. The plans were divided into three stages—(1) advances up the Solomons, (2) advances along the northeastern coast of New Guinea, and (3) attack the Japanese base of Rabaul on the island of New Britain. The first stage of its target was Tulagi, Guadalcanal.

On August 7th, 1942, American marines landed on Japanese-held territory and took control of an airbase, which they renamed Henderson Field, after a pilot that had been shot down on Midway. The Japanese navy mounted an assault on August 9th and inflicted heavy damage, sinking one Australian and three American cruisers, and damaging another.

The battle for Guadalcanal became a long, drawn-out struggle on an island that was covered with almost impenetrable tropical jungles. The men suffered from the usual jungle diseases of malaria, dysentery and damp-rot. There were critical shortages of food, medicine and supplies. Insects and snakes added to the discomfort that had to be endured. Patrols moving through the jungle had a difficult time in identification of other patrols due to the density of the jungle. It was easy to mistake friend for foe, or foe for friend. There were nightly fights with mortars and small arms. All in all, the conditions were such that it sapped the energy of the fighting men as they tried to maintain the slim hold they had on the island.

On September 13th, the Japanese landed fresh troops and attacked again. The American marines could barely hold their lines—but they did not give. In late October, the Japanese attacked again, only to be hurled back again. This was their last major land effort.

Between August and November seven naval battles took place in the waters surrounding Guadalcanal. There was a carrier battle in October when the *Enterprise* and the *Hornet* intercepted a Japanese task force approaching Guadalcanal. The *Enterprise* was badly damaged and the *Hornet* was sunk.

The American forces were replaced with fresh units and supplies in December 1942. The Japanese, realizing they could not win, evacuated the island on the first week of February 1943.

The battle for Guadalcanal became a psychological victory for the Allies and was the first time the Japanese had experienced defeat after they had had an unbroken string of victories. The threat to Australia had been removed. Sad, but true, every victory has its cost, and Guadalcanal cost 4,407 lives.

It soon became evident after the Pearl Harbor attack that the war in the Pacific was going to be fought with greater ferocity than the war in Europe. In the United States, the political cartoons, the movies, and the fiction writers were increasing the feeling that the Japanese were fanatics. But Japan was doing the same thing about the American people. In both countries racism and cultural differences were intensified. As these ideas permeated the American culture it made the military fight harder and it made the people on the home front more fearful.

After the Japanese attack on Pearl Harbor, there was fear that the Japanese people living on the west coast of the United States were involved in sabotage or espionage. The fear developed into panic, regardless of the fact that no Japanese-Americans were proven to have been involved in any subversive activities. The Japanese-Americans became scapegoats as unsubstantiated rumors were circulated. Lieutenant General John L. DeWitt was ordered to oversee the evacuation of 110,000 Japanese-Americans being transported and placed in internment camps that were located in seven different states. Sixty percent of these people were American citizens, and 40,000 of them were children. Most of the Japanese families were forced to sell their property and possessions at ridiculously low prices and then were taken to one of these camps to live in inadequate housing behind barbed wire fencing.

The program of relocation began to be phased out late in the war. Most of the government officials that participated in placing the Japanese-Americans in the internment camps later regretted their actions. In 1982, forty years after the Executive Order 9066 on Wartime Relocation and Internment of Citizens became law, the Congress of the United States issued a report condemning the relocation policy. They placed the blame on racial prejudice, war hysteria, and actions of political law-makers who did not comprehend the inhumanity of the law they passed. In 1988, Congress compensated the Japanese-American internees each $20,000, but no amount of money and no governmental apology can compensate the internees for the humiliation and the unjustified treatment they received.

# China Unstable Ally of the United States

President Roosevelt was very much aware of the problems involved in keeping China as a strong ally that would vigorously support the United States. Chiang Kai Shek presided over the unstable Chinese Nationalist government and was constantly being challenged by the communist movement within his country. After the Japanese attack on Pearl Harbor, Roosevelt believed that America needed to help China remain strong in order for China to provide air bases for America to launch a final assault on the Japanese home islands.

Chiang knew the Americans were going to fight the Japanese, regardless if China helped or not. Chiang did just enough to pacify the United States and to insure that China would continue to receive lend-lease aid.

The Japanese had taken control of large areas in northern China and many of China's coastal cities. The Chinese were not able to force the Japanese from their tenacious grip on part of China's territory. The inability of the Chinese to show the required strength to take a leading position resulted in Roosevelt sending General Joseph W. "Vinegar Joe" Stilwell to China, as commander of the United States forces in the China-Burma-India theater. Stilwell was to also act as an advisor to Chiang and his Nationalist government.

Stilwell had been chosen for the position of commander because he spoke the language, he was a capable officer and had been in China before. He was very outspoken, but was unable to persuade Chiang to mount offensives against the Japanese. The two men quarreled and Stilwell could not hide his lack of respect for the weak Chinese leader and his inept army, which was badly trained, poorly equipped, underfed and completely lacking in motivation to fight. The Chinese officers frequently beat their soldiers, which might have accounted for their lack of motivation to fight. Chiang could not be moved to take the initiative against the Japanese and it was obvious that all he wanted was more and more aid from the United States.

In the 1930s Chiang had hired General Claire Chennault to command China's air forces. Chennault had retired from the United States

Army Air Force prior to his appointment in China. In 1941 he received permission from Roosevelt to form the American Volunteer Group, also known as the Flying Tigers (AVG). The Flying Tigers fought on the side of China's Chiang Kai Shek against Japan. The Flying Tigers soon developed an impressive reputation because of their numerous successes in their encounters with the Japanese after the attack on Pearl Harbor.

Chennault made exaggerated claims to President Roosevelt of what he could accomplish, such as defeating the Japanese in one year. The result of this was that supplies that were to go to Stilwell were instead diverted to Chennault. Chennault was given the command of the newly formed Fourteenth Air Force and was given first priority of the supplies coming in over the Himalayas, the "hump," as the Americans called it.

American fighter pilots outperformed the Japanese when they were confronted by an equal number of planes, but they did not achieve control of the air. Fuel for the heavy bombers was scarce and repeated Japanese bombing raids forced Chennault to give up airfields.

In April 1944, the Japanese successes in their offensives in eastern China were very alarming to General Marshall and he requested that Roosevelt demand that Chiang place Chinese forces under Stilwell's command. Chiang agreed, but he insisted that the forces be placed under a different general's command.

Roosevelt, not wishing to alienate Chiang, recalled Stilwell and replaced him with General Albert C. Wedemeyer. Although Wedemeyer was able to get along with Chiang, the Chinese forces still were not motivated to fight. General Wedemeyer quietly removed Chennault of his command after Roosevelt's death.

The United States sent engineers, construction personnel, and air units to China, but only a small number of ground forces. The famous 5307th Provisional Regiment, known as Merrill's Marauders, consisting of all volunteers under the command of Brigadier General Frank Merrill, were sent to help the British and the Chinese clear northern Burma. In 1944 the Marauders marched one hundred miles and surprised the Japanese by blocking their only supply line into the Hukawng Valley. The success in north Burma shortened the air supply route to China. There were newly built pipelines running parallel to a new road which were carrying much needed aviation fuel. The increased delivery of supplies did not seem to help improve the Chinese military performance.

The biggest benefit that came from the United States sending supplies to China was that it kept the Chinese fighting the Japanese. The fact that the Japanese needed to expend resources and men against the Chinese diverted some of their supplies and attention away from fighting the United States.

Chiang appeared to be unable, or perhaps unwilling, to reform the Chinese Nationalist Party, which was plagued with corruption. Chiang received much of his power and money from rogue-type warlords who abused and took money from the Chinese peasants. The United States military planners realistically knew that no matter how much financial aid they gave to China, they could not depend on the Chinese when their help would be needed. Therefore, they discarded the idea of using China as a staging area for the intended invasion of Japan. Eventually, the Chinese Communists became successful in unifying the people within China and they chased Chiang and his disreputable followers from mainland China to Formosa (Taiwan).

# Pacific Encounters 1943–1944

America's production of necessary wartime equipment was now increasing at a phenomenal rate that the Japanese would never be able to match. America had to come from behind in this war, but was now moving ahead. The powerful fighter planes such as the P-38 Lightning, the F6F Hellcat, and the F4U Corsair were coming out of the defense plants in unbelievable numbers and were being delivered quickly to the military. The Navy was beginning to receive faster aircraft carriers and battleships. About this time the proximity fuse was developed which was radio controlled and it made shells explode if they came even close to the target. Also, at this time the cryptographers were working constantly on decoding enemy messages, which gave the Allies a heads up on critical enemy plans. The Japanese and the Germans did not know that the Allies had this decoding capability.

The Allies discovered that Germany was perfecting new weapons of mass destruction that could easily defeat the Allies. The knowledge of this possibility made Roosevelt, Churchill, and Stalin that much more determined to have the primary military objective be that of eliminating Hitler first. Most of the commanders understood the reasoning, but that did not prevent MacArthur from attempting to get as much as he could for his troops in the Pacific Theater.

The war in the Pacific Theater had to be waged over vast expanses of land, oceans and air, and traditional military procedures would not apply in routing the enemy out of their strongholds. The shipping and transportation of food, munitions and medicines to the scattered Pacific Theater outposts was a very difficult job, but these critically needed supplies were now arriving in a more timely manner.

By January 1943 with the seizure of Guadalcanal and the Papuan peninsula accomplished, the Joint Chiefs of Staff planned the campaign, code named CARTWHEEL, for the next offensives in the Pacific Theater. General MacArthur was put in command of this operation and was to proceed up the eastern coast of New Guinea. Admiral Halsey was to advance up the Solomon Island chain to Bougainville. While these plans were being made, the Japanese were also making plans.

They sent eight troop transports and eight destroyers to reinforce their positions on New Guinea.

On March 2nd, the Americans attacked the incoming Japanese reinforcements with B-17 bombers and sunk two of their transports. The next day General George C. Kenney sent in a force of medium bombers and fighters against the Japanese convoy. The American pilots sank four destroyers and all the Japanese transports. This battle was named the Battle of the Bismark Sea, and General Kenney's innovative tactics were used during the rest of the war. The Japanese soon realized that they needed to change their way of supplying their troops, and thereafter they began using submarines, air transports, and barges for those purposes. However, the Japanese were feeling shortages during the rest of the campaign.

Admiral Yamamoto launched air strikes against the Allies, but his pilots were inexperienced and they did little damage. The Japanese squadrons reported back to their superior officers and exaggerated the results of their raids. Yamamoto was very pleased with what he thought were excellent achievements by his airmen and he planned a visit to personally thank them. American intelligence decrypted the reports and they set a trap. As Yamamoto's plane and fighter escorts approached the island, eighteen American P-38's greeted him, and the bomber he was in went down in flames. The Japanese people mourned the loss of their hero and it was a significant loss to the Japanese high command.

In late June CARTWHEEL began with American and Australian forces going up the eastern coast of New Guinea. Admiral Halsey's first objective was the Island of New Georgia. Both MacArthur's and Halsey's objectives met fierce resistance. Again the fighting took place in dense jungles with the same tropical diseases, insects and heat taking its toll on the energy level of the military.

The Japanese at this time were fighting from fortified positions and they defended themselves down to the last man. Flamethrowers became the only way to remove the Japanese from their strongholds.

Summer came and then fall and MacArthur and Halsey were moving in closer to Rabaul. Halsey had the choice of which islands to cut off from their supplies and which islands to take and convert to air bases from which bombing missions could be launched.

The navy was now doing much better with their training in night operations and their use of radar, plus they were now receiving improved torpedoes. The American pilots were improving their performance against the outdated Japanese planes and inadequately trained pilots. The quality of the munitions being sent was vastly improved, thanks to the diligence of the people on the home front.

The Third Marine Division was put ashore on Bougainville on November 1st. The Japanese sent a task force from Rabaul to sink ships in the harbor and shell the beachhead, but the Japanese offensive was repelled by American destroyers and cruisers. Halsey learned from decrypted messages that the Japanese were amassing a large naval force to send against the Americans on Bouganville, and he began planning accordingly.

Halsey ordered a carrier attack on the large Japanese base at Rabaul and took out three Japanese cruisers and three destroyers. Again he attacked the Japanese base and they suffered such great losses that they retreated from the base. Within a short time American bombers were flying from airfields within the American perimeter and began pounding Rabaul.

In late December, MacArthur's soldiers and marines landed on the western end of New Britain and captured another airbase from which they could strike at Rabaul. At this time it became clear there was no need to seize Rabaul because it had been rendered inactive. There were a few clean-up operations and a few more islands to seize and the CARTWHEEL campaign was completed. Rabaul was no longer an objective and the new objective became the Philippines.

Another American operation was put into place before CARTWHEEL was finished, and that was the objective to seize a chain of islands in the central Pacific that would be within bombing range of Japan and that could be used as staging areas for an invasion. The rapidly increasing numbers of carriers and battleships being built and ready for use made these objectives feasible.

There were more than a thousand islands and not all needed to be fought over, only those which had air bases already on them, or where bases could be easily built. With the Americans strongly entrenched on a portion of these islands, it would cut off the supplies to the islands the Japanese held and would render them useless. However, the islands that had strategic value were heavily fortified. Most of these islands were clustered around lagoons where the beaches were located, making it difficult because incoming landing parties would have to advance directly into their firepower.

The first objectives were two islands in the Gilbert Chain, Tarawa, located in the center, and Makin located at the northwestern end. Tarawa was the most heavily fortified of the two islands and there were

69

approximately 5,000 Japanese troops on the atoll, most of them on the island of Betio. Admiral Raymond A. Spruance commanded the Fifth Fleet and was in charge of the operation. Shortly after midnight on November 20th, a force of three battleships, three heavy cruisers, five escort carriers, twenty-one destroyers, seventeen troop and cargo ships made an awesome display of power. The Second Marine Division carried out the assault.

At dawn the battleships, cruisers, and destroyers began bombing and shelling the atoll. The bombardment would lift just long enough to allow air strikes from the carriers. The barrage was timed to end just before the landing craft were to begin hitting the beaches.

Very little went according to plan. The first salvos fired by the flagship, *Maryland*, knocked its own communications center out, which rendered the commander unable to communicate with the other ships. The landing craft did not reach the beaches according to schedule and the commander could not restart the bombing or the air strikes to give cover to the landing parties. High winds, strong currents, and rough seas gave the men on the amphibious landing tractors (LTVs) a lot of trouble as they struggled to reach land. The Japanese opened fire on them and hundreds were killed or wounded.

The men following the first wave, because there were not enough landing craft to go around, had to wade ashore, and many drowned because of the weight of their packs. Succeeding waves met the same fate. A thin beachhead was established, and luckily the Japanese could not launch a counterattack that night because their communications center had been destroyed by the earlier bombardment. The marines suffered 1,500 casualties out of 5,000 men.

The battle for Tarawa continued for three more days. Reserve forces were sent on the fourth day and they also had to wade ashore under heavy fire. The Japanese were located in heavily fortified positions and could only be chased out by using flamethrowers and hand-thrown explosives. On November 22nd the Japanese surprised the marines with a suicide charge up against the marine lines. Small pockets of resistance were quickly eliminated and the island was declared secure by 1:30 in the afternoon of November 23, 1943.

Inexperienced National Guardsmen were sent into the battle of Makin and they were not trained for this type of warfare. It took them four days to accomplish what they should have done in two days, had they been better prepared. The extra two days resulted in the loss of an escort carrier that had remained offshore to provide them support. It was sunk by a Japanese submarine.

The American people were very disturbed when they heard about the slaughter at Tarawa. The marines had suffered 3,000 casualties on an atoll that was only a speck on a map. Pictures of mangled bodies of America's fine young men lying on the beaches were a grim reminder of the actualities of being in combat. The shocked Americans were made aware that the war in the Pacific would not be easily won without costing more human lives.

Tarawa gave the military commanders some bitter lessons to keep in mind as they prepared for the Marshalls, the next chain of islands to be secured. Future campaigns would improve fire control, there would be directing of traffic on the beaches, they would use more effective equipment, and the LTVs would be armored. It was obvious that they had underestimated the tenacity of the Japanese and that they did not realize the strength of their fortifications and their ability to sustain continuous air and sea bombardment.

The planning for the invasion of the Marshall Islands had begun before Tarawa and Makin were secured. Admiral Nimitz decided that the huge atoll of Kwajalein would be next. He ordered air strikes against the Marshalls from Tarawa and Makin to prevent interference from the numerous Japanese bases that were within striking distance. In January 1944 Admiral Mark A. Mitscher was given command of the Fifth Fleet, Task Force 58. He had twelve fast carriers under his command and they bombed Japanese installations throughout the islands and eliminated Japanese air power that could be a threat to the planned American invasion of Kwajalein.

Many lessons had been learned at Tarawa that proved helpful in the assault against Kwajalein. Aircraft carriers, cruisers, destroyers, and battleships were offshore for three days of continuous bombing of the Japanese on Kwajalein. The timing was precise with bombardments moving inland only minutes before the arrival of the first waves reaching the beach. The entire atoll was secured by February 4, 1944. The Japanese lost more than 7,000 men and the American casualties were 400 killed in action and 1,500 wounded.

The fact that the operation at Kwajalein went so well resulted in the date to invade Eniwitok, at the northwestern end of the Marshalls, being moved from May to February, thereby not giving the Japanese time to build up their defenses.

A possible dangerous situation existed in attacking Eniwitok, which was a very large Japanese naval base at Truk, which was less than 700 miles west. This base could handle 400 planes, and it contained submarine facilities. The location of the islands and the coral reef at Truk gave protection and anchorage against surface attacks. Mitscher's Task Force 58 was given the job of neutralizing Truk, which would be the first major assault operation carried out exclusively by carrier-based aircraft. On February 17th and 18th he made thirty strikes at Truk. Fighters were sent in first to take out those enemy planes that would try to intercept, and then they bombed and strafed the landing fields. After the Japanese could not use any of their air defenses, the American airmen went after the ships that were at anchor. The American battleships and cruisers that were waiting outside the harbor sank any Japanese ships that attempted to escape. Truk was in ruins and could not be used as a naval base again. The Americans lost thirty aircraft and one carrier sustained minor damage.

While Mitscher was busy pounding Truk, the American forces went in on Eniwitok in a smaller version of what happened on Kwajalein. The Japanese fought fiercely but they were outnumbered and out matched in firepower. The entire Japanese garrison of 3,000 men was killed. America lost 184 men and had 540 wounded.

Planning immediately began for an offensive against the Mariana Islands, which are located 1,000 miles northwest of Eniwitok. Three large islands, Saipan, Tinian and Guam are located in the Marianas and their capture would provide airfields from which American B-29 Superfortresses could bomb Japan's main islands.

The previous military advances had been rapid across the Pacific, better than anyone had predicted, but now the men had to be rested, replacements trained, equipment repaired and supplies brought in. The commanders in the Pacific were still having to compete with the European Theater for their supplies, and the closer they got to Japan, the more critical it would be to have all the supplies they needed delivered to them in a timely manner.

The American successes made the Japanese change their thinking. They had suffered heavy losses and they now realized that they could not defend their far-flung empire. They would now create an "absolute national defense sphere" of much smaller proportions and they would defend it at all costs. Within this inner ring they could consolidate their naval, air and ground forces. The Mariana Islands lay within the "absolute national defense sphere."

In June 1944 the American forces rendezvoused in the middle of the Pacific Ocean and then began to head for the Marianas. Admiral Spruance was in charge of this operation, which consisted of 500 American ships carrying 127,000 men and was to be the largest amphibious assault against the Japanese. Saipan was only 1,200 miles from Tokyo and would prove to be a challenge in many ways. After four days of air strikes and naval bombardment the troops went ashore and ships provided fire support. Intelligence had underestimated the number of Japanese troops on the island. Their fortifications were not ready because the Americans had arrived before they expected them.

Saipan was six miles long and four miles wide and was another one of the ubiquitous Pacific islands that was covered with an amalgam of jungles, swamps, and steep mountains honeycombed with caves, and surrounded with coral reefs.

General Holland M. (Howlin' Mad) Smith was commander of the ground operation. There were 32,000 Japanese men that had been dispersed to several possible landing sites. Smith's plans did not go well. The Japanese artillery was a serious impediment to the Americans to get to the beach and then to establish a beachhead. There were heavy casualties and it took a week to extend the beachhead, to bring in reserve units, and to prepare to go on with the assault.

Saipan became a bloody battle. Due to a division commander not moving as fast as he was supposed to, it left some American troops exposed to enemy fire. Eventually, Smith, with Spruance's approval, relieved the commander of his duties. Army officers were infuriated that a marine general thought he could sack an army division commander, and the dispute had many repercussions all the way back to the United States and the press.

The Japanese were gradually pushed to a far corner of the island. On the night of July 6th the Japanese staged the largest banzai attack of the war, as thousands of screaming Japanese soldiers charged the sector that the 27th Army Division occupied.

They had no chance of victory so they charged into the American lines and created a massacre of monumental proportions. When daylight arrived the American soldiers counted 4,000 dead Japanese bodies. The United States lost 3,400 men and there were 13,000 wounded. Japan lost their entire garrison of 32,000.

Many Japanese civilians had moved to Saipan because they wanted to stay in Japan's "defensive perimeter." As the end drew near for the Japanese soldiers, the civilians began committing suicide before the stunned Americans. Although the Americans tried to stop them, they could not. Some used guns, or hand grenades, some jumped off cliffs and others just waded into the ocean. Parents killed their children who were too young to know what was happening. There were approximately 9,000 civilians that died this way.

On the 16th of June an American submarine reported seeing a Japanese battle fleet heading for Saipan. The fleet was commanded by Vice Admiral Ozawa Jisaburo and consisted of five heavy and four light carriers, five battleships, thirteen cruisers, and twenty-eight destroyers. Admiral Mitscher's Task Force 58, consisted of four carrier groups, one battleship, seven heavy and eight light carriers, twenty-one cruisers and sixty-nine destroyers. The battle between the two fleets began on July 9th.

The American pilots shot down more than 300 Japanese aircraft and only lost thirty of their own. Formally the battle is named "The Battle of the Philippine Sea," informally it is known as the "Great Marianas Turkey Shoot." This battle practically destroyed the Japanese naval air strength. The Japanese lost more than 400 planes, and about the same number of pilots. When the Japanese fleet left the water near Saipan, they had only thirty-five usable aircraft.

The Japanese had taken possession of Guam several days after their attack on Pearl Harbor on December 7th, 1941. The Americans now invaded Guam on July 21, 1944. The combined forces of the Third Marine Division, the First Provisional Marine Brigade, and the 77th Army Division encountered fierce resistance from the 19,000 Japanese men stationed there.

On July 26th, the Japanese launched an all-out banzai attack on the American lines. They broke through the lines in a few places, but the suicide charges drained any hope of success to oppose the Americans. There was some clearing out of pockets of resistance that took until August 10th. The United States suffered casualties at Guam of 8,000 and the Japanese were almost totally annihilated.

There was an unexpected bonus with the battle of Guam as the Japanese had used the island as a supply depot for alcoholic beverages in that part of the Pacific. The American soldiers and marines were delighted with the capture of thousands of cases of whiskey, sake, and beer.

Tinian had fallen a week earlier. The Americans had feinted an attack near Tinian Town where the Japanese expected an assault because of suitable beaches there, but then the Americans landed on the other end of the island. The Japanese assaults were hurled back with heavy losses. They then retreated to the southern tip of the island where the inevitable suicides began all over again with only a small number of prisoners taken.

The capture of the Marianas pierced Japan's inner ring of defense and gave the United States air bases within range of Japan's home islands. About the same time the British in Burma started the first B-29 raids from China. On July 18th Togo Hideki was forced to resign as premier and a new Japanese cabinet was formed. There were Japanese politicians who realized the war was lost, but the military people had the control and the power and would not permit these sentiments to be expressed publicly.

General MacArthur continued his advances northward during the spring and summer of 1944. Again, he was aided by code decryptions that kept him informed about the location of the Japanese troops.

The Allies had captured many landing sites as they advanced, but many were on soft ground and were unsuitable for the large bombers. Biak had conditions more suitable for airfields that could accommodate the larger bombers. The 41st Army Division was scheduled to invade Biak on May 27th, 1944. The Japanese troop strength had been underestimated by the intelligence and the American troops got caught in an ambush. There were steep cliffs pocked with many caves that looked down on the airfield. The Japanese pinned down the attackers and inflicted heavy casualties. Reinforcements arrived and one battalion was evacuated at night by amtracs, and it took one week to capture the airfield. After constant exhortations from his superior officers, the commander asked to be relieved of his assignment.

The Japanese had built a task force around their giant battleships *Yamato* and *Musashi* and had sent them to defend Biak. Fortunately for the American troops there, the Japanese canceled their sortie because at this time Task Force 58 had been launched in the Marianas and the *Yamato* and *Musashi* were ordered to go to the Philippine Sea.

President Roosevelt traveled to Pearl Harbor in late July to confer with his Pacific Theater commanders, General MacArthur and Admiral

Nimitz. Roosevelt had just been nominated for a fourth term and he wanted to appear to be an active commander-in-chief of the American forces advancing on many fronts. MacArthur had always managed his own publicity very carefully, and gave the impression that he was almost single handedly winning the war. MacArthur detested Roosevelt and he felt that at this meeting his popularity was being exploited by the president.

The main topics discussed at the Pearl Harbor meeting were about the future operations against Japan. There were three sites possible, the southern coast of China, Formosa, or the Philippines. China was eliminated because the Chinese Nationalist government was unreliable. Nimitz argued for Formosa. He thought seizing more bases in the Philippines would be too costly in men and resources. MacArthur spoke eloquently on behalf of the Philippines and stated that the United States had an obligation to liberate the Filipino people and the American prisoners of war there as quickly as possible. He claimed that when he was alone with Roosevelt he told him that bypassing the Philippines would anger the Americans and could negatively affect Roosevelt's election in November. It cannot be corroborated, but Roosevelt did go with MacArthur's ideas.

MacArthur had promised the Filipino people, "I shall return," and in fact the invasion of and operations from the Philippines would fall directly under MacArthur's jurisdiction.

The decision was to bypass Mindanao and to assault Leyte in October in the central Philippines. Before moving against the Philippines the United States conducted a series of carrier raids, but the air battles were very one sided and the Japanese could not match the American equipment and forces. The Americans attacked Peleliu, a coral atoll, and the Japanese were entrenched in caves. The fighting went on for months and 6,000 American men lost their lives.

The invasion of Leyte on October 20, 1944 involved 160,000 men on four separate beachheads and the Japanese only put up light resistance because they were saving their strength for counterattacks later. In the early afternoon General MacArthur went ashore, and because the landing craft he was in drew too much water to make it to the beach, he and his landing party had to wade the last few yards. Many pictures and movies have shown this historic moment throughout the United States. After arriving there he made a radio broadcast beginning with the words, "People of the Philippines, I have returned!" A dramatic

76

moment to be sure—but it also showed that modesty was not one of MacArthur's stronger characteristics.

The Battle of Leyte Gulf began on October 23rd and lasted for two days. The Japanese had four aircraft carriers left with only a few planes on each. They planned to lure the American carriers to where they had two task forces and then they would sink them. Their plan almost worked.

Admiral Halsey's Third and Admiral Kincaid's Seventh Fleets outfoxed, out-maneuvered, and out-equipped the Japanese, and again the Japanese suffered tremendously high losses. Japan lost four carriers, three battleships, ten cruisers, and eleven destroyers. The United States lost the carrier *Princeton* and a number of smaller ships. The Battle of Leyte Gulf broke the viability of the Japanese fleet.

On the last day of the battle, Japan employed a new weapon that had ominous implications for the future—the "kamikazi," which means "divine wind" and refers to a typhoon that came at the fortuitous time to prevent a Chinese invasion centuries earlier. The kamikazis were suicide units who would fly their bomb-laden aircraft directly into American ships, they preferred aircraft carriers, or troop transports. The advantage of using kamikazis was that little flight training was needed, obsolete planes could be used and they had to be blown out of the air to be stopped. The Americans realized that squadrons of kamikazis would be difficult to deal with. America felt that the use of this type of weapon reinforced the feeling that the Japanese were a fanatical race.

The Japanese were sending reinforcements and supplies from Luzon to the port of Ormac. Bloody fighting took place at Ormac and it was December 10th before the resistance ended, although there were still some Japanese in the mountains.

The victory on Leyte had taken longer than anticipated and had caused critical losses in the navy. Before Leyte was secured American forces had taken Mindaro, a smaller island just south of Luzon. Landing of troops was virtually unopposed, but the fleet had taken a severe battering from land-based kamikazis. The end of 1944 saw the United States preparing for the final campaign in the Philippines, where they had suffered a catastrophic defeat in 1942.

# Frederick Mills, Music Teacher, Serves in the Pacific Theater

Frederick E. Mills was born in Mount Vernon, Ohio. He has two sisters, one older and one younger than he. He received a Bachelor of Arts degree in Music Education from Ohio University and was teaching instrumental and vocal music in Dunkirk High School, (Hardin-Northern). Despite the fact he was the sole support of his widowed mother, he was drafted into the United States Army Infantry, on May 11, 1942.

From the time I went into the service I thought I wanted to be a warrant officer, but I never made it. They said I didn't weigh enough, but I did make it as a tech-sergeant and was trained in radar installation and repair. I was sent to New Guinea and was assigned to a radar unit.

Most of New Guinea was covered with dense tropical jungles, but there was a high mountain range running down through the center of the island. The climate was hot and humid. Our radar equipment was made in Canada and it did not work well in the hot humid climate. We had a lot of trouble with it.

The Japanese occupied New Guinea and were mainly up in the high mountains. They had plans to use New Guinea as a base to help them invade Australia. The American soldiers were sent into New Guinea to help protect the Americans in the 5th Army Air Force there. I went in on the third wave and the Japanese were hiding and then they let loose on us. Oh, it was bad! The youngest guy in our outfit was killed on Wakde Island. That was terrible! He was standing right behind me—he should have been behind our big truck.

The jungle warfare created specific problems. Sometimes it was difficult to get needed supplies to us. Transportation was very difficult. There were debilitating jungle-related illnesses and fevers. I had some fevers and was jaundiced for awhile. Sometimes our senior officers would get us lost. There is nothing like being lost in a jungle and not knowing where your enemy is. And this went on and on.

We kept going from one island to another. We had moved into the Trobriand Islands close to Rabaul. One day I heard singing. The voices blended beautifully in four-part harmony. It sounded very good. I discovered a group of about fifteen native workers taking a break. They were sitting around in a circle and were singing. I thought, *what am I getting into here?* I was fortunate to be able to carry my clarinet with me, so I got my clarinet out and started to play. I played with them—they acted as if they enjoyed it. For me, that was a very unique and wonderful experience. I later discovered that missionaries had been in the area before and had taught these people a few hymns.

With some encouragement, I was able to persuade the natives to sing for me. Can you imagine what it looked like there in a clearing in the jungle, an American soldier accompanying a group of native voices singing, "Onward Christian Solders" and also other well-known hymns? I was then able to persuade these very modest people to sing some of their own songs. They had a greeting song, which if translated in English, seemed to be a greeting to the "Dim Dim" (white soldier).

There was a vacant mission located on the side of a mountain, and it was a very interesting place. There was a lot of teakwood there and some of the men wanted to take a piece of that wood with them as a memento and a carving project for in the future. I didn't take any because the wood was very heavy. While up at the mission we had a good view of the sea below. One day we saw ships coming. They just kept coming, more and more of them, and then a naval battle began between the U.S. Navy and the Japanese Navy. It was unbelievable to be able to watch all that action from our safe vantage point high on that hill. I don't know any particulars about that battle.

While we were up at the mission, the commanding officer (C.O.) of our unit came riding up on a small Japanese horse. He said the horse probably belonged to a Japanese officer and he had left it there. Our C.O. showed us how he could make the horse kneel down to help the rider dismount. He always knew something about everything. Eventually, the horse just wandered off.

We kept getting sent on to different islands, always going farther north, we were at Hollandia, and as usual, there were Japanese there. We always had to contend with the Japanese—it was a never-ending job. Eventually, after much bitter jungle warfare by the American and Australian troops, we broke the Japanese hold on New Guinea.

Later some of us were sent to a rest camp at Orando. A bunch of young, green soldiers were there. They talked all the time. They hadn't been anyplace in battle. They were told they had to do KP and they said, "No, this is a rest camp." They didn't understand anything about duties and security. Our radar group had been through a lot and the young talkative kids got on our nerves. I didn't mind doing KP.

When I got back to my radar outfit I found out that my latest request for warrant officer didn't get approved, although my C.O.'s recommendation stated that I had integrity, intelligence and a sense of responsibility. I had tried to be a good soldier, but two years on the islands and in the jungles made me think I needed a change. I applied for Special Services and was transferred to the 11th Special Services Company.

I had to give up my rank as tech sergeant when I joined Special Services. All I now had was my clarinet. I was in a band of about twelve men. Many times we performed on a makeshift stage on the back of an army truck. Most of the time I played a baritone saxophone, and sometimes I played clarinet or flute. There were times we performed very close to battlefields. One time when we got off a ship in Manila we had to run for our lives because we were being strafed. I thought to myself, "I left a good outfit for this!"

About this time, I began having very painful toothaches. If there would be a military dentist nearby I would go see them. Their only treatment for me was to extract the aching teeth. I left quite a few teeth in the Pacific Theater during WWII.

Once our band was going into Luzon to play. We were on a troop ship. The ship's officers had received word that there was trouble ahead and that they should speed up and hurry the disembarking process. We heard over the speaker system, "Now hear this—Now hear this—disembark immediately!" The problem was a kamikaze plane. It was too late! There was a loud noise as the plane dove into the troop ship and its nose was buried through the upper deck. A prayer of thanks went up because the Japanese pilot delivered a torpedo that was a dud and it did not explode. The Japanese pilot was dead and I can still see his face and his ceremonial scarf laying across his shoulder. Just as we realized what all had happened, the engineer from below decks, came running up on top deck with blood on his head and running down his face, yelling, "Please, Sir, we need some help down below! We have men injured down below." This was the period of time that the Japanese kamikazes were making every effort trying to keep the American troops from landing in the Philippines. I was extremely lucky in this case.

The band went to Clark Field and other places in the Philippines. We also played in Okinawa after the Americans liberated it. Once during Christmas time, the band was playing for a group of paratroopers. They had just experienced a really tough assignment and had lost some of their men. When we started to play the Christmas songs they got very quiet. Soon the exhausted and heavy-hearted paratroopers were becoming emotional and beginning to cry. It was all the band members could do to keep on playing because they too were feeling emotional. It was a sad time.

I saw the *Enola Gay*, the plane that was on its way to drop the atomic bomb. When we heard that Japan had surrendered, our officers called us together and tried to get us to enlist in the occupation army. I jumped on top of a table and I told them, "I have the points and I'm going home!"

I'm glad I served, but I was ready to go home. I did my part, but war always leaves mental scars that can't be erased. I often think about our radar outfit. It was a great bunch of guys. We were on our own—but we got the work done that we were assigned to do.

I served three years and seven months and was honorably discharged on December 4, 1945. My discharge papers noted that I was awarded a total of five Bronze Stars: four Bronze Stars for serving in the Asiatic-Pacific Theater and one Bronze Star for serving in the Philippine Liberation.

✽　　✽　　✽

Upon re-entering civilian life, Frederick enrolled at Columbia University and received his Master of Arts Degree in Instrumental Music Supervision. At Columbia University, Frederick Mills met the very talented and accomplished pianist, Berniece June Warner, and they were married a year later. They were blessed with two sons, Frederick and Richard. Son Frederick is a molecular scientist at Bethesda, MD. Son Richard is a composer, private music teacher and instructor at the American Continental University in Atlanta, Georgia.

Frederick and Berniece moved to Lima, Ohio, in 1948, and became very active in the music organizations of that city. Frederick was a member of a committee of four, in 1953, that organized the Lima Symphony Orchestra. He played the cello in the symphony orchestra for forty years. He also taught music at Shawnee Local Schools for thirty-two years. He won the praise of hundreds of young parents when he taught their pre-school and elementary age children to play the violin by the Suzuki method. Mr. Mills is "Mr. Music" in the Lima area.

Two quotes that reflect the thinking of Frederick Mills:

So long as the human spirit thrives on this planet, music in some living form will accompany and sustain it and give it expressive meaning.
—Aaron Copland

No education is complete without awareness of music; music is an essential expression of the character of society.
—William J. Bennett

# Mr. X, U.S. Navy, Torpedo Man on PT Boat

My interview with Mr. X was granted with the understanding that I would not reveal his name or take any pictures. When I asked if I could take a picture of his Silver Star award, I received an emphatic reply of "No!" With these understandings agreed upon, the interview proceeded.

Mr. X began his story, as follows:

My mother emigrated from Czechoslovakia and my father emigrated from Serbia, Yugoslavia. My father died when I was four years old. I'm proud to say that I am an American!

Later my mother remarried, we lived on a farm and I learned about hard work by helping with the farm work. It was during the depression years and there was very little money. I tried to earn extra money by helping farmers, but I only earned about $1.00 a day. I went to St. Gerard School, but I became discouraged and dropped out of school in ninth grade. It was 1935, and I enlisted for four years in the United States Navy. In the navy I earned $21.00 a month and received board, room and uniforms.

I was in boot camp at Norfolk, Virginia, and then I served two years on a 4-piper, called *The Zane*, six months on the destroyer, *The Tucker*, and then six months on another destroyer, *The Porter*. Destroyers are called tin cans and I liked serving on the tin cans. In 1939 when I got out of the navy, I tried to find work and I decided that since I knew a lot about ships, I would go to California and work in the shipyards. I was sure I could earn more money there than I could earn working for farmers. Immediately after the attack on Pearl Harbor, Uncle Sam came looking for me and wanted me back in the navy, so I went back and signed up for another four years. I was sent to torpedo school in Newport, Rhode Island.

After torpedo school I was sent to the South Pacific and became part of a crew on a PT boat, at the PT base in Tulagi. Tulagi is a small island, next to Florida Island and just seventeen miles north of Guadalcanal. We saw a lot of action in Iron Bottom Sound between

Tulagi and Guadalcanal. Our PT boats were eighty feet long, made of three-quarter inch laminated plywood and they were equipped with various armaments and torpedoes. We sometimes carried four torpedoes and sometimes just two torpedoes. The navy was making us use up their old torpedoes before they would send us any new ones. The old ones would not travel straight to the target. With the risks we were taking, I thought they could have sent us the newer torpedoes. I was the Torpedo Man, First Class.

Things weren't going that well for Guadalcanal when I arrived there. We had nightly encounters with the Japanese. They would always come out at night and would try to sneak men and supplies in at that time. It was the objective of the PT crews to keep this from happening. During this time we also rescued quite a few downed American flyers, and ditched American sailors. At first, when we had an encounter with the Japanese and they would end up floundering in the water, we would try to rescue them. But they would swim away from us, or maybe even shoot at us. They did not want to be rescued. They felt it was an honor to die for their emperor, and to be rescued would have been a disgrace for them. We soon learned to let them alone.

There were down times at the base and sometimes we would drain the alcohol out of the torpedoes, distill it, run it off, mix it with coconut milk or orange juice, and drink it. I guess, when you don't have any of the real stuff, you improvise. It was awful stuff and could give you a terrible headache.

When we went out at night in our PT boats it was for the purpose of harassing the Japanese and sinking as many of their ships as we could. These were not easy assignments, as we had to hit-and-run quickly, all the while dodging and zigzagging away from the Japanese searchlights and five-inch salvos. It was sort of like David and Goliath—we were little David with our smaller wooden boats, and the Japanese were Goliath with their larger and heavily armored destroyers. The odds were really stacked against us.

One thing in our favor was that the natives liked us Americans because we were friendly and kind to them and our doctors treated them when they were sick. The natives hated the Japanese because they had been cruel to them and treated them as inferiors. The natives would act as lookouts and report back to us, and when they would find injured and lost Americans they would get them safely to our base. We appreciated what they did for us.

In December 1942, our CO received a message stating that a very important Japanese officer would be arriving on a Japanese sub at a specific time and location. Since we were the only navy in the area, we were given the task to sink the sub. It is my understanding that these orders came from two different admirals, and that this was an important assignment. The plans were carefully made. Two PT boats would be used, and I was in the crew of one of the boats, along with our CO.

Our two boats proceeded parallel with each other toward the target area. It was late and very dark. Just then the skipper on the other boat broke radio silence and asked our CO if he saw the submarine on the surface of the water. The submarine immediately dove. Just then the other PT boat sighted a barge close to it, and the skipper asked what to do about it. Our CO told him to wait until we got out of the way and then strafe it.

Our CO maneuvered our boat out of the way and the other PT boat proceeded to strafe the barge. Just then the sub resurfaced and we immediately sent two torpedoes and sunk the sub. One of our torpedoes passed under the other PT boat on its way to the target. The Japanese only had five I-class subs, and we had just eliminated one of them.

Our CO was awarded the Navy Cross and our crew was each awarded the Silver Star for sinking that sub. Between fifty to sixty men were lost on the Japanese barge, and between eighty to ninety were lost on the submarine. That's all I'm going to say about that.

These were terrible times and I lost a lot of friends in the Pacific. I also left all the blood, guts and gore in the Pacific. I don't want to talk about that. I've spent the rest of my life trying to forget about it. I feel that I'm lucky to have survived the fighting.

Before I went into the navy, I ran around with several guys, and one of them had a younger sister that I liked, but I couldn't get her to go out with me, because she said I was a wildman. When I came home on a four-month furlough, after serving in Tulagi, I discovered she had been writing letters to me which I had never received until I was back in the States. I had changed after my Tulagi experiences, and so had her opinion of me, and we were married in Newport, Rhode Island.

My furlough was soon over, and I was assigned duty on a ship that was working in the Mediterranean area and I was at North Africa, Southern France and Italy, nice duty after my experiences in Tulagi.

When I came back to the States I was happy to be with my wife again, and then I got the news that I was going to be shipped back to the Pacific Theater. I had this nagging thought in my head that I could not shake, that if I went back there again, I would not make it back home alive. I was packing my gear—my wife was crying—and then we heard the news about the dropping of the atomic bombs and that Japan had surrendered.

I'll not forget the day I came home and told my wife that the navy wanted me to sign up for another four-year hitch. She looked into my eyes, and in no uncertain terms said, "Honey, you have to choose—it is either the United States Navy or me!" It was not a hard decision to make because by then I was a happily married man, I had one child and another on the way, and I was ready to become a civilian. I had had my fill of war.

For some reason, I never felt that I deserved the Silver Star. I guess I feel that way because I know other people that deserved it more than I did and some of those people didn't make it back. I feel I was just plain lucky to have come out of the war alive. I see young people today and they don't seem to take the right to vote seriously and that worries me. Maybe they don't really know what we fought for in WWII. But, I feel that if they faced the same circumstances that we did in that war, I think they would rise to the challenges—just like we did.

In closing my story, I just want to say that the Silver Star is not what was important in my life. The important things were that I had a good marriage and three wonderful children, that we had a nice comfortable home, and that I was highly respected as a craftsman in my field. Thanks to my wife, I found peace in going to church with her.

# Another Version of JFK's PT Story

*The following PT story appeared in the book,* Tales of Tulagi, Memoirs of World War II, *as written and published by CDR John M. Searles, USNR, (Ret.) Copyright 1992.*

And then the Kennedy fiasco, PT 109! I have a few thoughts about this collision and here they are for what they are worth. It certainly wasn't Jack's fault that he was assigned to a three-boat patrol, and it may not have been entirely his fault that he became lost from the other two boats, as rain squalls in that area were blacker than the ace of spades. However, later when his radio, which he said was malfunctioning but was working well enough for him to hear his fellow PTs engage the Japanese destroyers, and when he saw all this action a little farther down the Slot from him, he failed to employ sound reasoning. When his ears and eyes had painted this picture for him, he had no choice but to call General Quarters. Then he had two choices of action. Run his PT down the Slot and join his fellow PTs against the DDs (destroyers), or stay in the area he was in, with all engines going and at General Quarters, and hope to get one or two torpedoes into a DD as he retreated up the Slot.

But what did he do? He let most of his crew hit the sack. Apparently he had no lookouts, and whether his engines were turned off or not, I don't know. The impression we got back at Searlesville was that Jack had secured for the night as if he were on a cruise on Long Island Sound. And then the DD cut PT 109 in two. Not the finest hour in World War II PT combat. It has been said that General MacArthur thought Jack should have been court-martialed, but most PT officers believed that was too heavy a punishment and thought he probably should have been transferred out of the PTs.

Then there's the Kennedy myth about how he saved most of his crew and brought them back to my base. Although he was quite resourceful and courageous in his efforts to save his crew, the truth is that they would still be out there on that island if we had not contacted our coast-watchers to send all the natives in the area out searching for them. The fact is that the natives finally found them and brought them back.

The book *PT 109* turned out to be a successful political stepping-stone to the White House. However, it was difficult for a PT skipper to read without raising an eyebrow or two.

# Part Four
# WW II Generation Makes Decisions

# Friends Pondering Their Futures
# in 1942–1943

In 1942, when I was a junior in high school, a friend introduced me to a man named Art Miller. Art was five years older than I and was a graduate of the Los Angeles Trade School in California where he had majored in electronics. He had been raised on a farm about ten miles away from where I lived. He had a great sense of humor and we had a lot of fun together. After several months of dating, we decided not to date anyone else.

Art had two close friends, Willis (Bill) Early and W. James (Jim) Byerly. I observed this triumvirate of Bill, Jim and Art to be the epitome of America's strong healthy young men, each had been raised on a farm, religiously nurtured in a pacifist religion, the Church of the Brethren, and were in their prime time of manhood. When a group of us would get together, Bill and Art would regale the group with tales of their many adventures. Bill and Art were the most daring with their stories of their mishaps on their motorcycles. Jim, a little older and wiser, didn't join his two compatriots on the two-wheeled Indian and Harley Davidson monsters. The bond between these three fellows was strong and they were always there for each other. I admired their energy level and their positive approach to life, and as I got to know them better I was convinced that I wanted to go to college and be as all knowing as I thought they were.

Bill was enrolled at Manchester College at Wabash, Indiana and was in love with a girl named Betty Jane Schul, whom he had met at college. Jim had graduated from college and had his first job as a chemical engineer. He was getting serious about a girl named Barbara Jean Levering, from Middletown where he worked. I had become a part of this group by virtue of dating Art. All three of the guys felt that the draft board would soon be looking for them and they needed to explore their options.

Bill went into the U.S. Air Force Reserves and was studying to become a pilot. Jim went into officer training in the U.S. Navy. Art, with

91

his background in electronics, and knowing that radar was an important technology for the military, enlisted in the Army Reserves in an accelerated and concentrated radar course. Bill married his college sweetheart, Betty. Jim married Jean, his longtime girlfriend from Middletown. I promised to wait for Art until the war was over. In the meantime, I would enroll at Bowling Green State University and major in education. There was a national shortage of teachers and I hoped that I could get into a cadet two-year program and begin teaching at the end of two years. Surely, the war would be over by then and we would get married. But first I had to finish high school. I would come to realize that in wartime, future plans are written in the sand. As the poet Robert Burns said, "The best laid schemes o' mice and men . . ."

# Pacifist Mother Prays When Sons Enlist

Elsie Altstetter married Perry Miller on November 25, 1909. They both came from successful farming families in the Allen County area, and they both had ancestors that settled in Allen County in the early 1830s. Perry and Elsie's farm was located on the historic Lincoln Highway, about ten miles north and east of Lima, Ohio, and had been in the Miller family since 1883. Shortly after the birth of their first child they built their farmhouse from lumber they cut from their own woods. Each year improvements were made and a large barn and other buildings were constructed. The livestock on the farm consisted of ten to twelve cows, three work horses, six brood sows which usually produced a total of approximately forty-eight hogs to market each year. Elsie always raised a large flock of chickens and the eggs she sold provided her with her own spending money. The lifestyle of this hardworking couple was simple and frugal and their social life revolved around their family and church activities.

Elsie and Perry had two sons, Walter and Arthur (Art), and a daughter, Lelia. Everyone in the Miller household inherited a strong work ethic, perhaps coming from being expected from an early age on to assist with the work on the farm. Perry contracted to farm additional acres and expected his sons to assist him with the additional farm work, and the money they earned from this farm work was turned over to their father. After the boys graduated from high school they were each given the opportunity to go on for further schooling. Walter chose the Brethren-related College of Manchester, in Wabash, Indiana, majoring in mathematics and secondary education. When Art's turn came, he chose The National Schools in Los Angeles, majoring in electronics. Perry was upset that Art had chosen a school that far away and that he chose electronics as his major. Perry admonished his son saying, "I do not know why you want to study electronics! You'll starve to death! There is no future in electronics!" However, Perry financed his sons' education in their chosen fields without uttering any more complaints.

Elsie and Perry gave their daughter Lelia the same option for further schooling as they gave their sons. She chose the same college her brother Walter attended. About this same time, Elsie became ill and needed extra help around the house. Lelia dropped out of college to go back home and help her mother. It was not long until she and her fiancé, Robert (Bob) McDowell, decided to marry. Bob would eventually be deferred from military service because he was a farmer. They lived on a farm close to Elsie and Perry's farm and attended the same church and many church functions together. Close family ties were very evident.

Elsie and Perry were devout members of the Pleasant View Church of the Brethren, which is located on Thayer Road, east of Lima, Ohio. The Church of the Brethren was founded in 1708, and stands with the Quakers and the Mennonites as a "peace" church. The Church of the Brethren has opposed war since its beginning in 1708. The Brethren exemplify their belief by the manner of their living, their service to working for peace, advocating justice, serving basic human needs and maintaining the integrity of creation.

Although Elsie and Perry were informed about the war news from Europe, they were hoping that the problems would be settled without the United States sending men over "there" to fight. They had faith that President Roosevelt could keep America out of war. The depression in the 1930s had created financial hardships for them, as well as many other families, and now there was hope that the economic conditions for most families were about to improve. However, everything changed on December 7, 1941, when war came to the United States out of the skies over Pearl Harbor.

The peacetime draft was immediately stepped up to wartime draft status with men being drafted for the "duration" of the war (whenever that might be). Young men of the Brethren faith assessed their religious beliefs, looked in their hearts and tried to make decisions that would agree with their conscience. The young men of Pleasant View Church, and other peace churches, faced this problem in different ways. A small percentage of men acquiesced to the demands of the draft board and were placed in combat within a short period of time. A greater number were farmers and were exempt from serving in the military because the government realized the need for monumental amounts of food to feed the growing numbers in the military forces. A small percentage declared themselves to be conscientious objectors and they volunteered to work in military hospitals and as medics on battlefields, or anywhere they could save lives. The people who possessed certain technical and vital skills enlisted in their chosen branch of military service with the hope they would have at least a limited amount of control over their own destiny. Naïve as this thinking was, they soon discovered that once in the military, there were very few, or no, options left to their own discretion.

Elsie and Perry waited to see what decisions their two sons would make. They did not try to influence them. All around the neighborhood they saw young men being drafted and leaving for military service. The newspapers and radio newscasts were filled with ominous descriptions of the battles taking place in towns and countries they knew little about. Statistics of Americans being killed in action were increasing. The entire country was geared for war, and the time came when Elsie and Perry, pacifist parents, had to face the fact that the country they loved would soon be conscripting their sons to go to war and fight for their country.

By now, Walter was married and had a wife and two toddler sons. He was a math teacher at a high school, but he knew that time was running out and that soon he would be drafted. After searching his heart, he went to his draft board and told them he was actually a conscientious objector, but he told them he wanted to serve his country and help in the war effort in the United States Navy if possible. He passed the physical and was quickly inducted into the Navy. After boot camp, he was trained to install and repair sonar equipment on submarines. His work was almost always in a port, and most of the time he was stationed at Pearl Harbor. At Pearl Harbor he was quartered in a docked submarine, with his bunk next to a torpedo.

Art was working in a factory designing special motors for unusual jobs. He was single and he knew he had better enlist before he would be drafted and not have any control over which branch of the service he would be placed. Art had heard about the highly secret radar technology and the vital part it was playing in England's war with Germany. He thought he would investigate this, thinking his previous training in electronics might be a skill the military needed. His thinking was correct and when he enlisted he was immediately placed in the reserves, in a nine-month concentrated and accelerated course in radar installation and repair. At this time, he was not in uniform and his work was classified, so people had no idea what he was doing and he was not permitted to discuss his training with anyone.

When the time came, Elsie had to face the fact that her two sons, of their own free will, had enlisted in the military and were being prepared to be sent overseas to fight in a war. She experienced the same terrifying fears that other mothers felt when their sons went off to war. And there was that gut-wrenching fear that she might never see them alive again, which she likened to something gnawing at her stomach every waking hour.

Elsie was perplexed because she could not keep from telling other people with a tinge of pride in her voice that she had two sons somewhere overseas who were serving their country. Elsie wondered if she was wrong to be pleased that they were doing their part in fulfilling the military demands placed upon them by their country. Deep in her conscience she worried if what her sons were doing and her own feelings would pass the approval of God. This was a test of faith that Elsie feared that they might all be failing.

Once Elsie's sons were overseas the censors checked all their mail and blackened out every attempt they made to tell their mother what they were doing and where they were. There was no way that Elsie's sons could tell their mother that they had each been given non-combatant duties, and everyday Elsie continued to pray for their safety and for the war to end.

Elsie and Perry were good citizens and they valued the freedoms the people have in the United States. They might have been pacifists at heart, but they supported the war effort by buying war bonds and helping with scrap drives. Perry continued farming but he also took a job working in a factory that was working on government contracts. Elsie worked with the women of the church sewing blankets to be sent overseas. Elsie and Perry participated in the Brethren Heifer Project by raising heifers that were sent overseas to farmers whose farms and cattle had been destroyed.

The WWII years brought forth very sensitive issues to be faced by preachers in peace churches. Where congregations had been loving and accepting of all their members, there were now isolated cases of non-acceptance because some men chose a path that did not strictly adhere to the "peace" doctrine of their church. An example: The oldest son, from a large family that belonged to the church, had been away on a tour of duty and had been granted a leave and was back home visiting with his parents and siblings. He had achieved the rank of an officer and looked very handsome in his uniform as he walked into the church with his mother and several of his siblings. Three of the older members of the church walked up to him as soon as he entered the church and severely chastised him for wearing that military uniform in God's house.

He was dumbfounded but remained polite, and he and his mother remained for the preaching service. When the service was over many of the people greeted him warmly and wished him a safe return. It is sad to report that the original rebuff hurt him deeply and he could not forget it and he never returned to that church again.

During the World War II years, there were similar isolated cases where members in "peace" churches did not know how to accept or relate to a youth who had grown up in their midst and had responded to the pressures of conscripted service. Elsie saw what happened that Sunday in her church and she was devastated that this fine young man had been severely chastised by three of the older members of the church. Elsie questioned, "How would Christ have greeted him that day?" She cried for him and his mother. She wondered if her own sons walked into the church in their military uniforms, how would they be treated? Sadly, she thought she knew the answer to that.

Young members in "peace" churches during the turbulent World War II years struggled to find ways to help their country and remain true to their church's peace doctrine. The pressures were intense as the draft boards were looking at each person of eligible age. The eligible men of the peace churches did not all choose the same path, but their faith in God steadied them and helped them traverse through the turmoil and confusion of this horrible time in the world. In the meantime, the pacifist mothers continued to pray, and they not only prayed for their own sons, but for every mother's sons.

## The Cattle of the Brethren

### Robert D. Abrahams

One of the Brethren sat under a tree,
And thought of his home across the sea.
There was little to view abroad that year
But men in anger and children in fear.
At home it was harvest time these days,
A time for thanksgiving and songs of praise,
But here in Europe the children were crying,
Their mothers were hungry, their fathers dying.
And what could a lone American do
But weep for the torture the world went through?

97

The Brethren are a quiet folk,
    With time to think of others.
They do not boast of what they do
    For some who are not brothers.

"I have to do something," vowed the man from the West,
"The question is this: what can I do best?
My people at home are farmers all.
I think they would help if they heard the call.
The kids over here are starved for milk;
A cow or two would be fine as silk.
I'll ask each brother to find some way
To raise me a heifer to give away
To a farmer somewhere else in need--
A fine fat heifer to start the breed."

Go forth, O cattle of the Lord;
    God send you peaceful grazing.
The Brethren blessed their offerings
    With song and feast and praising.

They all said "Yes!" and they bred their cattle,
And after the horrors of any battle,
A plundered farmer may send them word
For a heifer free to start the herd.
    And strangely enough, the Brethren never
Ask him a single question whatever,
As, "What is your color?" or "What's your Creed?"
All they ask is; "Are you in need?
If the answer is yes, and you'd like a cow,
We'll send you one freely, and send it now."

Let him who doubts that men are good,
    This simple tale recall;
Only the small in heart believe
    The heart of the world is small.

Note: In the 1930s there was a civil war going on in Spain, and a
young farmer, a Church of the Brethren youth worker by the name of

Dan West, was helping feed children in the war-torn country. He realized that the families needed milk for their children and how having a cow of their own would help them feed their children for years to come.

He asked his friends back home to donate heifers (young cows that have not borne a calf), to help the people be more self-reliant in supplying much-needed milk for their children. The recipients of a heifer would then donate female calves to other families and this would be a chain reaction to help many more people.

The idea of giving a source of milk instead of a cup of milk was an idea that quickly caught on. The people were also trained on how to care for their heifers. Families from 115 countries have received heifers in this manner. The Heifer Project has expanded and continues to this day. Now, the project includes not only heifers, but also chickens, goats and ducks. Sometimes children in Sunday school classes will collect money to send heifers to families that have suffered losses due to natural disasters or war.

# Gloria Graduates from High School, Weds Soldier

In the fall of 1942, I began my senior year at LaFayette-Jackson High School. I had attended this school since seventh grade and I had enjoyed every year there. The faculty at the school seemed very genuine in their caring for their students, and the friends I had made there were an important part of my life. I had no reason to believe that my senior year wouldn't be my best year at this small, rural, consolidated school.

If I could manage to stay on the honor roll, I should not have any problem getting enrolled at Bowling Green State University (BGSU) for the next year. Art would be leaving for the reserves on September 19th, and I knew I would be missing those Saturday night dates and those Sunday afternoons just hanging out at his parents' home or with his friends. We planned to write to each other every week.

School started and I continued to enjoy playing the flute in the band and orchestra, and singing in the girls' glee club and the mixed chorus. Our gym teacher offered to teach us how to dance, and this turned into a big issue and ended up before the school board. Some of the parents in the school district considered this to be risqué behavior. After discussing whether this would be a proper activity at school, or not, it was finally approved by the school board. Each day the teacher took her noon-time break and played swing music on a phonograph in the gymnasium. Girls danced with girls because none of the boys were brave enough to join us, but they were brave enough to sit in the bleachers and watch us. The music selections the teacher played the most were "Tuxedo Junction," "String of Pearls," "Elmer's Tune," "In the Mood," and "Pennsylvania 6-5000"—mainly Glenn Miller recordings.

The availability of a lot of products that we normally took for granted was affecting some of the programs at school. There was a shortage of paper available to our school, therefore the high school classes would not be getting a yearbook at the end of the year. The teachers had a limited amount of paper to use in classroom assignments so there was more use of the blackboards. Gas rationing eliminated most field trips on buses except for music *eisteddfods*, and basketball games. Lunches in the school cafeteria remained at fifteen cents and the cooks did an excellent job varying the menu and adjusting to rationing and the changing availability of staple items. I must confess that most of the time I walked with girlfriends at lunch time to a little store on Main Street in the village and bought a fifteen-cent lunch consisting of a hot dog sandwich, a Clark candy bar, and a Coke. Each item cost a nickel.

Graduation time was drawing near and the senior boys were all beginning to think about what would happen to them after they graduated. Would they enlist? Would they wait to be drafted? What branch of the military did they prefer? Would they have a choice? The war was always on everybody's mind and it affected everyone in the country, even if they didn't talk about it.

The school superintendent, Mr. Calvin Early, taught our senior history class and when the topic turned to current events the discussions became very serious. He understood the importance of the decisions the senior fellows were facing in a few short months, as soon as they graduated. I am reminded of how very young everyone looked. How naïve all of us were.

As a girl, I didn't have to face being drafted into the military so I could only briefly understand the extent of the fear that some of the fellows might be feeling. The daily news was a constant reminder of battles being fought all over the world. It was difficult to comprehend, but we all knew we didn't dare get too complacent in our quiet microcosm in northwestern Ohio.

Art's training in the reserves consisted of accelerated courses of technical information and involved a considerable amount of studying. He was dealing with classified information and could not discuss it with anyone. All his classes were at night and he was not yet required to wear a military uniform. The curriculum consisted of three different three-month courses at three different universities. He was given a seven-day leave between each three-month assignment. One leave was at Christmas time, and one leave was in March. When he was home in March of 1943, he gave me a diamond engagement ring, which concerned his parents that we were planning on getting married soon. He assured them that our plans for marriage were for after the conclusion of the war.

101

I graduated from high school in May 1943 and I went immediately to work in the office at the Lima Tank Depot. The Tank Depot/Ordnance Depot, was a large defense plant that had a government contract to build army tanks. I planned to work until fall at which time I would quit my job and begin attending B.G.S.U. I had money saved to cover my first year's expenses. I was enrolled and had my dorm room number assigned, as well as letters from the person who was to be my "big sister" on campus. It was late spring and my father came to me and said he had an emergency. He asked to borrow my college money with the promise to pay it back before I would need it for college. I was apprehensive about taking my money out of the bank, but there was no way I could say no to my father. After all the things my father had done for me, I could not refuse him.

On July 8th, 1943, Art finished his reserve training and was inducted into the U.S. Army Air Force and was sent to Miami Beach, Florida, for basic training. He and thousands of other soldiers were quartered in the large hotels along the beach. They marched in the streets everyday and received rigorous physical training on vacant lots or on the beach under the hot Florida sun.

My routine every day consisted of getting up early, eating breakfast with my father, and then he dropped me off at our friends, the Stoners. They had three daughters around my age and they had their own car pool and I joined them in riding to town. I gave them my gasoline ration stamps and I was thankful for getting to ride in their car-pool with them. It was always a lively ride because when you get four young women together it can be talk-talk-talk as you go down the road. I would arrive early enough at the Stoners that they would be having breakfast and Mrs. Stoner was always trying to feed me. This was such a very pleasant way to start off each day.

The summer passed quickly and soon it was time to send my first payment to B.G.S.U. I asked my father for the money he had borrowed, and he said, "I'm sorry, Gloryann, I don't have it to pay you back." And then he added, "It shouldn't matter about going to college because as soon as the war is over you'll be getting married. And besides, you have a good job right now at the Tank Depot."

I thought to myself, *What did he mean it didn't matter? He knew I had been making these plans for quite some time!* And then I found out what the big "emergency" was. My college money that I had saved was used to purchase building supplies for the farmhouse that he and

Lucille were remodeling. I was devastated and too embarrassed to tell anyone why my plans to attend college had changed, but I did tell Art when he called me long distance that evening from Miami Beach.

When I told Art what had happened, he was upset because he knew how much it meant to me to go to college. He said, "Let me think about this and I'll write you a letter since there are people listening to us on both ends of this telephone conversation."

The letter came and in it was the proposal to get married within a couple weeks. Our plan was to not tell anyone, but I would buy a large suitcase and begin to put things in it that I would be taking to Florida. I would purchase my train tickets and get everything ready. I would quit my job and I would tell my father that I was spending a weekend with a girlfriend. I told my good friend Waneta Stoner about Art's and my secret plans.

In the meantime, just several days before I was to leave, Art called me from Florida and said, "Gloria, I think you should tell your father what we are planning on doing. If you don't he'll be very hurt."

I told Art, "I will tell my father tomorrow about our plans. I don't know if he will be upset. You know how he sometimes reacts when things don't go his way—he gets hurt and then makes you feel guilty."

The next day after work, Dad stopped to get me at the Stoners' house just as he usually did. This had been my last day at work at the Tank Depot. I got into my father's car and as we were going down the road toward home, I said, "Dad, I have something to tell you." He never took his eyes off the road and he just kept driving.

I took a deep breath and said, "Dad, Art and I are planning on getting married this weekend. I have my tickets bought and my suitcases are packed."

Without taking his eyes off the road, he just reached in his pocket and pulled out an envelope and handed it to me. In it was an affidavit stating he gave consent to our marriage. He said, "I'm giving this to you so that you don't have to lie on your records. After all, you know you are only seventeen years old."

I couldn't believe what was happening. I leaned over and gave him a hug.

Then Dad continued, "But I also had a private detective hired to bring you back if you didn't tell me before you left. There is just one thing, I will not take you to the train station." And he started to cry.

I then asked him, "How did you know?"

He said, "You told Waneta, Waneta told her mother, and her mother told me."

I secretly said a prayer of thanks to Waneta. If she had not told her mother, this whole scenario would have had a much different and probably unpleasant ending.

On the morning of my departure, Dad dropped me off at my Aunt Annie's house in Lima. Annie was a very special person to me because she had helped take care of me for nine years after my father and mother's divorce.

Annie and I had bonded early in my life so she was like a mother to me, and I knew she was very concerned about me going on a train by myself to Florida. She gave me a hug and said she had to go to work and she left the house. I tried to sleep for a couple hours, but with the excitement of everything I could not sleep. Soon it was time to call a cab and get to the B. & O. Railroad Depot.

I was early and I was sitting on the wooden benches in the depot when Annie walked in. She had quit work early to come to see me off. I think, basically, she wanted to give me a few final words of advice, such as: "Gloryann, I want you to promise me you won't talk to any strangers on your trip to Florida. And you know how to be a lady, so always act like a lady down there in Florida. Most of all, I want you to know that if things don't work out with you and Art, you can always come back and stay with me."

So we sat there, holding hands, and I kept reassuring her that I would be okay, that I wouldn't talk to strangers, and I would always act like a lady.

We heard the train coming into the station and Annie had to say one more time, "Gloryann, remember, don't talk to any strangers." She walked with me out onto the loading area and watched me board the train. Tears were streaming down her face. I found a window seat and waved through the window to her. Now tears were streaming down my face, and I began to wonder if I was really as brave as I had let on to everybody about my trip to Florida.

The time went quickly and before I realized it the train was pulling into the Cincinnati terminal. I needed to make connections with a train going to Atlanta. A kindly looking black redcap asked me if I needed help and I told him that I needed to catch the train to Atlanta.

He said, "Missy, if you want to catch that train you is going to have to hurry because it is ready to pull out any minute. If you trust me, I know a shortcut, and maybe we can catch it."

So I followed the redcap out one of the big doors of the terminal, out into the yards, crossing track after track and it was getting dark. I was beginning to wonder if I knew what I was doing following this man out in the railroad yards. Annie's final warning to me was ringing in my ears. Just then my small carry-on suitcase that the red cap was carrying fell open and my lingerie and toilet articles fell on the ground between some railroad tracks. The red cap stopped and began picking up the dropped items and stuffing them back in the suitcase. I stopped, ready to go back and help, and he yelled at me, "Don't stop now—we're almost there!"

Finally, we were back on concrete beside a train, and there stood a conductor who was picking up a step stool and he was ready to signal the engineer to go. The conductor saw us and thankfully waited for us. I quickly reached into my purse and gave the redcap a fifty-cent piece for a tip. He looked at it with a look of disbelief on his face. I immediately felt guilty and wanted to give him more money, but the conductor was pushing me up the steps and there was no time to find more money in my purse.

As I turned and started walking into the coach I noticed most of the people were wearing military uniforms. There were only a few civilians in the coach. Also, there were people sitting on suitcases in the aisles and I quickly realized that all the seats were taken. The same situation existed in each coach.

The thought of sitting on my suitcase, in the aisle, all the way to Atlanta, was very depressing. As I chose a spot and was ready to sit down on my suitcase, a soldier stood up and offered me his seat. He then quickly disappeared into another coach. I felt very grateful and I said to myself, "The days of chivalry are not dead—and I'll bet that young man's mother taught him a lot about manners."

It was now very dark outside the windows of the train, and the conductor came through the coach, checked and punched the passengers' tickets, dimmed the lights and disappeared into the next coach. I settled back in my seat thinking how lucky I was to have caught the train at literally the last minute and I was now on my way to Atlanta. I was hoping to get some sleep. Dad had made me promise that I would get married the same day I arrived in Miami, so everything this far had gone as planned. The train just swayed and rumbled on and on through the night.

Just as I was about to drop off to sleep, I heard two soldiers arguing—one was in the seat in front of me and the other was in the seat behind me. It seems they had purchased a bottle of whisky together and the one wouldn't give up possession of the bottle to the other one. Their argument became more heated. Suddenly, the two men rose up out of their seats and started to climb over my seat to punch each other out.

At that moment, two strong arms reached across the aisle and pulled me out of my seat and out of harm's way as the fists began flying. Simultaneously, four soldiers came running to this melee and grabbed the two drunken men and dragged them to opposite ends of the coach. They dropped them unceremoniously onto the floor and told them, "Sleep it off!"

One of the four soldiers took the whiskey bottle and threw it off the train. The people in the coach clapped their hands and cheered to show their appreciation for peace and quiet being restored.

I thanked the sailor with the strong arms for helping me in this wild situation. We introduced ourselves to each other. The sailor seemed to be very shy, but he began to tell me that he was from Wisconsin and that his parents had a dairy farm there. He had finished his navy boot training and was going to be shipping out when he got to Florida.

I told him I was also from a farm in Ohio, and that we had two cows, two horses, two hogs, and ten sheep. He laughed and I don't know why he thought that was funny, but maybe he thought it sounded like a little farm compared to his parents' dairy farm.

The coach was now quiet and everyone was trying to get some sleep as the train moved swiftly toward Atlanta.

By early morning the train reached Atlanta. The sailor was catching the same train I was to Miami, so he said he would look for me at the gate to make certain I was okay. I guess my 5-foot-2 inch stature, and my 106 pounds didn't impress him that I could take care of myself. He looked surprised when I told him I was getting married that evening and I didn't want the train to be late.

When the train pulled into the Miami station the sailor picked up my small suitcase and carried it down the steps for me. I looked around, and there stood Art waiting for me. Art could not understand why a sailor was carrying my suitcase. I told Art, "It's a long story, I'll tell you later."

It was Saturday and Art told me we only had an hour to get to the Dade County Court House and get our marriage license because they would close at noon. We caught a cab and just made it in time to get the license. I had no trouble by having the affidavit stating parental consent, but Art was nervous and he kept dropping all his identification papers on the floor. The very pleasant lady at the marriage license bureau just kept smiling at us.

Once we had the license we then had to immediately return to the train station and retrieve my larger suitcase that I had checked through. In our hurry we had neglected to notice the sign on the wall that said the baggage claim area would close at noon on Saturday and would open again on Monday A.M. That suitcase had the dress in it that I was planning on being married in! We asked a man who worked at the station if he would get my suitcase for us. We could see my suitcase on one of those large four-wheeled carts behind a locked gate. Our pleading that it was our wedding day meant nothing to the man. There was nothing for us to do but to go shopping for a suitable dress for me. My traveling clothes would certainly not be appropriate to wear to my wedding.

With the help of a very understanding owner of a dress shop, I found a dress in a dark blue crepe that was perfect. We then hurried on our way to the apartment that Art had rented for me. On the way we stopped at a deli and bought a can of soup, some sandwich meat, a loaf of bread, a quart of milk, and some Oreo cookies. But there was no time to eat as Art had to return to his company at the hotel and I had to get a bath and get dressed for our wedding.

Shortly before seven o'clock, Art arrived with two army buddies and Chaplain DuBose who was to perform the ceremony. Art introduced every one to me. He then pinned a white orchid corsage on my "wedding" dress and we got into a typical nondescript olive drab military vehicle. As we rode to the church the soldiers kept a continuous line of chatter going, I suppose it was meant to keep me calm and at ease.

In about fifteen minutes we arrived at a Methodist Church that had a sparkling white exterior of stucco and looked beautiful in its simplicity. The interior of the church had a special glow as the late afternoon Florida sun shone through stained glass windows. I felt calm as the five of us walked down the red carpeted aisle toward the altar of the church. And then my mind began to race with all kinds of thoughts—

*I just wanted to pause and absorb the moment, I wonder how many brides would like to stop in front of the altar and yell, "Everybody! Freeze!" because they knew it was all going to be over too quickly.*

But the chaplain was busy telling everyone where to stand and he looked at me and nodded and asked, "ARE YOU READY?"

I answered, "Yes." Because I never like to keep people waiting. I'm thinking—*I must focus—I must remember everything that I see and hear today. What is the hurry?*

The chaplain is speaking, "We are gathered here today . . . join in holy matrimony . . ."

*I had thought that the words of Ruth, "Wherever you go, I will go . . ." would be appropriate for the wife of a military man about to follow him wherever the military might send him in the United States. While we were on our way to the church, why didn't I ask the chaplain to use that verse somewhere in the ceremony?*

" . . . Arthur, do you take this woman to be your wife? . . . "

*Oh no, nobody brought a camera with them—how will I ever be able to remember how everyone looked?*

. . . . Art just said . . .. "Love, honor and cherish" . . .

. . . . *I just heard myself say, "Love, Honor, and OBEY" I had wanted to substitute another word for "obey." It's too late now! Oh well!*

. . . . The chaplain just said . . . "I now pronounce you man and wife. You may kiss the bride."

*I looked at Art, with this pleased look on his face, and I knew we loved each other. I knew he wanted the same things in life that I did, such as a good marriage, a home and children. I also knew that the war put a big question mark on our plans, so we were determined to enjoy whatever time we would have together before he would be deployed somewhere overseas.*

In just a few short minutes we were back in the chaplain's car and we were soon at our apartment house. Art wanted to pay the chaplain, but he refused the money saying, "This is one of the pleasant parts of my job."

Our wedding was a typical wartime wedding. None of our family and friends were there. There was no music, there was no beautiful scripture or poetry read, there were no pictures taken, but none of those things affected the commitment that was made there. It is difficult to imagine in retrospect, but there was so much uncertainty at this time for our generation, and yet, we did not have any assurance that the United States would be on the victorious side.

# "Honeymoon" in Stuart, Florida

September 19, 1943, the day after Art and I were married, was spent getting me acquainted with Miami Beach. We went to the hospital to see one of the guys in Art's company who had been injured in a self-defense judo lesson on the beach. At first the doctors thought he had a broken neck, but now the doctors were not certain. He laughingly said, as he pointed to the brace on his neck, "This might keep me from having to go overseas."

Next, Art wanted to take me to the Post Exchange (PX) and the Commissary and show me the types of merchandise they stocked. He planned to purchase some shaving cream while we were there. When we looked in the door of the PX, it was obvious we would need to push our way through a sea of khaki so I decided to wait on the sidewalk in front of the PX. I said to Art, "Wouldn't it be funny if I saw somebody I knew here?"

Art laughed and said, "Fat chance of that happening!" and he disappeared into the PX. As he walked in, several soldiers walked out and there was a young man who had graduated a year earlier than me from the same small high school.

We stood there looking at each other, not believing that in that crowded place, so far from LaFayette, Ohio, that we would ever see someone we knew. It was that strange feeling of coincidence and of how sometimes the world can be so small. A few minutes later Art returned from the PX, and I introduced him to Randall Clum, a former student at LaFayette Jackson High School.

Later that day Art and I went to the beach and the sky and the ocean were both a heavenly pure blue color. I felt that this was a beautiful tropical paradise. We went into the water and it was warm and felt so good and then we heard people screaming. It seems that a lot of Portuguese Man-of-War and jellyfish came in close to the shore that day, and everyone was trying to avoid their poisonous stings. There were a lot of soldiers at the beach taking a break from their rigorous basic training. One of the surprising sights on the beach was a number of overweight older women wearing corsets under their swimsuits, with

110

garters hanging out of their suits and the garters were flapping against their legs as they walked up and down the beach. All of these things were fascinating to me.

One of the unique procedures for the soldiers at Miami Beach was that they had to do their marching in the streets. Each company sang a song as they marched and the rhythm of the song helped them keep the cadence of the marching. The song Art's group sang was "Someone's in the Kitchen with Dinah." I could hear that song when he would be marching to the drill field and then when he would be coming back from the drill field to go to the mess hall for lunch. He would be at the back of the marching unit, and would fall out when they reached the corner close to our apartment. He would fall out of formation and dash upstairs where I would have lunch ready for him. After lunch he would listen for his company's song and he would run down to the street and fall in on their way back to the drill field. He never got caught. Nobody ever told on him. And we had a few extra stolen minutes together.

The next week we had the usual routine. Then one day I didn't hear the "Dinah" song by any of the units marching down the street. Around dinner time there was a phone call for me on the phone in the hallway on the first floor. It was Art, he said, "I'm being shipped somewhere, don't have any idea where. Just stay where you are and I'll call you. Don't panic, I don't think we are being sent overseas, just yet."

*Don't panic, he says! He doesn't realize how easily I get frightened! He doesn't realize that I get lost easily, as I have no sense of direction! Here I am alone in this very different and strange place!*

The streets of Miami Beach were always a sea of khaki and very crowded with military men, and a girl walking alone was certain to be noticed and flirted with. Sometimes the military men were a bit rowdy when off duty, so I felt it was safer to stay close to the apartment house. It was the Jewish holiday, Rosh Hashanah, and most of the tenants in the apartment house were Jewish. There was a beautiful courtyard in the center of the apartment house with a profusion of green plants, a lovely fountain, and some white wrought-iron benches. I thought I would go sit there, but there was a group of people gathered around a rabbi, or a cantor, who was chanting and the people were sitting quietly listening and praying. It was comforting to listen even though I did not understand the significance of what they were doing. I lingered awhile on the walkway that overlooked the courtyard. I just wanted to take advantage of the moment—it was so peaceful. I knew I should not intrude, so I quietly walked up to my apartment and closed the door. I felt forsaken. I almost let thoughts of doubt about me being in this strange environment by myself enter into my mind. And Art was going to who knows where? But then, I told myself, "I'm okay, I can figure out what to do. I'll just go to bed, get a good night's rest, and see what tomorrow brings."

The next day Art called to say he had good news. He was just two hundred miles up the coast at Camp Murphy. He told me to take a Greyhound Bus to Stuart, Florida. He had determined that Camp Murphy was located about halfway between Palm Beach and Stuart, and that the cost of living would probably be cheaper in Stuart, so that was where I was to go.

The next morning I packed my two suitcases, called a cab, bought my bus ticket and I was soon on my way to Stuart. After riding for several hours and the bus making many, many stops along the way, the driver stopped again and turned to me and said, "Here's your stop, Miss."

I looked out the window and asked the driver, "I don't see a town, are you sure this is it?"

The driver said, "Yep, this is it. Across the road is the Chamber of Commerce, they'll help you."

I stepped off the bus and the driver retrieved my luggage from the outside storage compartment. He hurriedly set my suitcases by the road, hopped back in the bus and quickly drove away. I still could not see a town!

I was thinking *Art Miller, what have you gotten me into*? But there in front of me was a rickety old building the size of a garage, with no paint left on its siding, but on the front of this building was a faded sign that said, "Chamber of Commerce." I carried my two heavy suitcases over to the building, left them outside the door, and walked in. I asked the man sitting at a desk, "Where is Stuart?"

He laughed and said, "You are here."

I told him, "I don't see it."

He laughed again and said, "It's over there, beyond that large bunch of trees. Do you need some help?"

I told the man I needed to find a hotel. By now it was late afternoon and I wanted to be in a safe room before dark. He understood my predicament, and called a cab for me. I think there was only one hotel in the small town of Stuart, and there was a room available. As soon as I was checked into a room, I went in search of a place where I could get something to eat.

I called Camp Murphy that night, and was informed that I could not speak with Art, but a message was delivered to him with a phone number where he could reach me. I later learned that upon arriving at Camp Murphy, Art was immediately involved in orientation and screening procedures, as were the other newly arrived buck privates. They were all restricted to the base and could not receive any phone calls or leave the base for an unknown period of time. The realization hit me that I was on my own again.

Several days later, Art called to say I could catch a bus that carried military men and their wives to and from the camp. I caught the bus and rode to the camp, which was about a half-hour ride. We had enough time to get a snack at the PX, talk for a bit, but soon I needed to get on the last bus back to Stuart, and to my hotel room. Art told me to look for an apartment, as it was going to be too expensive to keep living at the hotel. I thought, *Just what made him think I was capable of doing all these things! He had so much faith in me! He didn't realize that after dark, I could barely find my way from the bus stop back to the hotel. I am such a wimp!*

The next day, after walking around town all morning and not finding any apartments for rent, I stopped at a quaint little diner for lunch. I asked the waitress there if she knew of any apartments for rent. She was very friendly and told me to check at the Riverview Apartment House and gave me directions on how to find the place.

I found the two-story apartment house and they did have an efficiency apartment that was vacant. The rent was $22.00 per month, which seemed reasonable, so I signed the renter's agreement and hurriedly moved in. That night I again went out to the camp to visit Art. He was delighted that I had found a place to live in such a short time. I gave him our new address, and told him not to be disappointed when he saw our new home.

I was beginning to worry about how we were going to meet expenses. My money was beginning to run low and as yet I had not received a military allotment check. The very next day I went job hunting, and because Stuart was a town with a population of approximately 8,000, I feared that with so many army wives in town, there might not be any jobs. I walked by a laundry and saw a "Help Wanted" sign in

113

the window. I went in and told the manager I was applying for the job. He looked me over and told me to report to work in the morning. Talk about being a green kid from the country—I never asked for any details about the job!

When I arrived for work the next morning, I was told I would be a "sheet shaker." I was led to a large, hot, steamy room where there were large commercial washers and dryers. My job was to take sheets out of the washers and put them in dryers. When the dryer stopped I was to take the sheets out, and fold them "just-so" and start them through a large Mangle ironer. There was somebody else on the other side of the ironer and she was to fold the ironed sheets a few more times and stack them on a table.

The person on the other side of the ironer was always yelling at me to "hurry up," but I couldn't work any faster. The sheets were wet, tangled, and twisted together when coming out of the washer and I was supposed to untangle them before I put them in the dryer. And then when the sheets came out of the dryer, I had to fold them just so and then start them through the ironer. All this time my arms were flying around over my head as I was trying to hold the sheets up off the floor. The room was hot and steamy, my legs and feet hurt because I did not own comfortable shoes for standing all day on concrete. I thought if that lady on the other side of the ironer yelled at me one more time I would scream something profane back at her. I don't know what I would have said, but for certain, my job was more involved than her job. There were times during that awful day that I thought I was going to faint.

Art was still not permitted to leave the base and I had promised him I would come out to see him that night. Actually, I was nearly exhausted, and all I really wanted to do was take a bath and crawl into bed. When I arrived at the camp, we went to get our usual dessert snack. Art looked at me and said, "What's wrong with you tonight? You aren't talking."

I started to cry and then I proceeded to tell him about my " sheet-shaking" job. He became upset and told me to quit that job the very next day. He said, "We'll be okay on the money. I don't know why you took that kind of a job. That job would be too hard on you physically. Didn't they tell you ahead of time what the job entailed?"

I confessed, "I forgot to ask what I had to do and I also forgot to ask what it paid. How could I have been so dumb?"

Art put his arms around me and we walked to the bus stop, then he started to chuckle. I asked him what was so funny. He said, "I was just thinking about my little wife and her 'sheet-shaking' job." The bus was there and he said as I got on the bus, "Remember—quit that job tomorrow morning!"

The next morning I called in sick at the laundry and made another attempt to walk around Stuart's business district to see if I might find another job. By sheer luck, I walked into an abstract company to inquire about a job and a typist had just quit because her soldier husband was being sent overseas. The owner of the business was quite abrupt and he told one of the three young women working there to give me a typing test. I was handed a sheet of descriptions of land with most of the typing consisting of numbers, fractions, and abbreviations. I made two errors. The owner, Mr. Kennedy, then called me into his office and said, "Do it over again when you aren't so nervous." Actually, I was more nervous the second time, but I did it with no errors.

Mr. Kennedy then told me I could have the job and he wanted me to start the next day. I couldn't believe it and I knew it had to be better than shaking sheets all day! I went back to the apartment and realized I had forgotten to ask what the salary was. When would I ever learn! (The salary turned out to be $15.00 per week. On my third week I received a raise and then I received $17.00 a week.)

After finding the typing job, I thought I should walk over to the laundry and tell the manager that I had found another job, but before I could open my mouth he fired me. This was not an ego-crushing event in my life—but I do have to chuckle when I think of my short-lived career as a "sheet shaker."

About the time that I got the typing job, Art was permitted to live off base. He received a small amount of extra pay for the meals that he missed at camp, and I began receiving my allotment check for being married to a man in the military. With careful management we knew we would be able to cover our expenses. We opened a bank account and kept enough money in it so that when Art would be deployed, I would be able to get back to Lima.

We lived within our means and our apartment was ugly, but Art never complained. It was a one-room efficiency, the room was adequate in size and served as a living room and bedroom. There was a bed that was on casters that slid out of the wall. The furniture was nondescript, consisting of a small wooden table, three unmatched kitchen chairs, a daybed that served as a sofa, one occasional chair, and an end table with a lamp on it. There was a walk-in closet with a built-in dresser at the end, shelving on one side of the closet and on the other side there was a rod for hanging clothing. The kitchen was smaller than the walk-in closet and had a two-burner kerosene stove on which to cook. For baking there was a metal box with a big hole in the bottom of the box, and this box was to be used like an oven. You were to put the box over a lit burner to suffice as an oven and there was an unstable shelf in the box on which to place the food to be baked. But there was no thermometer to register the temperature inside the box, so the cook had to "guess" how hot it might be. Rather than possibly waste precious food, most of the cooking was done on top of the burners. Everything was tiny—there was a tiny refrigerator, a tiny sink, three feet of counter space, and a makeshift cabinet on the wall. The floor of the entire apartment was covered with badly worn linoleum in an indescribably ugly dark color.

There were no bathrooms in any of the apartments. Each floor of the apartment house had a large men's bathroom and an equally large women's bathroom in the center of each hall. The bathrooms were each complete with two toilets, two lavatories, and one bathtub. The elderly tenants who were accustomed to coming each winter and staying in this apartment house, were now afraid to use the bathrooms because they thought all soldiers had venereal diseases, so they figured their wives would also have venereal diseases. Therefore, the older people could be seen every day and night carrying chamber pots down the hall to empty in the bathrooms. We always had a good laugh at night when a certain elderly gentleman would be carrying a chamber pot down the hall and invariably the lid would come off and go rolling on the floor to the end of the hall, clanging all the way.

The apartment house had traditionally been a place where a lot of railroad retirees came each winter, and with the influx of army wives in the town, their favorite apartments were not always available now. There was a lot of resentment coming from the older tenants toward the military couples staying there. However, the army wives in the building developed strong bonds and helped each other whenever they had an emergency.

Rumor had it that since all the soldiers at the camp were working on radar equipment, they were being made sterile. However, only two

116

of us army wives out of approximately twenty that left the apartment house that year were not pregnant, one other army wife and myself.

Certain foods were rationed at this time, so I had to learn to use our food stamps wisely. If I would have been a better cook I could probably have conquered that two-burner kerosene stove. Art's parents sent us their meat stamps because they butchered steers and hogs and they canned a lot of their meat and did not need their stamps. Art's mother sent me some of his favorite recipes to help me in the cooking department. Although Art received a little extra money for living off base, he did not get any food stamps, so we had to get along with just my food stamps.

Stuart had been a small quiet southern town before the war and the influx of the military men and their families. We could tell that some of the town's citizens resented us being there, even though we probably helped the economy of the town. The business district was small with a sprinkling of necessary stores, such as grocery, hardware, clothing, pharmacy, gas stations, etc. We enjoyed going to the diner in town because the waitresses were always very pleasant to the military people, and they served good food at reasonable prices. There was a jukebox in the diner and Art would hold my hand while he played our favorite song, "Paper Doll," by the Mills Brothers. There was one movie theater in the town and we would try to go there about once a month. We found a place that rented bicycles and often on Sundays we would ride out in the country, eat a picnic lunch, and enjoy looking at the different vegetation and the citrus groves.

We particularly enjoyed the backyard at the apartment house because it sloped down to the banks of the St. Lucie River. The St. Lucie is a large river that begins in central Florida and flows to the Atlantic Ocean. We spent a lot of time just sitting and watching the river and the wildlife around it. We were told that there were alligators in the river. We never saw any swimming past us or sunning themselves on the bank, but one night a seven-foot alligator crawled out of the river and was captured on the sidewalk just a few short blocks from our apartment house.

Admittedly, our apartment was not attractive by any stretch of the imagination, but it gave us a place to shut out the rest of the world. The war news was not good at this time, and all the soldiers knew that on a moment's notice they could receive orders to be shipped to another camp stateside or overseas. We just made the most of each day that we had together. I have jokingly called the six-month stay at Stuart during the winter months in sunny Florida, "our honeymoon," with compliments from Uncle Sam.

In March 1944, Art received orders that he was being transferred and was given a ten-day travel pass to Camp Warner-Robbins, near Macon, Georgia. Ten whole days! That meant we could go to Warner-Robbins via Lima, Ohio.

# Part Five
# War Spreads to the Mediterranean Area

# Africa Campaign—Desert Fighting—1943

In 1939 Benito Mussolini watched as Hitler invaded France and just six days before the French asked for a cease-fire, Mussolini declared war on them. He had greatly exaggerated his military strength, his weapons were poorly made, and his transportation system was inadequate. Mussolini's armies were no better because they lacked skillful leadership, and the Italian soldiers were not motivated to fight. To no one's surprise, his operations against the French were ineffective. Actually, Mussolini had a hidden agenda because he really wanted to take control of the Mediterranean area and the Suez Canal. His first main target was Egypt. In Libya, which bordered Egypt on the west, Italy had 250,000 troops assembled, under the command of Marshal Rudolfo Grazani. Great Britain only had a small garrison in Egypt.

Great Britain already had its resources stretched to the limit in fighting Hitler elsewhere on air, land, and sea. Winston Churchill was barely able to send 30,000 reinforcements made up of Indians, Australians, and New Zealanders to Egypt to fight against Graziani's forces of 250,000 men. The British definitely knew that if the Suez Canal fell to the Italians they would probably not be able to win the war.

Graziani had made his military reputation with having troops under his command that fought against Ethiopians who were armed only with spears. Realistically, he knew that he was not ready to fight the British in Africa. Mussolini pushed Graziani to go into Egypt and the Italians met little resistance. The Italians stopped after advancing fifty miles into Egypt and were planning on waiting for more supplies to arrive.

British General Sir Archibald Wavell seized on the brief period of calm, and launched an attack on December 9, 1940. The British armor attacks quickly demolished the Italian fortifications and the Italians retreated, leaving behind 40,000 prisoners. The Italian cannon was no match for the British "Matilda" tank.

The British, under field commander General Richard O'Conner, chased the retreating Italians into Libya. By January 1941 the British had taken several fortified ports and Tobruk. Two weeks later the retreating Italians became trapped between British forces. The British had 2,000 casualties, but 125,000 Italians surrendered.

In February 1941, Mussolini attacked Greece and eventually had to retreat back to Albania. At this point, Mussolini's blunders brought Hitler to his aid. Hitler sent an armored division and a motorized infantry division under General Irwin Rommel to North Africa. Rommel proved to be a cunning foe in the desert warfare. He forced the British to retreat back to Egypt, but he could not take Tobruk. The Italians captured General O'Conner, which added to the humiliation of the British.

The blowing and whirling sand of desert warfare takes a heavy toll on men and machinery. The extreme temperatures of the heat in the daytime and the cold at night were draining the energy level of the soldiers. German U-boats and aircraft harassed the ships bringing supplies for the British troops. However, Italy's navy was timid after the British used carrier-based torpedo planes to attack their naval base at Taranto. In March 1941 an Italian task force tried to intercept a British convoy of reinforcements to Greece. A battle took place off Cape Matapan and Italy lost two destroyers, three cruisers, and suffered heavy damage to a powerful battleship. After this date, Italy's warships offered no challenges and stayed close to their port, but their torpedo and submarine boats continued to operate.

The British military had code-breaking abilities that gave them an advantage in World War II, which was called the "Ultra Secret." In 1920 the Germans had constructed an encoding machine called the Enigma, and they did not know that one of the Enigma machines had fallen into the hands of some Polish authorities and was replicated before it was delivered to the intended receiver. Polish mathematicians discovered how to break the Enigma's complicated patterns, and they then shared the information with the British. Ultra started to be used by the British in the desert campaign and the rest of the war.

The story is told that when German Wilhelm Ritter von Thoma was captured and was invited to have dinner with British General Bernard Montgomery, he expected to be questioned for information. Instead, Montgomery told him, "I am going to tell you the state of your forces." Von Thoma said he was "amazed at Montgomery's knowledge of Germany's deficiencies and shipping losses. He knew as much as I did about our position."

The British had also broken the Italian naval codes, which was crucial to the attack on Taranto and the Battle of Matalan.

General Claude Auchinleck replaced Archibald Wavell in the fall of 1941. The British Eighth Army and the Afrika Korps under Rommel had many skirmishes with neither being declared the victor. After the Japanese attack on Pearl Harbor, on December 7th, 1941, the Eighth Army lost strength in numbers when the Australian divisions and others of the Eighth were pulled out to defend British positions in Australia and Singapore. Auchinleck had gained some ground, but Rommel's superior tactical skills took a heavy toll on the British.

The Afrika Korps struck the weakened Eighth Army in May 1942, resulting in Rommel capturing Tobruk in June. Tobruk provided Rommel fuel and supplies that they desperately needed. Rommel now had the British on the run and chased them back into Egypt, to El Alamein.

At El Alamein, the British had the defensive advantage of controlling a forty-mile passage between the Mediterranean on the north and the Qattora Depression. Rommel's maneuverability was greatly restricted at this point. Again several battles ensued with both sides suffering heavy losses. During this time, Hitler had refused to send Rommel the resources he needed to secure a victory.

Churchill, upset over the stalemate, removed Auchinleck and placed General Bernard L. Montgomery in charge of the Eighth Army and General Harold Alexander commander of the Middle East. Within two weeks, Montgomery had to face an offensive launched by Rommel. The British took advantage of the lull and received tanks, much-needed supplies, and more troops. The use of Ultra gave Montgomery the information he needed about Rommel's plans to strike.

Rommel's attack came on the night of August 30th–31st but was abandoned after several days. Montgomery took the credit for the defensive strategy, which had really been devised by Auchinleck.

Montgomery reinforced his troops with men, guns, and airplanes. Under Montgomery the troops showed an improvement in morale and discipline and they mounted an attack against Rommel with superior numbers.

Rommel and the Italians offered formidable resistance but they were outnumbered. On November 2nd, Rommel wanted Hitler to let him retreat. Hitler refused his request and told him, "Fight to victory or death." Rommel disobeyed Hitler's orders and left the Italians to fight on their own as best they could.

The Eighth Army chased the Afrika Korps into Libya. The Allies invaded the French Colonies of Algeria and Morocco. It was November

1942, and this force was made up of mostly American troops and it was the first time for the Americans to enter a battle with Germany and Italy. Back in the United States the people wondered why American troops were fighting in Africa when they were already occupied with fighting the Japanese in the Pacific.

At this point, Joseph Stalin of Russia told Churchill and Roosevelt that he wanted the Germans to be forced into fighting on another front to give Russia some relief from the German offensives against them. Russia had been subjected to brutal assaults by the German armies, and the Russians were suffering extensive casualties. Talks began about a cross-channel invasion, but Army Chief George Marshall claimed the United States was not ready for that plan in 1943 and so it was postponed until 1944. A diversionary plan, TORCH, was agreed upon by the Allied leaders to strike at Sicily and Italy.

General Dwight D. Eisenhower was a West Point graduate and had served under Generals John J. Pershing and Douglas MacArthur. By the time of the Pearl Harbor attack, he had advanced to the rank of Brigadier General and was working mainly in Washington D.C. Eisenhower possessed exceptional organizational and logistical planning skills and had been noticed by General George C. Marshall. Marshall was thinking about selecting Eisenhower to be in charge of the American build-up in Great Britain. However, when the decision needed to be made about the person to be in command of TORCH, the leaders were cognizant of the bitter feelings between the French and the British over Churchill's ordering an attack on French warships moored near Oran to prevent them from falling into German hands. Unfortunately, more than 1,250 French men died. Therefore, it was felt that the commander for TORCH needed to be an American, and Marshall's choice for that position was Eisenhower.

When France fell to the Germans, Charles de Gaulle fled to England and established himself as the leader of the Free French Movement. As commander of the North African Campaign, Eisenhower dismissed any idea of placing de Gaulle in charge of the 120,000 occupational French troops in Morocco, Algeria, and Tunisia. Eisenhower made Jean Darlan Chief of French Military Forces and head of the civil government. This was a controversial appointment because Darlan was the head of the Vichy government and considered to be quasi-Fascist and anti-Semitic. The appointment greatly concerned General

Marshall, President Roosevelt, the British, and the Free French. It nearly cost Eisenhower his job.

Eisenhower explained that the French troops in Morocco, Algeria and Tunisia would be more likely to recognize Darlan as their leader and would listen to him regarding a cease-fire in case the Allies had to move in to be conquerors. Eisenhower said that he made this decision in the effort to save lives. The concern over the advisability of Eisenhower's choice was moot, however, because a month later in December, Darlan was assassinated and General de Gaulle was then included in the North African government.

January 13–24, 1943, Roosevelt and Churchill, along with their military staffs met at Casablanca. Stalin was invited but could not be there because he was needed to make critical military decisions pertaining to the German invasion of Russia. Stalin made it clear that he wanted the leaders to consider an invasion of France to remove some of Hitler's war resources away from their invasion of Russia. By the time the conference met it was obvious the Allies would win in Africa, but they could not set a definite date.

At Casablanca, Eisenhower was made supreme commander, with General Harold Alexander in charge of all ground forces, Air Marshall Arthur Tedder was put in command of the air units, and Admiral Andrew B. Cunningham was put in charge of naval operations. It was decided that a stable French government needed to be established in North Africa. Despite his egotistical personality, de Gaulle would appeal to the free French people. Generals Giraud and de Gaulle were to work as a team, but soon de Gaulle was in complete control.

It was decided that the next target would be Sicily, which meant the cross-channel invasion would not be until 1944. This was a disappointment to Stalin. Churchill was very forceful in arguing that the Mediterranean region was the "soft underbelly" of Europe and that control of that region was vital.

Roosevelt, with Churchill at his side, surprised everyone by announcing to the press after the Casablanca Conference was over, *that the Allies would prosecute the war to the unconditional surrender of Germany, Italy and Japan.* Although Roosevelt did this on his own, no one stood against this doctrine. There are historians today that say this doctrine made the war last longer. It permitted propaganda people in Germany to tell their people that the Allies wanted to enslave their people. In Japan the propaganda people were saying that the Japanese would not be able to keep their emperor. The end result was that the German and Japanese people fought harder.

The war in North Africa proved to the American troops that they had not been prepared for that type of fighting. Eisenhower accepted a lot of the blame for poor decision making and inept performances by some of his subordinates. Eisenhower learned from the North Africa campaign to be more forceful. He started by replacing the commander of II Corps and replacing him with George Patton. Eisenhower ordered Patton to clear out the dead wood, instill discipline in the troops and toughen the troops with realistic training. Patton did not need much urging.

# Sicily and Italy Campaigns—
# Mussolini Inept Leader

The invasion of Sicily, code named HUSKY, was in the planning stages before the North Africa campaign was finished. Originally HUSKY called for seven separate landings, but General Montgomery objected because he felt that was too many. Montgomery won the argument and the number of invasions was cut to two. It was thought that the seizure of Sicily would mean control of the Mediterranean and that possibly Italy would choose to get out of the war.

General Montgomery wanted to be in charge of the HUSKY operation with the American II Corps under his command. This was unacceptable to the Americans. General Alexander was put in charge of the Seventh Army. A compromise was worked out, but the result was that the British and the Americans did not cooperate with one another, and they actually functioned like two independent operations.

There was an interesting gimmick staged to throw the Germans off on the plans of the Allies. The British intelligence dressed a corpse in a British uniform, put it in a life preserver off the coast of Spain to make it look as if the body was a courier whose plane had crashed at sea. They had chained a briefcase to his body containing documents stating that the Allies were planning to invade Greece and Sardinia. The Spanish found the body with the documents, believed what they read, and turned everything over to the Germans. The Germans then strengthened the defense systems of Greece and Sardinia and neglected to do anything about the defenses of Sicily.

In the early hours of the morning of July 10th, 1943, the Allies began putting troops on the beaches of Sicily. The Allies faced weak resistance and within a few days eight divisions were put ashore. The Allied casualties that resulted were few and they were caused by inadequate fighter protection against German aircraft attacks.

It had been previously determined that Messina should be taken as soon as possible in order to prevent Axis troops from escaping to the mainland. Messina was located just two miles from the "toe" of Italy.

Montgomery had planned to send his troops on a road on the east coast up to Messina, but he did not calculate the trouble they would run in to with the terrain around the city of Catania.

Montgomery made some very bold decisions for a man who had a reputation of always being overly cautious. While he was dividing his troops to get around Catania, the Germans and Italians were concentrated at Messina to block the Allies' advance. Montgomery took over some roads in rerouting his troops that were supposed to be used by General Omar Bradley, who commanded II Corps, and General Patton. Montgomery's change of plans infuriated the two American generals. General Patton took it upon himself to go to Palermo, which had no strategic value. Patton then decided to make a name for himself and started toward Messina. Montgomery, at this point, in order to save the lives of his troops, let Patton get to Messina first. When Patton arrived in Messina, the Axis troops had been ferried across the Strait of Messina and were in Italy. Two generals with big egos fought the Sicilian campaign. Patton's aggressiveness and energy would be useful in fighting the Germans, but his uncontrollable behavior was sometimes a cause of embarrassment to the military leaders and to the country.

Mussolini had failed in his military strategy and had failed to inspire his armies and the people of his country. Toward the end of July 1943, the Italian Grand Council and the king dismissed Mussolini and put him under arrest in a secret hideaway. Somehow Hitler discovered where Mussolini was being held captive, and in a daring raid by the German SS rescued Mussolini and put him in charge of a "government" in northern Italy. But the government did little and with a broken leader such as Mussolini, it had no real power.

Field Marshal Pietro Badoglio, a former commander of the Italian army, headed the new Italian government. Hitler, upon hearing of Mussolini's downfall, sent army divisions to Italy. The big decision for Badoglio was whether to fight off the Allies alongside the Germans, or to join the Allies, or just offer passive resistance.

Eisenhower had been hoping to negotiate with Badoglio to help the Allies. The Italians were frightened of the Germans, and on September 8, 1943, Italy's king and Badoglio fled from Rome and the Italian soldiers laid down their arms before the advancing German troops. At this point, Eisenhower's hope of getting Italian cooperation was gone.

Churchill, Marshall, and Roosevelt could not agree on a strategy on what to do about Italy. German troops were quickly arriving in

Italy, and Rommel had been given command of the German forces in northern Italy. The German leaders were also having difficulty in agreeing on what to do about Italy.

On September 3, 1943, when a part of the British Eighth Army crossed into the toe of Italy, the German forces gave only light resistance because they were retreating to the north.

General Mark Clark commanded the Fifth Army and landed on September 8th close to Salerno. Other landings were spread out at such a distance that they could not bring their forces together quickly. The Germans were throwing a heavy attack at the Allied forces, and the situation became precarious until an airborne division and heavy air and naval bombardment came to assist. By September 15th, when forward units of the Eighth Army arrived, the crisis was over. The German Field Marshal Albert Kesselring stopped attacking and began retreating. The exhausted Allied troops took a brief rest and then moved on and took Naples on October 2nd.

General Marshall felt that by October the original objectives had been achieved. Actually, Italy had been knocked out of the war: The Foggia airfields were now under the control of the Allies, Naples had been captured by the Allies; and the Germans had to devote more than twenty divisions to defending Italy. The city of Rome became an objective that Churchill and Roosevelt wanted. Rome was more of a political rather than a military consideration, but the thrust was to go to Rome.

The Allied troops faced rugged mountainous terrain running down the center of Italy and the rainy winter weather had made the roads impassable and it was difficult to expeditiously move the men and equipment. The troops had to halt at the Gustav Line, which was a system of fortifications that ran eighty miles south of Rome on the west, crossing Italy and ending at the Adriatic Sea on the east.

Churchill, Roosevelt and Stalin met in November 1943 with their military advisors in Teheran. Stalin did not feel that Roosevelt and Churchill were acting in good faith. Stalin wanted the cross-channel invasion as soon as possible to draw some of Germany's forces away from Russia. Roosevelt named Eisenhower to command OVERLORD and the emphasis was now turning toward a future invasion of Normandy to take place in the spring of 1944.

The naming of Eisenhower to command OVERLORD, the cross-channel invasion of France, meant Italy was to take second place. Reassignments had to be made of key military personnel, British General

Henry Maitland Wilson took Eisenhower's place, Generals Bradley, Patton, and Carl Spaatz were reassigned to England and General Montgomery was to command the British forces in OVERLORD and he turned over the Eighth Army to General Oliver Lease. The remaining higher echelon of Allied officers remaining in Italy had to fight to get needed supplies because the main objective was to get a build-up of resources ready in England for the cross-channel invasion.

On January 22, 1944, landings at Anzio began and this operation was called SHINGLE. The Germans mounted heavy counterattacks, which inflicted heavy casualties on the Allied forces. If the Allies would have had more landing craft and more men, the landing would have fared better. Landing craft were in short supply because many had been designated for the OVERLORD preparations.

In January the Allied forces failed in trying to break through the Gustav Line. A large mountain, Monte Cassino, was used as a stronghold and the Allied troops that moved against Monte Cassino suffered heavy losses. The battle-weary American troops were replaced in February by a New Zealand corps commanded by General Bernard Freyberg.

There was a Benedictine monastery on top of the mountain, and an Indian Division thought the monastery was being used by the Germans as an observation post. In mid-February, after much deliberation by several generals, it was decided to bomb the monastery. Hundreds of bombers blasted the monastery to rubble and afterwards they discovered that the Germans had not been using the monastery after all. But, when there was nothing there but rubble, the Germans began to use it for fortification and could easily repel the Allied attacks. There were heavy casualty losses in this area of the war.

On May 11th, the VI Corps broke out of the Anzio perimeter. Ignoring plans to trap the Germans against an advancing Eighth Army, General Clark decided to move north to Rome and these were the first American troops to enter the city of Rome. On June 4th the great news of the Allies capturing a first Axis capital was in all the headlines and the news broadcasts. Just two days later on June 6th, the headlines and news reports were all about the Allied invasion of Normandy.

### Reported Statistics

| Sicily Campaign: U.S. Army | 2,572 KIA | 5,746 WIA | Navy 546 KIA |
|---|---|---|---|
| Italy Campaign | 36,169 KIA | | |

# Doyt Hanthorn, Captured in Italy, Relates POW Experiences

Doyt Hanthorn was raised on a farm and worked alongside his parents helping with all the work that goes into farming. He had a very pleasant disposition and had a penchant for mischief making. He was never unkind with the mischief, it was always just good-hearted playfulness. When Doyt was in the army he suffered from extreme frostbite on his feet. The results of the frostbite caused severe damage to his feet and have plagued Doyt with problems ever since. It is this author's opinion that the unpleasant experiences that Doyt faced in his combat duties, as well as his prisoner of war experiences, were made tolerable because he had been accustomed to hard work and maintaining an optimistic viewpoint in life. Doyt has been a successful farmer, a devoted family man, and a devout member of his church. His story was told the first time to his daughters on January 3, 2000. The author feels honored to be able to share his story with the readers of this book.

## Army Record— as dictated to his daughters on January 3, 2000

I was drafted into the army in March of 1943. I was sent to Camp Perry near Toledo, Ohio for about ten days, which was basically a time of orientation and induction paperwork. From there I went to Camp Wolters, Texas for about thirteen weeks of basic training (boot camp.) After this time, I was allowed to come home for a short furlough before heading overseas. After my furlough, I went back to Camp Wolters and from there was sent to Camp Shanago, Pennsylvania. On August 20, 1943, I began my journey overseas to Oran, Africa, and we arrived at their port on September 2, 1943. Upon arrival we noticed some Arabs sitting on the mountain tops watching us through field glasses.

When we left Africa we went across the Mediterranean Sea. The ship received orders to stop in the middle of the Mediterranean Sea, so we dropped anchor and we all decided to go swimming. Instead of waiting on the side of the ship where everybody else was swimming, I decided to try something else. I resolved to swim completely around the other side. I became very tired during this adventure and almost drowned before I reached the other side.

It was September 15, 1943, while we were in the middle of the Mediterranean Sea, that our ship received orders to go to Italy. We arrived in Italy on September 21, 1943, and it was there that I was assigned to Company F, 157th Infantry, 45th Division. From there I was sent to Salerno, Italy and into combat.

It was during this combat that some shrapnel entered my raincoat and ticked my arm. The sergeant came around to see if any of us were wounded and I showed him my raincoat. He made me take off my coat so that he could look at the flesh wound, because one cannot tell if there is actually an injury at first sight. This was the closest that I ever came to being wounded in battle. However, it was there at Salerno Beach that my feet got frozen. The date was December 15, 1943. We did not have supplies to treat such injuries, so I had to make do with Burma Shave to rub on my feet. This was a type of shaving cream.

When I arrived overseas, my mom wrote me a letter that helped me to feel closer to her and the family. She told me to look for a certain star in the West at night and wish upon it. I don't know if I saw the same star as my mom did, but it always felt as if it were the right one.

We were on the front lines at Salerno Beach for thirty days, and we had no baths and no shaves that entire time. After this time at the front, we were allowed to go back and rest for ten days at our base camp. Then we were again sent back to the front lines for approximately ten days. The terrain was mountainous country, which necessitated the use of mules to carry our food and ammunition.

Our next destination was Anzio Beachhead. We were happy to see that the British came to relieve us, however we were disappointed in the fact that they brought only tea and no ammunition.

We had just finished our shift on the front lines and were headed back to rest when the Germans counter-attacked us. There was a cave close by which had two entries into it. We all went inside it, but the Germans went on top of the cave and set off two dynamite charges. They ordered us to come out of the cave and we all feared that they would shoot us, due to the lack of food and necessary resources that POWs required. However, as we marched out of the cave we were relieved that no shots were fired, but they did come at us with flame-throwers, which kept us marching and obeying their orders.

The Germans marched us out from the cave and put us into box-cars. These cars took us to Naples, Italy where we were to spend the first part of our incarceration. They held us in a movie-making house for a few days and then they took us on to Rome. From here, we were put into boxcars again and were sent to Stalog 7A Camp. We were there for only a few days as well and then were sent on to Munich, Germany.

In Munich we were put to work cleaning up the debris from Allied bombings. We stayed in an old school house. The American planes bombed around us for fourteen days straight. Only one incendiary bomb hit our building through all fourteen days. The Germans accused us that the Americans knew where we were, but they had no idea that we were there in Munich. We stayed there for approximately three months.

In Munich, all we had to sleep on were straw mattresses. We soon found out that these mattresses were infested with ticks and fleas that quickly took up residence on our bodies. They would get so bad that we would take off our clothes and open up the seams to try to get them off our clothes. Before we started our march, my legs had big sores around my ankles where the ticks had bitten me.

After I was reported missing in action, the mailman brought another telegram to our home informing my parents that I was a POW. Mom and Dad were out husking corn in the backfield when the mailman saw them, he ran all the way across the field to give them the second telegram. He was so happy to be able to give them the telegram with the good news that I was still alive.

After being captured, we soon began receiving the International Red Cross packages. They contained a small can of salmon, cheese, Spam, margarine, a few crackers, a chocolate bar and fifty cigarettes. We received more than this but I can't remember all that was in the packages. These packages came every week until we started our march back across Germany at the conclusion of the war.

While we were in Munich our job was to clean breweries. The guard would say, "You watch for me while I'm back in the brewery drinking and then I'll watch for you." He would go home drunk almost every night.

Then they sent ninety-nine of us to an airport to clean it up. The first day we worked. Then we all decided we weren't going to do that hard work the next day. The Germans came in with fixed bayonets and changed our minds. The next day they took us to Stop, Poland, and we worked on a potato farm. We got potatoes once a day and once a week we got enough horse meat to make soup. We had a lot of rutabagas to eat as well, however they were not very tasty. We also received about three-quarters of a loaf of black bread a week. On Christmas Eve, the Germans brought us cookies and candy. We could hear plainly the Russian artillery.

There were nine of us in this camp. We were here approximately nine months. The farmers here had two big steam engines, one at each end of the field. They had a large cable that connected them. They would pull a plow with one engine one way and then the plow would turn over and they would continue plowing back the other way. The wheat would be cut and shocked. They would haul it to the barn and put it there for storage until it could be threshed in the wintertime. They also raised a lot of potatoes. They would boil potatoes and feed them to their hogs. There were also several horses on this farm.

There were nine of us who started out on this march. We kept picking up men from other camps along the way. We ended up with about three hundred men. On this march I met a neighbor from Ohio, Murry Shulaw. We were so surprised to see each other. This was the only time I saw a guy that I knew while I was in the army.

They started us on a march across Poland and Germany. I lost the heel from one of my shoes while on this march. We marched until we met the American lines. When we met the Americans we heard that President Roosevelt had died.

While we were on this march, it was nothing to see a dead horse with a couple legs cut off. People would cut them off to eat. It could have been the Germans or whoever was walking along these roads. The horses were from the German civilians retreating from our U.S. Army. One time on this march they made soup for us with a horse's tongue. Nobody wanted to eat it, so I took it, skinned it, and ate it. We had not had any meat for a long time. After I took the meat, several others wanted some of it. I did share a bit with them.

The day we were liberated, the Americans came to pick up the German soldiers who had been guarding us. The German captain in charge of us was mean, so we told the Americans about him. The Americans sat him on the bumper of one of the trucks and the driver would see how close he could come to the truck ahead of him as they drove us away. It was Friday, April 13, 1945, the day I was liberated.

The Americans put us all on airplanes and sent us to Le Havre, France. Here we all had physicals and were de-loused. They put us on boats and brought us home to America. It took us eleven days to come across the Atlantic. I was assigned to work in the galley, where they pass out food, so I had plenty to eat on this trip. I started to gain back some of the weight I had lost. When we landed in New York Harbor, we were so glad to see our homeland that we all stooped and kissed the ground.

We were given new army clothes and sent home to be with our families for thirty days. After this we were all sent to Miami Beach for another thirty days of rest. This was quite a vacation. We stayed in big fancy hotels that even had maids who would come in and make the bed in the morning. One thing I remember about this trip was the southern-fried chicken. I really liked this and ate it often, until one day I peeled back the batter to find chicken feathers underneath. I don't think I ate any more chicken on that trip.

After our vacation, they sent us to Camp Atterbury, Indiana, for a few days, then on to Morristown, Indiana, where we guarded German prisoners. They gave us a gun and a clip of ammunition. We weren't allowed to carry our guns loaded, so we took our guns and set them in a corner. We did not worry about the Germans leaving as they would have much rather been in America than in Germany. Some of them said they would be shot for treason when they were sent back home. The German prisoners were picking tomatoes and working in a cannery. We even sent them back to pick up our guns.

I was able to come home for a couple days on leave during my time in Morristown. I was hitchhiking home, east of Lima, when an automobile came up behind me and stopped. It was my mom and my two younger brothers. My mom had just said to my brothers, "Wouldn't it be funny if that soldier was Doyt?" Sure enough, she was right! Talk about a mother's intuition!

I was discharged from the service on November 14, 1945.

The girl I married I met on a blind date. We were each with different people. I called her a week or two later for a date. We were married on January 16, 1948. The Lord must have spared my life through all of this so I could have the wonderful family He has given me.

I have three beautiful Christian daughters, Saundra, Mary, and Susan. These daughters have given me seven lovely grandchildren who love the Lord—Christian, Jennifer, Kathryn, Alisha, Kara, Anna, and Kyle. I feel I have been blessed over and over even with my wonderful

Christian sons-in-law and even further as my grandchildren are getting wonderful Christian mates.

(Note: When the Germans counter-attacked us, they were successful in dividing our company. We, who were in the northern caves, were all taken prisoner by the Germans. Since December 2002, I have discovered that we who were in the northern part of the caves and divided from our regiment were very lucky to be taken prisoner, because most of the other men were killed.)

# Part Six
# Home Front Remains Strong

# A Visit Back Home in Ohio

Typical of the military men's wives in the apartment house, I cleaned out the cupboards in our apartment in Stuart and gave all the food items to other army wives in the building. There was no way that I could squeeze food items in my two suitcases and with rationing, you never wanted to throw anything away.

What few belongings we had were put in my two suitcases and Art's duffel bag. We said "goodbye" to our friends in the apartment building and to our dearly loved ugly honeymoon-suite and boarded the train at the Stuart depot. I must have been a little homesick and didn't realize it, because I was feeling very elated as we began the first part of our journey back to Lima, Ohio. How nice it would be that on this trip Art and I would be traveling together. Again, the train was crowded with mostly men and a few women in military uniforms. Thankfully, we found a seat where we could sit together and could relax a little and try to sleep. But again, there were a few people in some of the other coaches that were sitting on suitcases in the aisles.

I had put some snack food in my purse because I knew from experience on my previous trip to Florida that the dining car could never feed all the extra people traveling in the coaches during these war years. When we needed to change trains, we would quickly buy food in the train terminals, but no hot meals. By the time we reached Ohio, my sensitive stomach was upset.

When we finally arrived in Lima, Art's parents were at the station to meet us. The Miller farmhouse was a welcome site, and all the wonderful food my mother-in-law had prepared helped my stomach problems disappear. Although we were extremely tired that first night back home, we sat up late and talked about our wedding and our life together in Florida. My in-laws wanted to hear details of what our life was like with Art in the military and us living in a small southern town so far away from Lima.

Our tiredness began to show and so we all said good night. After we washed the traveling dirt off our bodies and crawled into the big antique bed upstairs, we enjoyed the best sleep that we had had for a long time. The war seemed to have temporarily disappeared from our thoughts.

The next morning we borrowed Art's father's car and went into town to see if we could find my father at work at the power plant in the B. & O. railroad yards in Lima. We wanted to surprise him. He was not at the power plant where he usually worked. We waited awhile, and then I saw him walking across the railroad yards toward us. I saw him stop and look toward us and when he recognized us, he began running. I ran to meet him and we threw our arms around each other and hugged and hugged. I didn't realize until that moment how very, very much I had missed him.

Dad kept asking me, "When did you get here? How long are you going to stay? Are you coming out to the house?"

I told him, "We just got in last night. We'll be staying with Art's parents, but we'll definitely be spending some time with you, Lucille and the kids. Richard was just five months old when I left for Florida, I'll bet I won't know him. Diane and Nancy were just toddlers, and Marilyn is enjoying being a freshman. We'll be glad to see everybody. We will call you and make some arrangements. We better go now because you probably need to get back to work." As we turned to walk away I noticed that Dad had this big smile on his face.

When Art and I got in the car, he laughed and handed me his handkerchief and said, "You better use this and wipe the coal dust off your face." I had forgotten that my father would get lots of coal dust on his face, hands and clothing while he worked in the power plant.

I then told Art this little story about my father: He had gone into a bank to cash his paycheck and he had gone directly from work and was wearing his work clothes. He apologized to the woman at the teller window and said, "I'm sorry I'm so dirty, but I just came from work and didn't have a chance to clean up before I came here."

The woman said to him, "Sir, that dirt on you is a badge of honor—wear it proudly!" Dad said, "When I walked out of the bank after cashing my check that day, I felt ten feet tall!"

I say, "God bless that woman, whoever and wherever she is!"

Art's mother cooked food on a kerosene stove, only a bigger and better one than we had at the Stuart apartment. She was of German heritage and was a wonderful cook. She arranged some family dinners so that we would get to see everyone at once. She invited my father's family for dinner one evening. This was the first time our two sets of

140

parents had really met. I guess you could say that Art and I had more or less eloped and there had been no prior meetings of the two families. Art's mother did herself proud with a wonderful meal that evening. A date was then set for my in-laws and us to go to dinner at my father's house.

Several nights later, Art's parents, Art and I were all sitting around the dining room table at my father's house. We had finished eating a delicious roast beef dinner, a rarity in times of rationing, the little kids had been excused from the table, and the adults were lingering over a second cup of coffee and my father said, "Just a minute, Art, I have something for you."

Dad left the room and came back with a poorly wrapped gift box and handed it to Art. Art opened the package and in it was an eight-inch, very sharp, knife in a leather sheath. Dad said, "I bought this for you to take with you when you go overseas. If you get into some hand-to-hand combat it might come in handy. I hope you'll never need it—but you never know."

Art was speechless. I looked at his mother and she had turned very pale and looked as if she was going to faint. His father cleared his throat and said loudly, "Well, I hope he will never need it!"

Art finally said, "Thanks so much, Louis, I hope I don't need it in any hand-to-hand combat, but it's certainly a nice knife, and I'll always keep it. Thank you."

I looked at my father, and I knew his gift was a show of concern for the welfare of this young soldier who sat across the table from him in this safe Ohio environment but who could be facing danger in maybe just a few short months.

My in-laws, on the other hand, who were steeped in the doctrine of their pacifist church, could not bear to think of their youngest son being sent into battle. Their other son, Art's older brother, was in the Navy on a submarine in the Pacific. They could not prevent their sons from going to war, they could only pray that they would not need to kill, or be killed. That gift brought to their minds thoughts of how repugnant and brutal war really is and how helpless individuals are who have no control over their own destiny in times of war.

Dad's gift seemed to end all the polite conversation and small talk. It wasn't long until we left with my in-laws and were back at their house. No mention was ever made to us about the gift Art had received earlier that evening.

Although we had received occasional letters from Art's friends, Jim and Bill, the military kept transferring everyone around and it was impossible to keep current addresses. Art and I went to see the parents of these two friends and obtained their latest addresses. Their parents seemed to appreciate our visit and said they were praying for everyone's safe and quick return back home. There was a touch of sadness in the way they talked about how they missed having their house full of young people. They said, "It is so quiet around here, everybody has gone off to war."

Of course, Art and I went to see my Aunt Annie, and my Aunt Minnie who was now living with her. Annie was full of questions because she had never been out of the state of Ohio, and just couldn't imagine us being so far away. Minnie had taken a job at a small boat factory that had a defense contract to make lifeboats. She looked frail and I wondered how she could handle a job in a factory. Annie worked at The Gro-Cord Rubber Company, where they were making soles and heels for military shoes. My two aunts had cooked a fine dinner for us and I wondered how many of their precious food stamps it had cost them. We had a wonderful visit. Annie reminded me when we were ready to leave that if Art went overseas, I could come and stay with Minnie and her.

We also had some wonderful visits with Art's sister, Lelia, her husband Bob, and their son Jerry. Bob was a farmer and exempt from military service. Jerry was about four years old and thought his Uncle Art's uniform was really great and had his picture taken in it. He was a delightful young child and we loved to hear him sing some of the silly songs that were popular then, such as "Mairzy Doats" and "Three Little Fishies."

What precious memories we captured on this short visit back home, but all too soon it was time to say goodbye to everyone and get on a train and go to Macon, Georgia.

142

# Gloria and Art in Macon, Georgia

It was a dreary rainy day in Georgia. We retrieved our luggage at the train depot, bought a newspaper, and we were sitting in a small restaurant, looking for ads in the paper that would give us a clue as to what was available in rooms for rent in Macon. We made call after call only to be told that each place was already rented. We were about ready to give up and find a hotel, when Art made one more call, and the pleasant voice of a young woman answered. He told her we were responding to her ad in the paper for a sleeping room with kitchen privileges. They talked for a little while and she gave him directions on how to find the address.

When the taxi pulled up in front of a well-kept lawn and home, Art told the taxi driver to wait for a few minutes. The lady came to the door, smiled and in her sweet Southern accent said, "You are here about the room, aren't you? Let me show you the room."

The room was located at the front of the house, it was immaculate, with beautiful hardwood floors and a gas fireplace. The room was attractively decorated and we both immediately liked it.

The lady hurriedly said, "My name is Sue Ellen Smith, and I want you to know I don't rent the room to just anyone. But I could tell you were nice people, and I want to do what I can for the war effort, so you just get out there and pay that taxi driver. Move your things right in here." She was breathless by the time she finished saying all that.

The rain had made the room chilly, and Sue Ellen went over to light the gas fireplace. Then she showed us around the house and explained where everything was in the kitchen. She had us sit down at the kitchen table and have some sweet tea and cookies with her.

Sue Ellen said, "My husband is a city fireman and he works twenty-four hours on duty and twenty-four hours off duty. He knows I don't like to be in the house alone, so he said I could rent the room out, if I was careful to whom I rented it. I can tell that we are going to get along just fine. We have a little three-year-old daughter and she'll be waking up from her nap real soon. I know you will think she is real sweet cause we just LOVE her to death! We also have a son and he's playing over at a friend's house right now and you'll like him too. He's ALL boy, which pleases his daddy."

Sue Ellen's bubbly personality and her Southern charm put us at ease right away. We hung our few clothes in the small closet in the room, and moved our other things into the dresser and chest of drawers. Sue Ellen knocked on the door, gave us some bath towels and wash cloths, and told us since we had just arrived in town and didn't have time to buy any groceries yet, we should just eat with her and her children. What a wonderful introduction to Macon!

The next morning Art needed to report in at Warner-Robbins. After getting directions on where to catch a bus out to the base, he hurriedly left the house. I immediately went job hunting that same day, not realizing that Art's time at Warner-Robbins would be very short because it was a "replacement" depot. I found a job working as a receptionist and assistant to an osteopath in a downtown office building. I was to start work right away as the doctor's previous assistant had abruptly left several days before. (That "abruptly" should have been a clue.)

When Art returned home that evening, he said he saw a notice on a bulletin board at the base that Civil Service Exams were going to be given the next day. He told me it might be a good idea for me to take the exams. I went out to the base and took the exam for clerk-typist before I started working for the osteopath. The testing official for the Civil Service Office informed me that in approximately four weeks I would receive civil service certification, "if" I passed.

It took several days before we met Sue Ellen's husband, Raul Smith. He was a big strong man, with a friendly smile, very much in love with his wife, and totally captivated by his children. We all hit it off right away, and soon they had us eating our meals with them. They only charged us a few extra dollars to furnish us two meals a day.

Little Betsy would wait at the window for Art to come up the sidewalk and then she would run and jump into his arms, and then she would look at me and say, "Look! I got your hubband! Look! I got your hubband!"

The Smiths were a perfect example of a happy American family and their children were a true delight. We were privileged to be the recipients of true Southern hospitality in the Smith home.

Two wonderful weeks went by, and then I received a phone call from Art saying he was being transferred, but he did not know where.

I was to continue with my job and stay with the Smiths. Art later told me that he and a large number of men from Warner-Robbins were loaded into ten railroad coaches that night and they commenced a journey to a "destination unknown." They were not told where they were going or what their orders were. That was the way the military did things in those days. They could only figure out where they were by reading signs out the windows of the train. They did not dare leave the train. Eventually I received a call from Art and he said that he had been assigned to Kelly Field Air Force Base, which was close to San Antonio, Texas. It would be awhile before he could get a leave from the base and look for an apartment for us.

The office in downtown Macon where I worked was on the second floor and close to the Marine Recruiting Office. The marines were very friendly and polite and always spoke to me when I passed their open office door, or met them in the hall. I felt secure there, like living close to a police station. Meanwhile things began to change in the doctor's office where I worked.

The doctor always had clean nurses uniforms delivered for me to wear at work. He began telling me that I did not need to go into a storeroom to change clothes. He repeatedly told me, "I have seen a lot of naked women, you don't need to be so bashful." I continued to change in the storeroom.

My office duties consisted of answering the phone, keeping track of appointments, and helping patients put on hospital gowns. I was also trained to administer colonic irrigations. I hadn't counted on that as part of my job, but I managed with the help of some very understanding patients.

The doctor began telling me about how unhappy he was in his marriage and that his wife just didn't understand him. I knew, with his daily reminders that I needn't change clothes in the storeroom, that I could not trust him. I had promised myself to keep his office open while he went out of town to a medical convention. I needed the money, and he had scheduled several colonic irrigations for me to administer while he was away. On the day before he was to return, I was going to put a note on his desk stating that I was resigning and that way I would not have to face his wandering eyes.

On my last day, I walked into the office building and went to the second floor. The marines were waiting for me to come to work, and told me to step into their office. They said there had been a murder in the building and the police would be there any minute. I told them about my plans to leave a letter of resignation on the doctor's desk and to quickly leave. One of the marines said he would walk with me to the doctor's office while I put my letter there. He then quickly escorted me out of the building. I thanked the marine, got on a city bus, and hurried back to the Smiths' house. I never found out who was murdered, but it wasn't the doctor because a few days later I received my final paycheck in the mail and it was signed by him.

When I told Sue Ellen about the doctor, she laughed and said, "That old fool, you are smart to get yourself out of there. You don't have to put up with the likes of him!"

I happily agreed with Sue Ellen. Within a few days the paperwork arrived stating I had passed my Civil Service exam, and then I knew that I had possibilities of finding a better job.

In the meantime, Sue Ellen and I had enjoyed our girl talks and spending time together. One Sunday I was invited to go along with the Smiths to Sue Ellen's parents' home and was treated to the most fabulous example of Southern cooking that I have ever had the privilege to partake. They always said that their kindness to me was part of their contribution to the "war effort." I felt safe at the Smiths' while I waited for Art to find a place for me to stay.

Early one evening Sue Ellen asked me if I wanted to go with her on an errand. She said, "I want you to see another part of Macon that you haven't yet seen."

As we drove along she explained, "We are going to the area where a lot of negroes live in little shanty-type homes, there are no paved streets or sidewalks, and very few street lights. We need to hurry before it gets dark. I have some things to take to the lady that works for me because it is too much for her to carry the things home on the city bus."

The streets of Macon soon turned into a section of hills and crooked red dirt roads, and eventually Sue Ellen stopped her car in front of one of the little houses. She had quite a few bundles of her children's outgrown clothing and several large sacks of groceries in the back seat. As we were putting everything on the porch, the Smiths' housekeeper appeared. She looked pleasantly surprised at the items we had just placed there. She and Sue Ellen talked for awhile and then Sue Ellen gave her some money and said she would see her the following Monday. As we drove away the lady's children were happily waving to us from the porch and they had already begun to investigate what was in the packages.

Ever since the first day Art and I came to Macon I had noticed the ubiquitous black kettles in the backyards of homes in the residential areas. We also noted that there was one in the Smiths' backyard. When I questioned Sue Ellen about this, she said that was the way most of the people did their laundry. She went on to explain that they filled the kettle with water, built a fire under the kettle and washed their clothes in it. She said that her white sheets always came out sparkling white. The housekeeper did the Smiths' laundry and Sue Ellen said her housekeeper always cooked starch on the kitchen stove and she used just the right amount to make their clothes look like new.

I gained a great amount of respect for the work that Sue Ellen's housekeeper did as I watched the meticulous way that she did the cleaning and the washing and ironing for the Smiths. The Smiths' house and clothing always looked absolutely perfect! Sue Ellen and her family were very kind and appreciative to their housekeeper and they paid her well. I saw no racial prejudice or mistreatment in the Smith home. How fortunate I was to become a part of this loving and caring family, even though it was for just a short period of time, just by Art answering the "right" ad in the Macon newspaper.

Meanwhile Art was very busy getting acclimated to his assignment at Kelly Field, but it took him about four weeks before he could find a sleeping room with kitchen privileges. And now it was time for me to join Art in San Antonio. Sue Ellen took me to the train station, we hugged each other, said goodbye, and we promised to write, but regrettably we never did.

# Saboteurs—Spies—Secrets

Important components in fighting a war against tyrants are saboteurs, spies, secrets and underground activities. Tyrants are people who have usually gained their power by force and illegal means. Subversive activities are many times the only way the oppressed people can fight back. Since tyrants gained their position of power by force, it usually takes force to unseat them. Quietly and secretly, moral and ethical people will join together and form resistance movements. Although these people realize they are putting their own lives at risk, they feel that they would rather be dead than to live under the oppressive rule of a deluded egomaniac. In the words of America's famous patriot, Patrick Henry, "Give me liberty, or give me death!"

There are numerous examples of spy activities dating back to Biblical times; one example is Delilah betraying Samson. Mata Hari was a Dutch woman dancer who was a spy for Germany during the World War I years and was executed by the French. Lieutenant M. E. Clifton James acted as a double for the English General Bernard L. Montgomery in World War II to deceive the Germans about the pending D-Day invasion. Spies will always be at work trying to ply secrets out of unsuspecting countries. Confirmed active enemy spying was taking place in Hawaii for at least a year prior to the Japanese attack on Pearl Harbor. It is unbelievable, but foreign spies traveled at will in the United States before December 7th, 1941. It is more unbelievable that the United States did not have spies working for the U.S. government in other countries.

As the Germans were invading France in 1940, the French Underground was placing money, ammunition, guns, and dynamite in secret hiding places. The French Underground was well organized and moved frequently when there was a danger of being discovered. The French Underground was divided into two groups, the Corps Francs, which compared to the American Rangers, and required nerve, strength and indifference to death. The other group was the Saboteurs, which could be made up of old men, women, and children. Records were kept of the names of the recruits, how many people they could lodge and feed,

148

if they owned a car or a bicycle, and if they enlisted for sabotage, transport, or commando duty.

New recruits to the French Underground were taught how to sabotage production in factories, how to handle guns, how to handle dynamite, derail trains, blow up bridges and factories, and how to use a garrote to strangle a man before he could make a sound. Maps were made showing which routes to follow to move people to safety. There was a list of German houses where friends of the Allies would be able to get food and a safe place to sleep. In some cases specific instructions were written on rice paper so that the carrier could eat the paper if they were in danger of being captured. The work of the underground required stealth and cunning.

After the occupation of France, the Nazis began moving trainloads of much-needed food out of France to Germany. The Underground chemists concocted a way to have the railroad workers in the railroad yards poison all the food. Hundreds of Germans died from the food that was shipped out of France.

Secret radios helped the Underground keep in touch with England. Secret printing presses printed leaflets and newspapers and circulated them to combat the Nazi propaganda. Several times the Nazis discovered the locations of the radios and the printing presses and killed the operators. The Underground retaliated by killing the people who killed their people.

When the time came, the French Underground notified the Allies they were ready for the invasion of Normandy. At the appointed time, the Underground cut German communication lines, and dynamited strategic transportation areas to prevent German reinforcements from arriving on time.

When Paris fell on July 2, 1940, Winston Churchill became alarmed that the Nazis might invade England, and he made the decision to ship all of England's gold and securities to Canada. Churchill said that if they had to, they would fight the war from Canada. Under the strictest security the vast fortunes of gold and securities were loaded onto ships and began their dangerous journey of crossing the Atlantic Ocean. Churchill knew the risks, but the ships arrived safely, and again under strict security conditions, the precious cargo was unloaded at night into a train that carried the treasure to the Sun Life Assurance Company in Montreal's Dominion Square. Meticulous records were kept and every item in the shipment was accounted for, which included

773 million dollars worth of gold bullion, plus 299 boxes of securities, with a total value of $1,750,000,000. In the next three months more gold and securities were received bringing the total to over two billion dollars. What is amazing is that during those three months 134 Allied and neutral ships were sunk in the North Atlantic, but not any of the gold-carrying ships went down.

At the beginning of World War II, Great Britain's ships sailed across the Atlantic Ocean in convoys that were carrying valuable war equipment and needed food supplies for the British, but German wolf packs were sinking a large number of the British ships. Also, many American ships carrying war supplies to Great Britain fell prey to the ruthless wolf packs. American and British ships were being sunk faster than they could build new ones. The Germans had built a code machine called the Enigma, which was difficult for the English and the U.S. to break. The Germans had the advantage of sending coded messages to the German submarine commanders that gave them the location of the English convoys.

By a quirk of fate, a German Enigma machine fell into the hands of several Polish scientists. Poland immediately began working on the German Enigma machine trying to break the codes. They had seen the value of this complex code machine and had hired the best cryptographers they could find. Poland figured that men with mathematical genius were needed to work on cracking the complexities of the Enigma. Much of Poland's successful work in this area was due to the extraordinary ability of Marian Rejewski.

Poland wanted to share the Enigma machine and their research data with Great Britain because Great Britain entered the war in their defense. Poland had soon come under the domination of the Nazis and the Polish scientists realized they needed to get the Enigma out of Poland and into the hands of their ally, Great Britain. A French playwright, Sacha Guitry, and his actress wife, Yvonne Prentemps, helped get the Enigma machine through customs without inspection and paying duty by claiming the large diplomatic bags were a part of their own monumental stack of luggage.

Britain's survival depended on her ability to control the sea, but as yet she could not read the Germans' naval coded messages. A number of German submarines were disabled at sea by the English navy and parts of their Enigma-coded message equipment, codewheels, and other information were removed by the English before the German vessels sank. These items were turned over immediately to the head-quarters of the English cryptographers working at Bletchly Park, an estate in the town of Bletchly, located fifty miles northwest of London. More than one thousand people worked extremely hard to read Enigma messages not only meant for submarines, but also for the Luftwaffe, the army, the SS and also pencil and paper cipher systems. Piece by piece, the cryptanalysts were solving the complexities of the Enigma.

The English had seized enough Enigma information that they could now divert their convoys away from the wolf packs that had formerly threatened their survival in the war. At this point Ultra became the cover name for the solutions of the Enigma intercepts. Ultra was the second greatest secret of World War II, the atom bomb being the first.

Ultra reduced the uncertainty surrounding the enemy and helped the Allies anticipate their enemy's actions and not be taken by surprise. The Germans would not face the reality that Enigma could be broken. Ultra brought peace sooner and helped to save many lives of the British, American and German people. It was a great intellectual achievement that the code-breakers at Bletchly discovered at a critical point in World War II. As the author David Kahn wrote in his book, *Seizing the Enigma,* "The unraveling of the Enigma was the equivalent of those endeavors that are awarded Nobel prizes. And like those, it benefited humankind."

The United States had a secret weapon that was originally put into use sometime during 1918 to 1919 during World War I. Fourteen Choctaw Indian men were assigned to the Army's 36th Division, and they helped the American Expeditionary Force send and receive orders faster and were instrumental in helping win important battles in the Meuse-Argonne Campaign in France.

One Choctaw was placed in each field company's headquarters. They handled military communications by field telephone, then they translated the radio message into the Choctaw language and wrote the field orders, which were then carried by runners between the companies. The Germans were never able to break the code, but they did capture about one in four runners.

This was the first example of the Choctaw language being used in an unbreakable code. On November 13, 1989 the French government recognized the valuable contribution of the Choctaw and were the first to officially honor the Choctaw with the Knight of the National Order of Merit, which is the highest honor France can bestow.

In World War II, seventeen Comanches were assigned to the Signal Corps of the Army and were trained in communication and their language was used, which could not be decoded by the enemy. They worked in teams with the regiments in the field and messages were sent back and forth to division headquarters. The French also honored the Comanches for their contribution on the same day they honored the Choctaw and they also received the same award. (Note: The Comanche code phrase, *posah-tai-vo* meant "crazy white man," which was used to designate Adolf Hitler. They had a word for airplane but no word for bomber, so they made up a word for "pregnant airplane.")

During WWII, a man named Philip Johnston, the son of a missionary, was not a Navajo, but was raised around the Navajos. He was very fluent in their language and he realized how they could become codetalkers for the military. He went to the U.S. Marines and convinced them of the advantages of using their language because it is unwritten and very complex because it uses pitch and tone of the voice, for the same word, but with different meanings. He set up a demonstration, which used encoding, transmitting, and decoding a message in twenty seconds, which would take thirty minutes on a machine to do the same task. The Marines were convinced and immediately Navajo code talkers were sent to all the Marine units in the Pacific Theater. They devised a Navajo dictionary of 413 military terms, e.g., chicken hawk = dive-bomber, humming bird = fighter plane, iron fish = submarine, etc. The code talkers provided an important service because they saved time as compared to traditional methods of coding and decoding messages. Usually the Indians did well in the military and they were well accepted by the other soldiers. Stereotyping did not appear to upset them. They were America's unique secret weapon and they also saved many lives.

# Gloria and Art Relocate
# in San Antonio, Texas

The sleeping room with kitchen privileges that Art found was in the home of an elderly, deaf widow named Mrs. Edith Baines. She evidently rented the room in her home to get a little extra money. The challenges she faced with her deafness created in her a fear of strangers, therefore, it took awhile for her to trust us. After awhile I realized that if I wrote notes to her, we could communicate fairly well with each other. For example, I asked her in a note if I could use her ironing board. Thereupon, she took me to a closet and showed me her ironing board and iron. She then wrote a note to me saying I could use them anytime I wished. Art and I both had difficulty understanding her speech, so the notes helped us all understand each other, and hopefully eliminated some of the fear she had of the "strangers" living in her house. Sadly, we seldom saw Mrs. Baines smile and we understood how trapped she was feeling in her very quiet world. I have often wondered what she would have done if I would have given her a hug. Perhaps it would have frightened her; I'll never know.

Mrs. Baines's house was immaculate and she made it known to us that we did not dare leave any crumbs of food in the kitchen because food left anyplace attracted ants and roaches. We soon discovered this when we had a small bag of potato chips in our room and left it open for several hours, and a line of roaches immediately marched in for a feast.

I was getting accustomed to living out of my two suitcases and adjusting to the lifestyles in different cities. The weather was hot in San Antonio when I arrived in May, and I immediately developed a prickly heat rash from my neck to my ankles. That heat rash stayed with me for my entire stay in Texas. When I took a bath it was like thousands of needles pricking my skin. I then understood how little babies must feel when they get a prickly heat rash and they cry when their mothers bathe them. There were times when I could have cried as I got into the bathtub and the bath water created the waves of pain associated with each little heat-rash blister.

Art's assignment at Kelly Field Air Force Base was working out very well and he was hitting his stride in airborne radar work. He had permission to live off the base, so he could come home each night. He received an extra $30 in his monthly military paycheck for off-base housing and food.

San Antonio was a large city with five military bases surrounding it, and there was a glut of military wives on the job market, therefore I felt lucky to get hired as a clerk at a dress shop that carried moderate to expensive women's wear. I was paid a base salary plus commission. The saleswomen that I worked with were mostly army wives. Everyone was very friendly and a strong sense of camaraderie existed among us. The store demanded that we dress well and wear hose. The hose hid my heat rash, but they might have also contributed to it.

One morning when I arrived at work, I found everyone, clerks and customers, all gathered around a radio at the back of the store. It was June 6, 1944, and the Allies had just landed in Normandy. The news commentators on the radio were announcing that the Allied Forces of the United States and Great Britain, under the command of General Dwight D. Eisenhower, were invading Normandy. The news commentators were explaining how the Allied forces were using an unprecedented number of men, ships, planes, tanks, etc., in this invasion. We all wanted to stay close to a radio because we didn't want to miss any of the news. It was frightening to think of what our fighting men were going through and we surmised that the size of this battle was beyond our comprehension.

A few more customers came into the store and joined our group around the radio. Someone in the group said, "This is a decisive battle our troops are in today. Going into Normandy is a big undertaking for the Allies. We are probably going to lose a lot of our men in this battle."

Then someone else in the group said, "Let's join hands and pray for our soldiers." Unashamedly we formed a circle, held hands with people we hardly knew, and we all silently prayed for the safety of our men in this momentous battle—the invasion of Normandy. At least four of the women that worked in the dress shop felt certain that their husbands were fighting in some capacity in the invasion and they were visibly upset.

For the next several days the news media gave accounts of the Normandy invasion. They stated that the invasion was a combined effort of navy ships and airplanes shelling the German fortifications behind enemy lines to soften their ability to fight off the incoming Allied soldiers onto the beaches. Many paratroopers had been dropped behind enemy lines the night before to take out strategic fortifications. Not everything went as planned, but within three days the news was encouraging as the beachheads were now under control of the Allies.

A rebroadcast of the message that General Eisenhower had read to the assault troops before they went into battle and to the airborne troops before they emplaned was later aired to the American people, as follows:

"Soldiers, sailors and airmen of the Allied Expeditionary Force: You are about to embark on a great crusade, toward which we have striven these many months. The hopes and prayers of liberty-loving people everywhere go with you. In company with our brave Allies and brothers in arms on other fronts you will bring about the destruction of the German war machine, elimination of Nazi tyranny over the oppressed peoples of Europe, and security for ourselves in a free world.

"Your task will not be an easy one. Your enemy is well trained, well equipped and battle hardened. He will fight—fight savagely. But in this year of 1944 much has happened since the Nazi triumphs of 1940 and 1941. The United Nations have inflicted upon the Germans great defeats in open battle, man to man. Our air offensive has seriously reduced their strength in the air, and their capacity to wage war on the ground.

"Our home fronts have given us an overwhelming superiority in weapons and munitions of war, and have placed at our disposal great reserves of trained fighting men. The tide has turned. The free men of the world are marching together to victory. I have full confidence in your courage, devotion to duty and skill in battle. We will accept nothing less than full victory.

"Good luck and let us all beseech the blessing of Almighty God upon this great and noble undertaking."

Soon the details began to emerge that gave the American people a glimmer of the awesome size of this undertaking. The sheer numbers of men participating, the astronomical numbers of munitions and supplies, the logistics involved in the planning—it was beyond our comprehension. It was obvious that it was too soon to talk about victories, because most of Europe still needed to be liberated from Hitler's grasp. But we all know that every march begins with that first big step—and we had just taken that first big step on the forward march to Germany.

# The Invasion of Normandy—D-Day

The planning for D-Day began two years prior to June 6, 1944, and ultimately the decisions rested on the shoulders of the supreme commander of the Allied forces, Dwight D. Eisenhower. The invasion of Normandy was a unified operation, called OVERLORD, and it required the cooperation of the all the commanders. Sometimes "territorial" disputes would arise between the different commanders and Eisenhower appeared to be the best leader to resolve the dissension. The British General Bernard L. Montgomery had more combat experience than the other commanders but was often accused of being overly cautious. Montgomery and Eisenhower continued to have differences of opinions throughout the campaign.

The secret stockpiling of supplies in England was rapidly growing. One and a half million American soldiers were arriving in Southern England and many had to be quartered in private homes. English girls began dating some of the American GIs, which did not please most of the British soldiers also quartered there. The English taunted the American soldiers by saying, "You are overpaid, oversexed, and over here." The American soldiers replied, "You British soldiers are underpaid, undersexed, and under Eisenhower." However, the English and the American soldiers eventually learned to work together for the common cause.

As the final days before the invasion grew near, the following equipment was put on alert: 5,000 ships, 4,000 landing craft, 600 warships, 2,500 bombers, 7,000 fighters and fighter bombers. Six divisions were to make the initial landings: three American, two British, and one Canadian. The target was a sixty-mile stretch of beach between Cherbourg and Le Havre. The British and the Canadians were to go ashore at landing areas called Sword, Juno, and Gold. The Americans were to land at Omaha, Utah, and the port of Cherbourg.

In the meantime, the Germans had been busy preparing for possible invasions along the entire coast line of Europe, General Irwin Rommel's plan was to meet the Allies on the beaches and chase them back into the waters. The areas were heavily mined, and bunkers and pill-boxes had been constructed. Obstacles, called "Rommel's asparagus," were placed in the channel waters, that could wreck the bottom of landing craft. Steel beams with mines attached were strategically placed in beaches and meadows to stop invaders. The Germans had sixty divisions with which to defend Europe's coastlines. Thanks to Ultra the Allies knew the locations of these divisions.

The British General Sir Percy Hobart had developed some unique equipment in preparation for the invasion. The Crab was designed to go through a mined area and clear paths for incoming troops. There were flame-throwing Crocodiles, and amphibious tanks, called the DD, that could propel themselves to shore. The weird looking inventions garnered the nickname of "Hobart's Funnies." For some reason the Americans did not make as much use of them as they could have. The Crab would have saved a lot of American lives had it been in use on the Omaha and Utah beaches.

May had been the original date for the invasion but was postponed until June 5–7. The deciding factors were the moon and the tides. Weather conditions on the first few days of June turned severe. The needed air operations would have been impossible. Eisenhower ordered a "stand down." Early on June 5th, the weather conditions improved a little with a possible favorable forecast for the next day. After consulting with his staff, Eisenhower ordered: "June 6th will be D-Day." He knew that the longer the Allies waited the more time the Germans had to improve their defenses. If he made the wrong decision, Eisenhower knew it would be disastrous for his troops. Each delay would move the invasion later and later and would give the Germans more precious time to prepare. What Eisenhower didn't know was that the German channel patrols, the key commanders, and Rommel had left their posts because they all thought the weather conditions made it impossible for an invasion.

On the night of June 5th, the Allied ships moved stealthily through the sea toward France. Overhead, airplanes carried paratroopers and towed gliders. These airborne units were to seize exits and bridges to prevent the Germans from getting reinforcements to the beaches. Through some errors, the paratroopers were dropped far from their planned targets. The silent glider pilots were dropped closer to their planned area and took most of their objectives and created a lot of confusion among the surprised German soldiers.

Shortly after dawn, the main landings began, with British Second Army troops under the command of General Miles Dempsey going ashore onto the beaches Sword, Juno, and Gold. They were able to quickly move on toward their goal of Caen and were temporarily stopped at that point. The American troops under General Omar Bradley were to go ashore on Utah and Omaha. The troops at Utah, after encountering a limited amount of resistance, were able to get established. The story of what happened at Omaha was nearly a disaster.

As the landing craft approached Omaha Beach they were being bounced around by six foot waves. The soldiers were getting seasick and weak at a critical time in the landing operation. Many of the landing craft unloaded their men too far out and these men drowned because they had heavy field packs of military supplies strapped to their bodies and were unable to quickly unload these in order to stay afloat in the water. The amphibious tanks were launched too early and most of them were at the bottom of the channel.

Once the American soldiers reached the beach they discovered that the German fortifications that lined the beach had not been previously destroyed by the American bombers, as planned. The Germans had the advantage of protection as they fired upon the invading troops. As veterans of the first several waves at Omaha described it, "We were like sitting ducks in a shooting gallery." To make matters worse, at Omaha the Americans faced the best of the Germany infantry divisions. It is a miracle that Omaha did not cave in to the German defenses.

On June 6th, D-Day, 2,500 Americans died at Omaha Beach; 2,499 died in airborne assault. Within three days the Allies linked up and the beaches were all theirs.

# San Antonio—
# The Countdown Before Deployment

The men in Art's company all knew that they would probably be sent overseas soon, and they tried to keep their spirits up and on the surface seemed to be enjoying each day as it came. The men in the company planned picnics for a number of Sundays. The picnics were a little disorganized but always fun.

One Sunday, the company planned a memorable trip to the San Antonio Zoo. Three of the guys stood in front of the chimps' cage and kept saying insults to the chimps. How the chimps knew they were being insulted, I never quite figured out, but the chimps got angry and picked up their dung on the bottom of their cage and threw it at the guys. The chimps' aim was very good and there were some big brown stains on three khaki uniforms. After a few swear words the soldiers laughed it off and admitted they had been outsmarted by a couple of chimps.

The city of San Antonio was an interesting city and offered many sightseeing opportunities. We enjoyed the River Walk downtown and we liked to rent a canoe on Sunday afternoons and just paddle around. On military pay you couldn't afford to do much.

One time on a military payday, we were sitting on a bench down by the river, and a drunken soldier came up to us and said, "You look like a nice couple, I want to give you some money."

Art told the man, "Keep your money, you'll need it later." The drunk was very insistent that we take it and he was getting angry and trying to stuff it in Art's pockets. We had to run to get away from the man, but he was drunk and it was easy to outrun him.

The city buses provided us with cheap transportation and we were able to get to scenic and historical areas, such as the Alamo. The Texans were always quick to point out their many battles with the Indians and the Mexicans in their early history and they took great pride in their state. Art and I always laughed when we would go into a restaurant and the menu would have all the statistics of how Texas was bigger and better than any other state in the United States.

159

There was a theater downtown called The Aztec Theater, which we tried to go to when our finances would allow it. The architecture in the lobby was of huge gray stones and it gave you a sense of entering a large cave. The carpeting throughout the theater was a dark red color, very thick, and looked expensive to my untrained eye. The dark ceiling in the seating area was very high and had little twinkling lights that resembled stars. Uniformed ushers with flashlights walked everyone down the aisles and showed the people where to sit. There was no popcorn sold in the lobby and no soda pop was consumed while watching the movie. The only things sold in the lobby were tiny boxes of mints and little hard candies. We watched the movie *Going My Way*, starring Bing Crosby, at the Aztec Theater.

There was a wonderful farmers market in San Antonio and Art would often stop there on his way home and purchase some fresh fruit or vegetables. On several occasions he bought a whole watermelon and carried it on his shoulders the ten blocks to our house. It was heavy and awkward to carry but it was a real treat to eat. We always offered our landlady a piece, but she refused. She would then get into the refrigerator at night while we slept and she would eat the entire center part of the whole melon.

I never think of Texas without thinking of bugs. Whenever Art was sent out on bivouac he would come back with a terrible case of chiggers. Quite often there were scorpions in the bathtub, and huge spiders would spin webs across the toilet seat, and roaches could find a tiny crumb of food in just a few minutes after it would be dropped on the floor. I understood perfectly our landlady's warning and kept my part of the kitchen and our room spotless.

Art received a seven-day furlough and that wasn't enough time to go to Ohio and back and have enough time for visiting, so we decided to go to Mexico for four days. That was the train trip from hell! The people on the train began opening the windows and all the heat and dust from outside came into the coach. There was no dining car and we were getting hungry. The train stopped at a small town and five women came out to the tracks and they were selling tacos and other Mexican food. We thought we wanted some coffee until we noticed the coffee vendor only had one tin cup and she wiped it out with her apron between customers.

We stayed in a hotel in Monterey and went to several restaurants and ate Mexican food, drank Mexican beer and listened to the Mexican

160

bands. We wanted to absorb as much of the culture as we could in this short period of time. In sampling the culture of the area we do not know how we missed "Montezuma's Revenge" but thankfully we did. There were interesting shops and we bought Art's mother a leather purse and we bought a soapstone box for the coffee table we would someday own.

In Monterey two little boys kept pestering Art to shine his shoes. Finally, Art gave in, and he asked me to take a picture of the boys shining his shoes. Just as I was ready to take the picture, three young men came running up to me and snatched the camera out of my hands and began yelling at both of us in Spanish. We finally understood they did not want us to take pictures of any of their people begging. We were lucky to get our camera back but we were quite shaken by the episode. Soon it was time for one of those miserable train rides back to San Antonio.

Less than two weeks after our return from Mexico, the dreaded phone call came. It was the 15th of October 1944, when Art called and said he was going to be restricted to the base. Preparations were being made to send a large group of men overseas from Kelly Field, and Art was one of that group. Of course, the soldiers did not know their destination, but they surmised that they were being sent to the Pacific Theater of Operations. The soldiers were ordered to make out wills before they shipped out. Unbelievably, Art was permitted one more night at home.

That last night we went to a little restaurant to eat dinner but we found it difficult to eat very much. We talked well into the night. We talked about where I should stay while he was gone. Art did not think I should try staying at my father's house. He assured me that his parents would want me to stay with them. We talked about trying to save money for when he returned as we would need to buy a car and some furniture. We never talked about me getting a car to drive while he was overseas. I had not driven a car very much before we were married and with gasoline and tires being rationed, I guess we thought it too much for me to handle. We talked about what kind of work I should look for, and Art laughingly said I should not try "sheet shaking" again.

That last night we laid in bed, our arms wrapped around each other, hoping that morning would never come. It was 5:00 A.M. and there was no holding back the dawn. Art did not dare miss his bus out to the base so he quickly dressed in his khaki uniform and I followed him to the porch. There had been no time for a last breakfast together, just enough time for one last kiss.

I'll never forget the look on Art's face as he walked down the sidewalk in front of the house, he stopped, turned around, and looked back at me. We both knew this was the last time we would see each other until after the war would be over. We had absolutely no idea how long this separation would be. It seemed frightfully final as I saw his back when he turned and walked away, going toward his bus stop. We had had approximately thirteen months together since our wedding. I needed to be thankful for at least that much time. I returned to our room and already I was feeling alone and sad. I tried to get a few hours sleep before the downtown businesses would open. I couldn't sleep so I started packing my suitcases.

It was soon time for me to call in to work and say I was leaving for Ohio. The managers understood because most of their clerks were army wives and were subject to being relocated at any time. I went to the bank and withdrew my "going home money," went to the train station and purchased my tickets, and checked the timetable for my departure. I had to write a note to my landlady because she could not understand that I was leaving. I told her in the note that she could have our supply of food staples in the cupboard and refrigerator. She seemed flustered and began to cry. I thought about giving her a hug, but instead I patted her arm and said "thanks," hoping she could read my lips.

I took a short nap, called a cab, boarded a train and I was on my way to Lima, Ohio. When I was out of Texas, my prickly heat rash miraculously disappeared.

# Gloria Returns to Ohio—
# Employed by U.S. Corps of Engineers

Riding on a train with most of the passengers being military personnel was not new to me anymore. Thankfully, the trains on this trip were not as crowded and noisy as on my previous trips. I settled down in my seat and was pleased I did not have to share it with a stranger. I began thinking about what I would do when I arrived in Lima. I made a list of priorities, (1) where I would live, (2) get a job, (3) make a plan to save money for when Art would return, and (4) get our few belongings all in one place and stop living out of a suitcase. The realization suddenly came to me that I no longer needed to ask my father for permission to visit with my mother and stepfather. I felt a sense of liberation as I made these plans for my immediate future.

I had picked up a newspaper in the train depot and began reading the latest news. There were many troublesome articles relating to the war in both the European and Pacific Theaters. I had a strong feeling that Art was heading into the Pacific Theater. As I read I began to feel very sleepy. I had not realized how exhausted I was from lack of sleep in the previous forty-eight-hour period and I slept quite soundly on the train, which made the time pass quickly.

I was thankful that I would arrive in Lima a short time after my father would be getting off work and his picking me up at the railroad station would not cost him extra gas. The train pulled into the station and there was Dad, with a big smile on his face. He was ready to welcome me back. We put my luggage into his Ford and headed out to his farm on Sandusky Road.

After eating and visiting with everyone for an hour I went upstairs to my former room to sleep that night. I did not want to waste any time and I wanted to go into town with Dad in the morning and be dropped off at Annie's house. I could walk downtown from there and I wanted to immediately begin job hunting.

Luck was with me, because I went to the State Employment Agency and asked if there were any office jobs available. I told them I

163

had a Civil Service classification for clerk/typist. That was all I needed to say and they told me the United States Corps of Engineers needed someone with civil service classification and that their office was in the plant at the Lima Locomotive Works. An appointment was set up for me in the afternoon. I met the colonel who was in charge of the Lima office and he hired me immediately. He took me to the police station to get fingerprinted, which was a requirement since I would be working with classified information. I was told I would begin working in two days, which gave them time to do a preliminary background check on me, and it gave me time to arrange transportation. I was elated and was silently thanking Art for encouraging me to take that Civil Service exam in Georgia.

I went back to my father's house that evening and excitedly told everyone my good news about getting a job. I called Art's parents and his sister, Lelia, to tell them about my job. Lelia said she knew that a neighbor worked at the Lima Locomotive Works and every day he drove past her house on his way to work. Before an hour was up I had a place in a car-pool that went to the same factory building where I would be working. The driver of the car pool only wanted two dollars per week and my gasoline ration stamps. He said he could pick me up at either Lelia's house, Art's parents' house, or at the end of the road at Annie's house, because he passed all three places on his way to and from work. My plans were to spend about two or three months at each place and keep rotating around until the war was over and Art came home. Hopefully, that way the people would not get tired of me being with them. How very fortunate I was to be able to get this all arranged in one evening.

When I left home to get married it was almost like an elopement, and I had left clothing in my closet and items in my chest of drawers and dressing table. I decided I should go upstairs and begin putting things in boxes in preparation for moving them over to Art's parents' house. It seemed important to me to get all my things in one place and in order. In going though my closet, I could not find my prom formal that Mother and Jimmy had bought for me. I went downstairs to ask Lucille if she knew where it was.

Lucille's curt response was, "I cut it up and made Easter dresses for Diane and Nancy."

My heart stopped, I was stunned, and all I said was, "Oh!" I turned and went upstairs to my room and cried. My beautiful dress that my mother and stepfather had taken so much pleasure in buying for me was gone. I had wanted to keep it forever. Our junior and senior proms were not elegant affairs, but they were well attended, there was delicious food served, and recorded music was provided for dancing. Everyone seemed happy and the boys all looked handsome and the girls all looked beautiful. There was an aura that permeated those two events that could never be duplicated. Knowing that my father and stepmother did not take any pictures of me in that special dress, I always imagined that at least I would have the dress to keep down through the years as a reminder of a special time in my life. I also imagined having a daughter that would want to wear it, and that would give me the opportunity to reminisce with her.

I tried to tell myself that a prom dress is probably not important in the total scheme of things when you think about the war that is engulfing the world. But also, civilized people need to hang onto and preserve the pleasing sounds of music, lines from great poets, and, yes, even a pretty dress that can remind us that all is not lost in times of war and strife, and that some day normalcy will return.

As soon as I regained control of myself, I called my father-in-law and asked him to please come and help me move my things out of my father's house. I knew I needed to leave before I said something that I would be forever sorry for. That night, all my worldly things, as few as they were, were moved into the spare bedroom at Art's parents' house. Art's civilian clothes were in the closet of his former room at their farmhouse. I had a comforting feeling that, at last, I was getting some order into my life.

I began my new job and I liked it very much. The U.S. Corps of Engineers had a government contract with the Locomotive Works to build power shovels and cranes which were shipped to military installations and maneuvers that required that type of equipment, both in the states and overseas. We also sent repair and replacement parts where needed to keep the equipment running.

I didn't know what to expect from a boss that held the rank of a colonel and who came to work in uniform, but I found him to be understanding, fair and very professional. I felt fortunate to have a job that was connected to the military and that in some small way I was helping my country.

I felt I needed to go to Detroit and spend a weekend with Mother and Jimmy and tell them in more detail about the various happenings after Art and I got married. I was planning to arrive there Friday night and return on Sunday afternoon. My train connections would work out well for this short visit. The day came to get on the train and I began having pains in my stomach. I thought the pains would go away and I didn't want to cancel my trip, so there I was on the train, heading for Detroit, and soon I was doubled over in excruciating pain. When I arrived in Detroit, Mother and Jimmy knew instantly that something was wrong with me. They called their doctor and he saw me immediately. Of course, everyone thought I was pregnant and about to miscarry. Then the doctor noticed my eyes and the color of my skin and he surmised I had hepatitis.

The tests proved positive for hepatitis and I was questioned about where I had been eating. I remembered that I always went to lunch with several women from the dress shop, in San Antonio. We usually ate at a lunch counter in a dime store not far from where we worked. Shortly before I left for Ohio, we discovered that the lunch counter had been closed because a hepatitis outbreak had been traced to it.

I dreaded making the call to the colonel and telling him I was in Detroit, Michigan and that I was sick and could not come to work for several weeks. He did not sound pleased or even as if he believed me. I was terrified that I would lose my job. I had been put to bed for a week at Mother and Jimmy's house and they took excellent care of me. Although I still felt sick and weak, I wanted to get back to Lima and back to work.

When I arrived in Lima, Art's parents took me to their doctor and he ordered me back to bed for another week. Finally, after another week, I was given the doctor's approval to return to work. On my first day back at work, when the colonel saw me, he had no doubt that I had been sick, as I had lost weight and my skin and the whites of my eyes still retained a yellowish color. When I told him how worried I was about losing my job, he smiled and assured me there had been no danger of that happening.

Letters began arriving from Art about a month later, but the letters had been censored, and when Art tried to write where he was, the censor blackened the words to where they were not readable.

Gloria Miller and her husband, Arthur Miller. This photo was
taken two months after their marriage.

James (Jim) Byerly. Jim was an officer in the United States Navy and was stationed at an Advanced Base Ship Dock—#1 (ASBD-1). This was a floating dry dock for the maintenance of ships that was located off the island of Samar, in the Philippines.

**Willis F. (Bill) Early was shot down over Berlin and taken prisoner.**

**John McNett served in combat engineers, landed on Omaha Beach, and fought all the way to Germany.**

**Doyt Hanthorn fought at Anzio, and was taken prisoner.**

# WESTERN UNION

1201

(19)

A. N. WILLIAMS
PRESIDENT

NEWCOMB CARLTON
CHAIRMAN OF THE BOARD

J. C. WILLEVER
FIRST VICE-PRESIDENT

The filing time shown in the date line on telegrams and day letters is STANDARD TIME at point of origin. Time of receipt is STANDARD TIME at point of destination

DWA343 33 GOVT=WASHINGTON DC APR 10 1143P

1944 APR 11 PM 6 21

MRS ANNA B HANTHORN=

ROUTE NUMBER TWO LAFAYETTE ALLEN CO OHIO=

THE SECRETARY OF WAR DESIRES ME TO EXPRESS HIS DEEP REGRET
THAT YOUR SON PRIVATE DOYT J HANTHORN HAS BEEN REPORTED
MISSING IN ACTION SINCE TWENTY THREE FEBRUARY IN ITALY
PERIOD LETTER FOLLOWS=

DUNLOP THE ADJUTANT GENERAL.

DOYT.

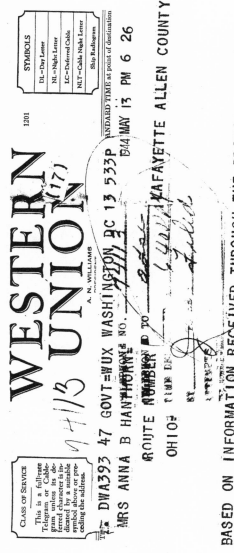

# WESTERN UNION

(17)

A. N. WILLIAMS
PRESIDENT

CLASS OF SERVICE

This is a full-rate Telegram or Cablegram unless its deferred character is indicated by a suitable symbol above or preceding the address.

SYMBOLS

DL = Day Letter
NL = Night Letter
LC = Deferred Cable
NLT = Cable Night Letter
Ship Radiogram

1201

STANDARD TIME at point of destination

DA393 47 GOVT=WUX WASHINGTON DC 13 533P

1944 MAY 13 PM 6 26

MRS ANNA B HANTHORN= LAFAYETTE ALLEN COUNTY

OHIO=

BASED ON INFORMATION RECEIVED THROUGH THE PROVOST MARSHALL
GENERAL RECORDS OF THE WAR DEPARTMENT HAVE BEEN AMENDED TO
SHOW YOUR SON PRIVATE DOYT J HANTHRON IS NOW A PRISONER OF
WAR OF THE GERMAN GOVERNMENT ANY FURTHER INFORMATION RECEIVED
WILL BE FURNISHED BY THE PROVOST MARSHALL GENERAL=

DUNLOP ACTING THE ADJUTANT GENERAL=

DOYT J.

THE COMPANY WILL APPRECIATE SUGGESTIONS FROM ITS PATRONS CONCERNING ITS SERVICE

Old telegrams of Dout Hanthorn

## ELSIE PHILIBEN MILLER

### A Mother's Prayer

GOD, FATHER of Freedom, look after that boy of mine, wherever he may be. Walk in upon him. Keep his mind stayed on Thee. Talk with him during the silent watches of the night, and spur him to bravery whenever called upon to face the cruel foe. Transfer my prayer to his heart, that he may know the lingering love I have bequeathed to him as an everlasting gift.

Keep my boy contented and inspired by the never-dying faith in his Mother's God. He is my gift to Freedom. May that Freedom forever remain untarnished, God.

Thru the lonely and confusing hours of training and combat, and throughout all the long days of a hopeful Victory, keep his spirit high and his purpose unwavering. Make him a proud pal to all with whom he comes in contact, and make his influence a noon-day light wherever his duty takes him. Nourish that boy of mine with the love that I gave him at birth, God. Satisfy the hunger of his soul with the knowledge of this daily prayer of mine.

To my country, and to world Freedom, O Heavenly Father, have I bequeathed this boy of mine. He is my choicest treasure. Take care of him, God. Keep him in health and sustain him under every possible circumstance of events. I once warmed him, God, under my heart. You warm him anew under his shelter and under the stars. Touch him with my smile and cheer and comfort, and my full confidence in his every brave pursuit.

Silent and alone, I pray, God, but I am only one of millions of Mothers whose prayers stream day and night to you. This is our Gethsemane. Lead us victoriously thru it, God. And lead that boy of mine thru his. Fail him not—and may he not fail you, his country, nor the Mother who bore him. That's all, God.

(Author Unknown.)

(Elsie Miller liked this prayer and she placed a copy of it in her Holy Bible.)

Elsie was the mother of two sons that served in WWII. Walter served in the U. S. Navy, and Arthur served in the U.S. Air Force. Elsie prayed daily for their safe return.

**Harold Barrick and wife, Helen. Harold was a Ranger, fought at the Battle of the Bulge, and all the way to Germany.**

Hannah, 4, (left) and Marian, 2,
Sondheimer, daughters of Elizabeth and Martin.

• All photos courtesy Elizabeth Sondheimer

Elizabeth and Dr. Martin Sondheimer on their wedding day.
They were married in her childhood
home on March 14, 1928.

Elizabeth Sondheimer was a ski instructor at this lodge in the Black Forest. Everyone she knew from there, all liberal Germans who were not Jews, were sent to concentration camps. All of the people in this photo were killed.

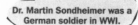

Dr. Martin Sondheimer was a German soldier in WWI.

The Sondheimers' home in Stuttgart shows war's devastation in 1944.

Hannah (left) and Marian wash their English bulldog, Joy, in their Lima backyard. The boy Ernest, was from Germany. The Sondheimers were housing him until his parents made their way from Germany.

All photos courtesy Elizabeth Sondheimer

Elizabeth and Dr. Martin Sondheimer on their 50th wedding anniversary.

Photos and text courtesy and permission Elizabeth
Sondheimer and The Lima News

# From 'Somewhere in the Southwest Pacific'

First place in this month's installment of letters from Camp and Sea and Oversea goes to Sgt. Frederick E. Mills. When last heard from, Sgt. Mills was in Australia. Now he writes to us from "Somewhere in the Southwest Pacific" under date of September 2:

The last bit of news you received from me came from "down under" in Australia. At this writing I am far removed from civilization as we know it. Since the Journal readers may be interested in native music, I will attempt to send a few items of interest on this subject. In general the native culture here is of a high order. Their decorative work is quite beautiful, particularly the work with native wood. My first musical treat came one day when some native workers relaxed from their duties long enough to sing and dance.

The missions here have taught some hymns, and I was relieved to discover that the hymns were well chosen. After some persuasion the natives began singing. I expected at the most a fair rendition in unison. What I heard was a beautiful performance in four parts! Their voices blended very well, and while these people lack some of the depth of tone which is characteristic of the Negro race, there was a softness about the tone which I find difficult to describe.

It is something I never heard in any race of people. Their procedure in getting started was most interesting. They were always careful to group themselves according to the parts and depended on one voice to lead them into each phrase. This leading voice was the highest voice, and as nearly as I could determine, sang a tenor part with the others. Thus, from a simple hymn, these natives had built a beautiful arrangement, retaining the basic structure but improving the whole with native embellishments.

Fortunately, I have been able to carry a musical instrument into this area, and it proved quite a curiosity to the natives. Can you imagine an American soldier accompanying a group of fifteen native voices in the singing of "Onward Christian Soldiers" and other hymns?

As you can expect, my curiosity to hear some of their native songs was very great, and again after much persuasion (these natives are a very modest people) they sang some of their songs. The key of E Minor seems to be the prominent tonality. I am enclosing a few bars of a song which seemed a kind of greeting song to the "dim-dim" or white soldier.

The English translation seemed to be "Hell-o-Dim Dim — etc." My native vocabulary is so limited that I was unable to get more than this main thought. I trust it will be of some interest.

I had intended to tell about the native dances and the drums, but this account has already reached a dangerous length. Out of sympathy to the censor I will close. — Frederick E. Mills, Sgt., 35403582, 710 Sig. Co. (Unit 2), A.P.O. 928 c/o Postmaster, San Francisco, Calif.

**This article was reprinted from "Music Educators National Journal" from November-December 1943.**

*Frederick E. Mills*
*Lima*
*Retired director of orchestras and string instruments, Shawnee Local Schools.*

*Fred was on the Trobriand Islands when he wrote this*

A rare peaceful moment.

**Frederick Mills, a music teacher, was drafted and served in the Pacific Theater.**

**Ivan Ross Clum fought sixty days on the lines and received the Purple Heart.**

**Duane Edgington was a Ranger, fought in Africa, Italy, and Germany, and helped liberate Nazi death camps.**

Special edition of *The Lima News*, dated August 14, 1945.

**Standing behind their parents: Reg, Lil, and Jim.
Seated: James and Sophia Cleal.**

# NOLAN C. CORE

During WWII the Coast Guard served as a specialized branch of the United States Navy. The Coast Guard handled explosives and other dangerous cargoes and acted as protection for port facilities. They were instrumental in many rescues at sea, and were a deterrent to saboteurs who tried to enter the U.S. via submarine drop-off.

The motto of the United States Coast Guard is *Semper Paratus*, or *Always Prepared.*

Nolan Core's extensive knowledge of marine engines and his meticulous pattern of care of the equipment on his ship were vital in a time of crisis and saved the lives of 25 people one stormy day at sea. He was **'prepared.'**

World War II was over and this was our first apartment. Art had not yet gained back the weight he had lost while serving in the Pacific. Also note the combination radio, record player, and ten-inch television. We had a lot of company who came to watch our television because it was one of the first in the Lima area.

Our first car after Art's return from the war, a used 1939 Plymouth Coupe.

# Home Front Meets Challenges of Rationing and Shortages

The shock of the sneak attack on Pearl Harbor sent the American people reeling and the people all across our great nation realized that everyone was going to be needed to win this war. We were not prepared to fight a war on such a wide scale across the Pacific and the Atlantic Oceans. The Americans knew that England had been receiving large amounts of war materials from the United States. We now had to think about producing supplies for our own armies. The sacrifices people were expected to make were made willingly, because the American people realized the survival of our democracy was at stake.

The American factories made a rapid transition from peacetime production to wartime production. Women and older men went to work in factories and built planes, ships, jeeps, tanks, munitions, and anything else the military needed. No one was more surprised than the women themselves at what they were able to accomplish. Due to the diligence and spirit of the workers on the home front, the American military units were getting equipped at a remarkable speed with the best munitions possible.

After the Pearl Harbor attack, extra precautions were being taken and air raid drills were practiced. Cities along our coastlines felt particularly vulnerable. Radios were silenced, blackouts were ordered and air raid wardens patrolled city streets and residential neighborhoods. Enemy planes had been sighted over San Francisco Bay on the night of December 8th, 1941, which reinforced the need for precautionary measures to be observed. On February 23rd, 1942, a Japanese submarine shelled an oil refinery near Santa Barbara, California. On June 22, 1942, a Japanese sub shelled Fort Stevens in the state of Washington. On September 9th, 1942, a Japanese plane dropped an incendiary bomb near Brookings, Oregon and ignited a forest fire. These intrusive acts on our West Coast obviously demonstrated that we are not impenetrable.

Gasoline rationing went into effect immediately after the Pearl Harbor attack. It was out of necessity that car pools were quickly formed, because the general estimate of the three gallons per week would only take the average car about forty-five miles. Many people began riding bicycles to work if it was within a reasonable distance and weather permitted.

Tires were also rationed because most of the rubber was being allocated for tires for military vehicles. Civilians learned how to fix flat tires with patches and a special cement. The goal was to keep a car operable because new cars were not available.

Sugar was rationed and cooks experimented by substituting honey. Coffee was rationed and people would use the coffee grounds over and over to extract as much flavor as possible. A substitute for butter was margarine, which resembled lard because it was white. Someone devised a capsule containing yellow dye that could be mixed with the margarine and then it looked like butter. Meat was probably the most serious problem for families that had been accustomed to having meat with every meal. Meat stretching ideas were shared, such as using ground meat and adding crackers or oatmeal to make more servings.

Shoes were rationed at two pair a year. This was a problem for young active children who were still growing. Shoe repair shops were kept busy helping parents keep their children in shoes. Shoes were resoled and repaired to extend their wear.

On December 31st, 1944, it was announced there would be greater belt tightening and people could only get one pair of shoes per year, the poultry allotment was reduced, and ALL good rubber would be allocated for military vehicles, and now even fewer tires would be available for civilian use. People drove more slowly now to extend the life of their cars and its tires.

Some things were not rationed but were difficult to find on the shelves in the grocery stores, and would disappear the minute the shelves would be restocked. The country's supply of wool was limited for clothing for civilians as most of it was going into uniforms and blankets for the military. Soap was in short supply and people would save every sliver of soap, put the little pieces in a jar, add a little water, and stir it into a form of liquid soap. It was more like a slime but it did have cleansing properties.

Children pulled their wagons around their neighborhoods and collected scrap metal and paper and took them to a designated recycle center. Aluminum and the foil wrappers on chewing gum were saved and turned in at the recycle centers. Silk hose and nylon hose were collected to be recycled to make gunpowder bags and parachutes. Children would walk through farmers' fields and collect milkweed pods that had dried. The white substance inside the pods was used as the stuffing for life preservers in the Navy. Many times when the children were working on scrap drives, gathering milkweed pods, or working in victory gardens with other children they would sing the song *"Just Remember Pearl Harbor."*

People were urged to buy war bonds and savings stamps. Some schools chose a particular day of each week and their students would bring in money to buy war bonds and savings stamps. Pauline Ingmire told of how her mother would tie a dime in the corner of her handkerchief each week so that she would not lose it on the way to school. She was very young to understand about the war, but she was eager to purchase a savings stamp with her dimes because she knew she was helping her country. Patriotism was at an all-time high, and soldiers were treated with great respect. Many times a man in uniform would order a meal in a restaurant and the proprietor, or other patrons, would not let him pay for it. A man in uniform that was hitchhiking would receive many offers for rides. The American people were proud of the people in the military and showed concern for their welfare.

Famous entertainers traveled around the country and put on programs to entertain the people and get the people to buy war bonds and savings stamps. Some entertainers went overseas to where the troops were and put on shows to give the soldiers a chance to enjoy a few minutes away from the war. There were times that the entertainers were performing close to the battlefields.

Families that had members serving in the armed forces would put a small banner in their front window with a blue star on it for each member serving. If a family had a son or daughter killed in action, their blue star would be removed and a gold star put in its place.

Women would volunteer to work at the Red Cross and would roll bandages. Every person, young and old, could find ways to help on the home front.

During World War II the railroads were the major mode of transportation and many depots had servicemen's canteens. The canteens usually provided free coffee, food, magazines, and cigarettes for the soldiers passing through on troop trains.

In 1942, Elouise Larsen and Charlotte C. Baker started the Lima Servicemen's Free Canteen. A small building was built by volunteers and was located at the crossroads of the Baltimore & Ohio Railroad and the Pennsylvania Railroad, in Lima, Ohio. The canteen served approximately ten trains daily from 10:00 A.M. until 10:00 P.M., 365 days a year.

Shafer's Meat Market consistently furnished meat for sandwiches for the canteen, and local groceries, bakeries and other businesses throughout the Lima and Allen County area provided food and other needed supplies. It was estimated that the canteen volunteers served 650,000 military personnel between 1942 and 1945. Pictures on display at the Allen County Museum show smiling soldiers hanging out of open train windows, reaching for the food snacks the canteen volunteers were holding up toward their outstretched hands. The only pay the volunteers received for their efforts were the smiles on the GIs' faces and the friendly waves as the trains pulled away from the station.

Every aspect of life on the home front in the United States during World War II, in some way or other, was touched by the needs of the military. The cooperation of the people to conserve essential items was expected and most people willingly complied with the government's rationing. But, sad to say, there were a few people that were involved in black-market activities. The black marketeers dealt in selling things such as rubber tires, silk hose, sugar, coffee, etc., at exorbitant prices. All these things were almost impossible to find legally toward the end of the war, and most people did not want to be involved in the illegal dealings of the black market. The black market people were corrupt and a disgrace on the otherwise patriotic and united home front. Luckily, they were few in number. The United States was not alone with this problem. The other countries involved in World War II also had to deal with black market criminals that procured goods by illegal means and became rich from their clandestine business dealings.

# Robert Polter Explains About Farming During WWII Years

I was born in October 1923 in Allen County. My father was forty-eight and my mother was forty-two years old when I was born. They also had a daughter who died in infancy. My grandfather Polter was a braumeister, as were his ancestors in Germany, but my grandfather emigrated from Germany to America when he was a young man. I'm told that my grandfather's last name was really "Poltergeist," and *polter* means furrier in German and *geist* means a noisy and mischievous spirit, or intelligence, wit, genius, soul, or ghost. I guess you take your pick on which meanings you like. Soon after entering this country my grandfather dropped the *geist* and our family name has been just "Polter" ever since. My father, Otto, was born on Kelly's Island where there were once a lot of vineyards.

My parents attended the Heidelberg Lutheran Church, which was a small church located in the country. Both my parents had feisty dispositions, but my mother could hold her own in an argument with my father.

My parents owned a 180-acre farm in Allen County, which required a lot of hard work. Although I was an only child I was not pampered and their expectations for me were to help them with the farm work. There were twenty-five cows to be milked every morning and night, and I started milking when I was five and a half years old.

I was seven years old when Dad would put the harness on a team of horses and would then hitch them to the farm implement that he wanted me to use that day. From there it was my responsibility to drive the horses and do the plowing and working the ground in preparation for planting. It was several years later, after I was older and taller, before I could manage putting the collars on the horses, and adjusting the harness, the hames straps, the tugs, the chains, the bits, the reins and all those other needed connections. It was very important to do all these things correctly so that the horses were comfortable while pulling the farm equipment.

189

The farm work probably contributed to me developing into a strong healthy young man. I was expected to do chores before and after school, which meant I could not participate in sports at school because of my duties at home. I did not realize it at the time, but I was learning a lot about farming from my dad and I was also developing a strong work ethic. I also realize that in this particular time in America, many farming families expected their sons to be involved in the work on the family farm, so my situation was probably not unique in the 1930s.

When I was in the eighth grade I had been hired by a farmer to do farm work for him and he was to pay me $1.00 per day. When the time came for him to pay me, he said, "You are only a boy and I am only going to pay you fifty cents per day." I told him, "But, I did a man's work and I deserve a man's pay." He refused and again said, "You are a boy and I'm only going to pay you fifty cents per day!" I then told him, "I will not be coming back to work for you again."

When I got home, I told my dad what had happened. He said, "I would have been upset if you had gone back and worked for that man."

In those days we had rings, made up of groups of men that worked together, helping each other on various large farm projects. We had rings for threshing, filling silos, buzzing wood, making loose hay, and butchering. When the ring came to a farm to work, the farmer's wife, plus some of the other wives, would help her and they would prepare a big meal for the men at noon. There was a lot of good fellowship that went along with the hard work.

In 1940 I thought I would ask my parents if they could pay me more money for all the work I did on their farm. We sat around the kitchen table and I told them I wanted to talk with them about giving me more money than the usual $1.00 a week that they paid me. My father looked at me and then at my mother, and then he asked me, "Well, what do you think you are worth?" I quickly replied, "I think I'm worth $3.00 per week." My parents looked at each other and pondered awhile and then Dad said, "Well, son, you do work hard for us, and we appreciate it, so your pay is now $3.00 per week." I felt good about this because I knew I had my board and room for free. My mother raised chickens and the egg money was her spending money, and she bought my clothing. I felt that I had made a good bargain with my parents.

We always had about ten horses on the farm, and we had several mares that we would breed. Dad was continually selling horses, but always keeping about ten horses for us to use on the farm. We had at least six horses that we used in the field. Horses could only be used for working in the field for about half a day and then they had to rest. We had other horses, so we always changed horses in the middle of the day. Even then, after working for an hour or so, we had to stop and rest the horses. Dad bought a new small Massey Harris tractor, which took the place of some of the horsepower on the farm, but we still needed the horses.

The mechanism used on a binder is intricate and can be very troublesome when it doesn't work right and you have sheaves of wheat or corn to bind. Ours had broken and was not working right at all. I had taken it apart, and had the parts all laid out on the barn floor when Dad walked up and said, "Just what do you think you are doing? Who is going to put that back together?" I looked at Dad and said, "I am." And I did! And it worked! Much to my dad's amazement!

We had a nine-hoe grain drill, seven inches apart and it was very narrow, just five feet across and it was pulled by two horses. It would take all day just to plant twelve acres. We planted corn with a two-drill corn planter, pulled by two horses, and it was also very time consuming.

When I was in high school I had a close friend, Richard Thornberry. He and I decided that we wanted to go to church together on Sundays, and we were trying to find a young men's Christian Education class that we liked. We spent quite a few Sundays going from church to church until we found the young men's class at the South Side Church of Christ in Lima, Ohio, that seemed to meet our needs. The discussions and activities at this church proved very meaningful for both of us.

In high school I belonged to the Future Farmers of America (FFA) organization for four years. I also was in all the vocational agriculture classes offered in high school. I learned a lot about more efficient and modern practices of farming. The VoAg classes and the FFA were very helpful as I pursued my career in farming.

The attack on Pearl Harbor happened on December 7th, 1941, in the middle of my senior year in high school. Young men had five days after their eighteenth birthday to get themselves registered at their local Selective Service office. After I graduated from high school the Selective Service Board (draft board) notified me that I needed to report for a physical. My dad worried about how he would ever get along without me to help him on the farm. I took the physical and was classified as

4-L (the L means limited service). I had a hernia and that was why I received that classification.

The attack on Pearl Harbor changed a lot of things for the farmers. The farmers had just begun to make changes and were gradually moving from horsepower to using tractors and mechanized power and then suddenly everything was rationed and farmers could not purchase new equipment. At this critical time our ring lost the big engine that ran the threshing machine, which was owned cooperatively by the ring. There was limited access to this kind of equipment, but we found a man who had a small combine and we were able to hire him when we needed to harvest grain.

Another problem we farmers faced was that the rings began to break up because many of the men that we counted on in the ring were being drafted into the military. With most of the younger men being gone the responsibility for continuing the farming was falling on older men and sometimes their wives. Also, we had to continually face the problems of equipment breaking down and figure ways to repair it ourselves. Replacement and needed parts were very hard to find.

The next most troubling part of rationing during the war was probably the rationing of gas. Many people thought farmers had lots of gasoline because they were allotted extra gas for farming purposes. Actually, we barely had enough gas to get our farming done.

Dad and I needed a grain drill. I went to an auction and bid $350 on a used drill. The older people at the sale knew that the drill only cost half that much when it was new and they thought I was just a young kid and didn't know what I was doing. The problem was that there were no new drills available and this used drill made it possible to double the number of acres I could farm. My dad just shook his head in wonderment when I told him what I had bid on that used drill.

Very soon after Pearl Harbor had been attacked my dad bought a 1942 Plymouth car, with the gearshift on the steering column. This was the last of the cars made until the war was over. Dad could not figure out how to work the gearshift, and I tried and tried to show him how to operate it. Since cars were not being made anymore he did not want to take the car back to the dealer, so he gave it to me. And that was how I ended up with a new car when I was a senior in high school. There might have been some kids envious about me getting that car, but they did not know the whole story and how hard I worked.

I had started renting land to farm on my own when I was in high school. I kept expanding my farming in both renting and farming. I used my dad's tractor when I made loose hay. I used some of dad's horses when I needed horse power. I had a good start at farming when I graduated from high school in the spring of 1942 and when I married June Parlette in June of 1943. June and I had dated for two years in high school and she understood about farm life.

I made a good choice when I married June. She learned how to drive the tractor and would follow behind me when I would be harvesting grain, and she would be preparing the soil for the next crop. She always laughed because she had difficulty making straight rows with the farm equipment. She drove the grain wagons to the grain elevators and would get in line with the other farmers. June was small in stature but she was certainly a big help to me. We were quite a team!

I was lucky to have a fair amount of knowledge of how machinery worked and how to repair the equipment when something was broken. I also had experience at working as an auto mechanic and would do that type of work for neighbors and friends, as well as myself. I did a lot of this type of work in the winter when there was no farm work to do.

An example of how the government kept records of rationed items in wartime would be when I purchased a farm wagon that had rubber tires on it, and I had to sign an affidavit agreeing that I would not remove the tires on that wagon and put them on a car.

The war years were full of uncertainty for our family. I was called several more times by the draft board to take another physical. Each time they classified me as 4-L. My parents and my wife worried about how they could manage the farming without me. These were uncertain times for everyone.

*When Bob was asked what he thought helped him to be a successful farmer, his answer was the following:*

First—I believed in good management of the farms, and I always planned ahead on what was the best thing to do to increase the productivity of the land.

Second—My knowledge of how to make mechanical things work and being able to overhaul the farm equipment saved me a lot of money. If I had had to pay for service calls on all the repair work that I did myself, I would not have lasted in farming during the World War II years.

Third—I must have been in the right place at the right time during the 1940s and the 50s, to get started in farming.

Fourth—I lived by this same advice that I would give to young people today—Be honest in all your dealings with people. Honesty is very important, and try to give a good day's work for a day's pay.

When Bob was asked to reflect on his life during the World War II years, he answered, "I have always felt that I was blessed by God to have been born into the generation that was called upon to help America in World War II. The people in this great nation of ours became totally united to work together in a way that was truly inspiring. I'm glad that I did not miss this part of America's history. Although I could not serve in the military, I worked as hard as I could to keep our farm producing up to capacity, because our armies needed the grains, the milk, and the meat. I was also blessed to be farming in the Midwest section of America where the soil is rich and productive for growing grains, and the pastures are lush and green for raising healthy cattle. I thank God that He gave me the skills to be a good farmer. I feel that God blessed our nation because our mission was to eradicate evil, and He guided us to restoring peace."

# Part Seven
# Local Men Relate War Experiences

# Ross Clum Fought Sixty Days on the Lines, Seriously Wounded

Ross Clum was born and raised on a farm near Ada, Ohio, and during his high school years he was very active in the Ohio Future Farmers of America Program. Ross's dream was to someday own a farm and be a productive farmer. By the time his high school sweetheart, Dorothy LaRue, graduated from high school in 1943, Ross had been classified by the Draft Board as 4-F. Ross and Dorothy were thinking he would not be going to war, so they decided to get married on June 27th. However, as Ross jokingly tells it, on December 18th, 1943, the Draft Board "reached out and touched him" and discovered a "warm body" and his 4-F classification was changed to 1-A and he was immediately drafted into the United States Army. He was nineteen years old. By this time he and Dorothy were expecting their first child.

Ross Clum first began his story on January 18, 2001 by walking to the corner of his kitchen and picking up a German helmet and a heavy leather belt that had a sheath attached. In the sheath was a very sharp bayonet. Ross pointed to the name of a German soldier in the helmet. Maybe anticipating a question, he said, "I did not kill this German soldier. I picked these up off a battlefield. I mailed them home for Dorothy to keep for me."

Ross dictated his story: "I was a buck private—that's all I ever wanted to be. I received my basic training at Camp Croft, South Carolina and further training in Mississippi. At this point we were put on a troop ship and landed at Glasgow, Scotland. From there we were sent to South Hampton, England and put onto a small troop ship and went across the English Channel. We landed on Omaha Beach, which had already been secured earlier in the invasion of Normandy. From there we were put on a train and headed for the front lines.

"We were then transferred into trucks heading closer to the front lines. We drove past St. Lo and Metz, and we observed piles of rubble caused by heavy bombing. There were some large craters in the road obviously made by bombs. The black man driving the truck I was in stopped two miles back from the lines and he said, 'Boys, you got to get out and walk now, cause this is a far as I go.'

"We walked the last two miles to the battle line. It was near Nancy, France, and the date was August 16th, 1944. At this point I was assigned to the Third Army, 35th Division, 320th Infantry, Company F. I was carrying an M1 rifle, an assortment of grenades, and a bayonet. I didn't know what to think. It was my first time to be in battle.

"We were in an area of rolling hills and the Germans were below us, so our position was better than theirs and our machine gunners soon knocked them out. This was the beginning of sixty days on the lines without rest. I was carrying a full field pack on my back and sometime during a machine gun attack my field pack was hit and my rations ran down over my neck and back. That was the last time I wore a full field pack. After that I just carried a shelter half and a blanket on my belt. Luckily that time I was low enough that they couldn't hit me—just my field-pack.

"During these sixty days we were constantly pushing forward and gaining ground. But these were sixty days without rest and decent food. Some of the men broke under the strain—some were hit—some died. You had to forget about personal hygiene. I never had my shoes off my feet for two weeks. Many of the men were getting trench foot. We tried to find foxholes or trenches that the Germans had already dug to conserve our own energy. We were surprised to find World War I shell casings in some of the trenches. We would get thirsty and would drink water from horse tracks by putting water purification tablets in the water. Life in the trenches was neither clean nor comfortable—it was a living hell!

"In another instance we were making an attack and the Germans opened up on us with machine-gun fire. My one buddy was shot in the head and killed at this time. Another buddy was hit by machine-gun fire through both of his calves and he couldn't walk. We had to keep low, but I was able to drag him back to an aid station. After I got him back there I started shaking and couldn't stop, so they kept me back there overnight so I got a little rest at that time. The next day I was back on the lines.

"It was a normal thing that you would have foxhole buddies and they would change every few days. You never got to know much about them—not even their names. We were all just 'buddies' and we tried to look out for each other as best we could. One day there was a new

198

recruit with me and we had decided to hang our damp blankets on the lower branches of a nearby tree hoping to get them dry. He was standing beside the foxhole that we would be sharing that night. I heard that special sound of an incoming mortar shell and I quickly tackled him so that he fell into the foxhole with me on top of him. The shell landed where he had been standing and our blankets were torn to shreds. There were so many close calls like that. There was an army saying that 'if you survive the first ten days in battle, you'll probably survive the war.'

"About this time I was issued a Browning automatic which had a clip of twenty bullets that could be fired in rapid succession. We were now moving closer to Germany. One night we saw a naked man hanging from a tree and we took him down. We could not tell if he was a German or an American. We wondered what was ahead. We didn't know what it meant.

"One night we were going through a wooded area, and when we stopped, a German came up to us and wanted us to take him prisoner. One of our guys volunteered to take him back behind the lines where some prisoners were being kept. It was only a few minutes after they had started back when we all heard a shot. Soon our man returned and said matter-of-factly, 'That German prisoner made a run for it and I had to shoot him.' You draw your own conclusions what really happened. You know, I can honestly say that I never knew if I shot someone. I was always in a group that was firing and I don't know if I ever hit anyone.

"Again we were in an area of rolling hills. We had just gotten a new company commander and you know the new ones always think they can win the war by themselves. Well, my platoon had all been killed except for two other guys and me. The commander had sent a reconnaissance man out to check the area and he came back and said, 'There is nothing out there.' We were then ordered to go over the hill, and we immediately got caught in the crossfire. It was November 19th, 1944.

"It was early in the morning when I was hit. Machine-gun fire had hit my upper left arm. I didn't dare call out for help. I jumped in a dead furrow of a plowed field and I was deliberately lying on my arm to keep it from bleeding out. The pain was not excruciating—it was more like a tingling sensation. I knew it was a serious wound, but I also knew that there were Germans close by ready to shoot at anything that moved. I played dead until dark. As I lay there I wondered *am I going to get out of this alive?* I did not lose consciousness and I was fully aware of what was going on around me. For some reason I was not afraid, but it seemed like a long long time before it got dark.

"After darkness came I crawled back over the hill and two guys in our outfit got on each side of me. They were really weak because they had also been wounded, but we held on to each other and started toward the aid station. There was a railroad bridge that had been knocked out so we had to go down one embankment and up another. We finally got to the aid station and three medics came running over to us and began working on me. About 10:30 or 11:30 at night I was put in an ambulance along with eight or ten other guys. The driver yelled, 'Everybody sit tight!' It was a wild ride but we got to the field hospital about midnight. This all happened within sight of the Rhine River and we were still in France.

"The next day I was moved to a hospital in Paris for surgery. This began a ten-month stay in various hospitals. One day a doctor stopped by to check on me and said he was also from Ohio. He asked me if I would rather go across the English Channel in a boat or as a litter patient in a plane. Naturally, I said I would rather fly. So I was flown to a hospital in South Hampton and was there for a month. From there I sailed on the ship *George Washington*, and landed in New York City. It took fourteen days to get across the Atlantic, but when I saw the Statue of Liberty it looked really good to me. I was then sent to Crile Hospital in Cleveland, which was a recuperating station.

"One of the good things about being at Crile Hospital was that Dorothy came to Cleveland and rented an apartment and I was permitted to go there and visit with her and our baby daughter, Shirley.

"I knew the time was getting closer that I would be able to go back home to Ohio with my family. But first I had to be transferred to a hospital in Atterbury, Indiana.

"I was awarded the Purple Heart for Wounds Received in Action on November 19, 1944 and was honorably discharged from the military with a 50 percent disability. I was released from the hospital and the military on August 31, 1945.

"I took several jobs upon reentering civilian life. I used the G.I. Bill for training in agriculture and bought farm land with a G.I. loan. Besides farming, I worked for thirty years as a federal employee in the Soil Conservation Service.

"My feelings about World War II are that I'm glad I was there and I did my part. I was fighting for my country and for the American people. Our freedoms of speech and religion are important and need to be protected. I have no regrets."

# The Winter of 1944–1945

I had arrived back in Ohio in mid-October 1944, and I was now staying with Lelia and her family. Everything was going well with my job and the car pool. I was picked up early each morning and taken to a parking lot close to the building where I worked. The people I worked with were all very congenial, and most days we ate our packed lunches together in the office. The atmosphere was task oriented, busy, but always polite.

Andy, our younger inspector was single, quite shy and was from Wisconsin. Mr. McElderry (usually called Mac), the other inspector, was older and he and his wife were also from Wisconsin, and they had rented an apartment in Lima. They invited Andy to stay with them in their spare bedroom. Andy had always appeared to be lonesome and withdrawn until Mac and his wife took him in. Mac said that Andy was like the son they had never had. Mac's wife packed lunches for her husband and for Andy. It was great to see Andy begin to open up and join in the conversations at lunchtime, in the office. The bonding between Andy and the McElderry's was very evident.

One day the Colonel, Ann, the Colonel's secretary, and I all looked up from our work when we heard a loud noise out in the plant. We were accustomed to hearing loud noises in the plant, but this was different because this was louder than usual, the building actually shook, and there was a lot of yelling after the noise.

A few seconds later, Mac came rushing through the door of the office with a very frantic look on his face, and he yelled to the Colonel, "Oh, Sir, Come quick! Come quick! It hit Andy! It hit Andy!"

The Colonel rushed out of the office and told Ann and me to stay there to take care of the phones. It wasn't long before the Colonel returned and his hands and arms were covered with blood up to his elbows. He told us that the large traveling overhead crane had dropped its load on top of Andy who was working directly beneath it. The Colonel shook his head and said, "The poor guy, he didn't know what hit him. Some others are hurt also, but Andy is dead. I need to wipe some of this blood off me and then get back out there. Mac is beside himself and he is going in the ambulance to the hospital with Andy—but it is no use."

Then the Colonel looked at Ann and me and said, "You ladies don't need to go out there. You don't need to see that mess." He then said, "Maybe you can clean some of the blood off the doorknob and my desk—I've made a mess of things in here." With that, he left, to find Mac at the hospital and drive him home so that he could tell his wife what happened.

The night of the accident I lay in bed thinking about how Andy had started changing and was becoming more outgoing and friendly. I thought about how Andy had responded to the kindness of Mac and his wife. I thought of Andy and how, in some odd way, he was a casualty of the war, only here on the home front. I thought of the McElderrys and how they were now grieving. I thought about the war and the killings and how unfair everything is. I thought that it was the beginning of the Christmas season and the Christmas Spirit was nowhere to be found.

An investigation followed the accident and it was discovered that the overhead crane had had a large boom attached by a chain and was carrying it to the far end of the building when the chain broke and caused it to drop its load. The chain's link that had broken had been welded and it broke at the weld point. This is a sad example of "a chain is only as strong as its weakest link."

In the middle of December, severe winter weather had come down on us with a vengeance, bringing deep snows, bitter winds, and below-freezing temperatures. For awhile the snow was three to four feet deep on the road in front of the house, my car pool could not make it through and I had to walk a half mile to the highway to catch my ride. Adding this to the fact that it was dark when I went to work and dark when I came home—it was a dismal time.

But then I would pick up a newspaper and read about our soldiers in the Ardennes Forest, who were experiencing the same bitter winter weather, and I felt ashamed for complaining. At least I had a warm bed and hot meals to eat. Our soldiers were sleeping two in a foxhole at night to keep from freezing to death. Their only food for this period of time was K or C rations. And worst of all, these soldiers were fighting the Germans every day. The fighting was fierce and many of our men were being wounded or killed. The news coming over the radio or in the newspapers carried very discouraging reports.

It was during this critical time in the war, that we were all asked to go to a certain place in the plant, because there was going to be a celebration of a contract completion for the Lima Locomotive Works. There was to be an important person there who would be speaking to everyone. They were going to have a short ceremony and break a bottle of champagne on one of our big power shovels. Workers and office people converged on the area and there was a man there who was telling the audience what a great job everyone had done.

I heard a strange noise behind me and I looked around and there was a woman trying to muffle her crying. Then as I looked around I saw more people crying. They were crying because they had loved ones who were off somewhere fighting, maybe in the Battle of the Bulge, maybe in the Pacific on one of the islands, and they had not heard from them for a long time. Several of the people had received word from the War Department that their sons were missing in action. They couldn't control their emotions—they did not feel there was anything to celebrate—so they turned around and went back to their workstations.

The alarming war news, the bitter cold weather, the gut-wrenching fear, the not knowing, all these things were so overwhelming this December 1944, and it was simply impossible to stand there and join in on what was called a "celebration." I also turned and walked back to my empty office. I put my head down on my desk and was ashamed that I wasn't strong enough to hold back my own tears.

Soon the other people from our office returned and someone said, with great irony in his voice, "Hey, Christmas is just a few days away, do you think we'll have peace on the earth and goodwill to men by then?"

# The Ardennes Forest—Battle of the Bulge

It was evident that Germany had suffered severe losses in France after the Normandy invasion. The Allies began their push toward Germany, but they did not realize that Hitler had decided not to listen to his military advisors and that he would now plan his own strategy and mount an offensive that he thought would divide the Allied armies. Actually, the Allies had the Germans outnumbered, but Hitler was refusing to face the realities that existed and he told his generals that they were to carry out his orders, exactly as he had stated, beginning on December 16th, 1944. Hitler went to great lengths to keep his plans a secret.

The Allies mistakenly believed that the Germans were incapable of mounting a large-scale offensive drive due to their previous defeats in France. They had received false information that they had not attempted to verify, and they even ignored an important intercepted Ultra message that would have revealed the coming assault. At 5:30 A.M., on December 16th, the surprised Americans were on the receiving end of a fierce German artillery attack. About the same time of this surprise attack, the weather turned bitterly cold and deep snows covered the area.

The Germans devised a clever scheme to further throw the Americans off balance. Three thousand German soldiers, dressed in American uniforms and speaking excellent English, infiltrated the Allied lines and played havoc with the American telephone and communication centers. They seized important transportation areas and misdirected American units. The resulting confusion lasted for several days until the Americans caught on that something was not right. When the suspected impostors were questioned for information about prominent American sports heroes or movie stars that most Americans know, and they could not answer correctly, they were immediately taken prisoner, or shot.

Once the element of surprise was over, General Eisenhower and General Bradley quickly moved in other units to help the beleaguered American troops in the Ardennes. The winter storms, the worst in fifty years, added to the difficulties that the American soldiers faced each day. Storms or no storms, the war continued on. There was no respite for our soldiers.

On the second day, December 17th, the Germans were partially successful in their offensive objectives. When the Germans reached St. Vith, a major crossroads, they were met by General Hodges's First Army, which had arrived to help defend St. Vith. The Americans had to evacuate St. Vith several days later, but while there they impeded the progress of the German drive at that point.

The Americans discovered a very disturbing incident that took place near the town of Malmedy. The Germans, under Commander Pieper, had taken 130 American soldiers prisoners and had them gathered in a field and guarded by two tanks. Supposedly, Commander Pieper left the area, and the two tanks machine-gunned the prisoners. Later German soldiers walked among the wounded and dead and shot anyone with any sign of movement. There is uncertainty if Pieper gave the order for this atrocity, but when word of what happened at Malmedy spread throughout the troops, it spurred even greater hatred for the enemy.

Bastonge was another city that lay in the path of advancing German troops. Bastonge was at the crossroads of two important roads and was virtually undefended, except for a few battle-weary personnel from the 101st Airborne, and a small number of people left from General Middleton's Headquarters. The next morning, December 18th, the Germans attacked the city with three panzer divisions and one infantry division. The unyielding men in the garrison held on and were able to repulse the repeated German attacks.

By December 21st, both sides in these confrontations were running out of needed supplies and munitions. They were all on the verge of exhaustion. The Germans had Bastonge surrounded. The Germans could have moved on, but Bastonge would have remained a blockage point for them to receive ammunition, fuel and other supplies.

## The Following Story Has Become a Legend in American History

Lacking heavy artillery that might have devastated defensive positions, the German commander resorted to bluff. He sent word to the besieged Americans that they must surrender or be wiped out.

General Anthony C. McAuliffe, commander of the garrison, sent a reply consisting of one word—"Nuts!" When the message was delivered to the German commander he was puzzled and asked if that meant a positive or a negative? The officer who delivered the message to the Germans gave a rough translation and added that "if the attacks continue, we will kill every goddamn German that tries to break into the city."

The impudent simplicity of "Nuts!" greatly appealed to American soldiers and civilians when they learned of it.

Although the Germans had been thrown off schedule by the tough resistance they had met at St. Vith and Bastogne, they were continuing to advance deep within Allied lines. It was now December 25th, and the bulge created in the Allied lines ran sixty miles deep and forty miles wide. The day after Christmas, Patton's advance units relieved Bastogne. The skies cleared and air strikes were now possible. The Germans now had to give up ground and the bulge was eliminated by the end of January.

One million men and thousands upon thousands of guns, tanks and other fighting vehicles were involved in the Battle of the Bulge. It is said that it was here that the American soldiers faced their strongest challenges of the European war. The survivors of the Ardennes offensive tell of the extreme cold weather, sleeping two in a fox hole to keep from freezing to death, no hot meals, always feeling cold, and yet always moving on and getting the job that they had been assigned to do done.

In retrospect, it has been stated that if the Germans had not been stopped at St. Vith and Bastogne, the Allies would have been delayed for months. German losses far exceeded the losses of the Allies in this campaign. The Germans never reached their intended goal of Antwerp. McAuliffe's insolent reply of "Nuts" will be remembered with a smile when, with his back to the wall, he out-bluffed the German commander. Memories of the cold-hearted atrocities at Malmedy cannot be forgotten or erased. And people began to wonder if the rules for the humane treatment of prisoners of war and the provisions for the treatment of the sick and wounded, as spelled out by the Geneva Conventions, had been forgotten, or intentionally ignored.

Stephen W. Sears probably described the American soldier the best in his book, *The Battle of the Bulge*:

"The greatest mistake Adolf Hitler made was to underestimate the fighting quality of the U.S. soldier. Like his forefathers in the Revolution and the Civil War and World War I, the average GI of World War II was at heart a civilian in arms. He cared little about the professional soldier's warlike bearing. He was careless about military spit and polish, casual about discipline, irreverent toward authority, and he did as little military housekeeping as he thought he could get away with. In his contempt for such 'softness and decadence,' Hitler utterly failed to see the fierce pride that was in the American fighting man. When the going was tough—and the going in the Ardennes was very tough indeed—the GI used his wits and his initiative and his independence of mind with an effectiveness that few soldiers in any of the world's armies could match."

"The American soldier had no monopoly on courage. But in those dark and savage days in the Ardennes he revealed, beyond courage, an extra steel-hard quality of mind and spirit that turned one of America's greatest battles into one of America's greatest victories."

# Ranger Harold Barrick
# Relates War Experiences

H. Harold Barrick was born on March 25, 1918 and was raised on a farm close to Johnstown, Ohio. During World War II he served in the 75th Infantry Division. Like many veterans of this war, he did not talk about his experiences until many years later. On November 26, 2000, he dictated the following information to the author about his experiences in World War II.

"On June 22nd, 1941, I married Helen Hollenbaugh. I was drafted in 1942, when I was twenty-five years old and was just finishing two years in ROTC, at Ohio State University. I was inducted into the U.S. Army at Ft. Hayes, Columbus, Ohio. After receiving training at Ft. Benjamin Harrison, Camp Atterbury, Indiana, and Ft. Leonardwood, Missouri, I was then sent on maneuvers in Louisiana for eight weeks in March until May. While on maneuvers I lived out in the open and slept in a tent at night.

"You see me now and I am a respected, well-behaved church-going person, but in the military I did get into some mischief. When our battery was stationed in Louisiana, a bunch of us went into a bar. There was a guy who kept pestering one of our men. Our first sergeant had been a professional fighter and had seen enough, so he picked up the bully and threw him through a plate glass window. We all got into a little trouble over that.

"After going through the rigorous training in Louisiana, I was then transferred to Camp Breckenridge, in Kentucky. My wife, Helen, was with me at the Leonardwood and Breckenridge assignments, and our daughter, Mila Jean, was born while I was stationed at Camp Breckenridge. When our daughter was four weeks old I was told I was to be shipped overseas, so Helen and the baby returned to Ohio. My war experiences were about to begin.

"I was assigned to the 75th Infantry Division, which had been formed at Camp Breckinridge. The 75th was the youngest division with an average age of twenty years. Now I was considered ready for battle

209

and was sent overseas on a troop ship. We landed in Glasgow, Scotland on Thanksgiving Day. The men of the 75th Infantry Division assembled at Cardiff, Wales, and from there we crossed the English Channel in LST boats. We landed at Le Harve, France and were immediately sent into battle. Our first contact with the Germans was at the Battle of the Bulge on Christmas Day, 1944. The ground was covered with two feet of snow and it was twenty degrees below zero.

"My assignment was in A Battery of the 897th Artillery Battalion, which was composed of about 550 men. Now, as a cadre man, I was also needed to help train new recruits coming in. We had four 105 Howitzer cannons. Specifically, I had a radio operator and a jeep driver working with me and I was called the forward observer. My job as the 'forward observer' was to go ahead and find where the enemy was and then send a message back on where to fire. We moved to St. Lo and St. Vith, taking ground and attacking all the time. The weather was bitter cold and it made the job we had to do that much harder. Besides always being cold, we only had K or C rations to eat most of the time.

"At St. Lo, two other soldiers and I got separated from our outfit. We hurried down into a cellar of a home for safety. We soon figured out that there were German soldiers upstairs, therefore we didn't dare talk with each other. We kept very quiet. On the second day the other two, who seemed to know each other, motioned to each other and then pointed toward the outside. I figured they were going to make a run for it. I shook my head 'no.' I decided not to chance it. They took off out of the cellar at a run and then I heard the machine gun fire. They were both killed. For me it was a test of nerves, maybe bullheadedness, but I vowed they would not get me.

"It was cold in the cellar. I had had nothing to eat for two days. I couldn't make a sound. There was wine there—every cellar had wine in it—I carefully drank a little, but what I needed was food. I slept fitfully. I didn't know if some of the Germans upstairs might come down to get some wine. It was now late in the third day and I suddenly realized I didn't hear German being spoken upstairs—I was hearing conversations spoken in English. Very, very, carefully I went upstairs and was greeted by American soldiers. What a relief!

"The closest call I had was in the Ardennes Forest, while in a battle, a ricocheted tracer bullet caught my coat on fire. I had to roll in the snow on the ground to get the fire out and then get back to my job of directing cannon fire. That was the only time when I was thankful for that snow on the ground.

"Once in France, our group was so hungry for some good meat, we stole a cow, killed it, and cooked the meat. The farmer, who owned the cow, came to our C.O. and he was really mad. He told our C.O. that his men had killed his good cow. We told our C.O. that we didn't do it. Our officer explained to the farmer that we were an honest bunch of guys, as he lined us up in front of the farmer. He then asked each one of us separately if we had killed his cow. We each answered, 'No, Sir.' The farmer believed us and left. It is a good thing he didn't look in our truck, because the cow's hide was in the back of our truck.

"My family didn't know until recently that I had been trained as a full-fledged Ranger while I was at Ft. Leonardwood. That's the same as a Green Beret now. I was trained to kill with my hands and to always know what was going on behind me. The training also included the handling of dynamite, nitroglycerin, primer cords, the clearing of mine fields and setting up tank barricades. This training saved my life several times. A basic part of the training was to always be very cognizant of what was going on and to never let myself get in a corner. I'm not proud of it, but I was trained to kill and I did.

"I was in a group that was selected to go into Holland to support some English troops that were fighting there. We were to help the English artillery units. The Germans were up in a belfry of a church using it as an observation tower. The English had been given orders to never fire on a church and they couldn't move because the Germans had them pinned down. When we got there, we saw the situation and shot the belfry off the church. We were in Holland for about a week to clean out a few more of the Germans that were there.

"It's strange that when people are fighting for the same cause, the people still don't respect each other. The English soldiers didn't treat us with respect. They acted as if we belonged to them—like we were from one of their colonies. The French vandalized our equipment all the time and they were no help. They didn't know who their friends were. After everything we were trying to do for them we couldn't under-stand why they treated us like that.

"We had gone through Cologne, Dusseldorf, Dortmund and then into a little town of Grevenvruck. We were there for about a month. We then moved on to Bredelar, in the Russian section. When we pulled out of there the Russians were right behind us.

"On May 8th, 1945, I saw the end of the war in Bredelar, Germany. There was a Polish concentration camp at Bredelar and I was shocked at the conditions that these people had had to live under. I helped draw and deliver rations for these starving people. The way these people looked, gaunt, emaciated, ragged, dirty—it is something I'll never forget! How could the Germans treat people like that?

"On July 4th, 1945, I was sent home on a one-month furlough. I was very happy to see Helen and my little daughter after being away for over a year. While I was home the Japanese surrendered and I received word to report to Camp Swift, Texas, and then to go to Camp Gruber, Oklahoma. I was a staff sergeant when I received my Honorable Discharge at Camp Gruber. Finally, I got home in October 1945."

"Oh, those were difficult years. I realize that I wasn't the first and I won't be the last to be called upon to fight and kill for our country. It is sad. It is hard to forget what I had to do. I have asked God to forgive me."

Harold Barrick served in World War II with honor, but in later years he admitted that he worried over the unpleasant tasks he sometimes had to perform as a soldier in the United States Army. When Harold entered civilian life he held a responsible position for many years with a large Ohio electric company. He was devoted to his wife and two daughters and he proudly assisted his wife as she pursued her career as a professional musician. He was active in civic and cultural organizations in the Lima area. Harold Barrick died of cancer on June 12, 2001.

older daugter Mila Jean
now Schaber b. 1942

# John McNett Lands on Omaha Beach and Fights All the Way to Germany

John McNett was the sixth child in a family of fifteen children. He was raised on a farm and was expected to help his parents with the farm work and to do daily chores. He graduated from Lima Central High School in 1940, and six months later was drafted into the United States Army. He went from Camp Perry, Ohio, to Camp Wolters, Texas, to Camp White, Oregon, and from there he was sent to England two weeks before D-Day. John served in the 35th Combat Engineers, attached to Patton's army and earned the rank of tech-sergeant. He was in the army for approximately four years and received his Honorable Discharge in August 1945. In 1948, he married Dorothy Rhoda and they had three children. John now lives on the McNett family farm.

The following is John's story in his own words:

"It was D-Day, June 6, 1944, and I was in the fourth wave of troops on the Normandy invasion and was being put ashore at Omaha Beach. I was lucky because when I stepped off the landing craft I only had to wade in water up to my waist to get on dry land. I did not feel the seasickness that some of the troops felt on the earlier landings. I was also lucky that I was able to keep my field pack and other gear dry.

"One complication we had was a lot of the big equipment that we were going to need was now at the bottom of the channel waters. The Germans had laid mines everywhere, and they had all kinds of obstacles built and lots of barbed wire strung around which hindered our progress. Also, the Germans were hidden behind some natural barriers and some pillboxes so they had an easy job shooting at all of us as we arrived on the beach. By the end of that first day, we had only gained one mile. It took us three days before we got hooked up with the men that went in on the other beaches.

"It was at Omaha Beach that I first faced enemy fire. We all considered everybody in our outfit as friends, and sadly, some of our friends did not survive the fighting at Omaha. But that was only the beginning of

213

spending sleepless nights in foxholes on the continual fight for German territory on the way to the Rhine. There was also the loss of comrades who were beside me one minute and shot down the next minute. And there was the constant nagging question of when will it be my turn to fall to a German bullet. We were all trained to 'kill or be killed', but fate also played a part in my survival.

"It was my job to drive a colonel and I always went first. But this one time, for some reason, I decided to go second. The lead vehicle, just ahead of us, hit a mine and all the occupants were killed. It was a terrible explosion. The bodies of the people in the jeep were blown to pieces. There were no recognizable parts of their bodies remaining to bury. The explosion was so violent that there were parts of the jeep hanging in the trees beside the road. I could have been in that lead vehicle. It makes me stop and think *why*?

"The Germans had been using Paris for their headquarters for Occupied France, but in August 1944 the French Underground Army chased the German soldiers out of the city of Paris and Paris was now free. In the meantime the Allies had been chasing German soldiers out of other parts of France. Surprisingly, the Germans did not want to fight in Paris and quickly surrendered, which was against Hitler's orders.

"Later in August, thousands and thousands of Allied soldiers entered the city of Paris and received a wild reception. It was an experience I'll never forget. We were in formation, carrying our field packs and weapons and we started marching down the street. I was excited to see the Arc de Triumph up ahead. People were lined up along the street and they were yelling and obviously happy to see us. All at once, the women began running out into the street and began throwing their arms around us and they were hugging and kissing us. It was impossible for us to stay in our marching formation. After we passed the Arc our officers had to stop us and get us reassembled. Later we were told that this was the greatest demonstration Paris had ever seen."

John then said, with a chuckle, "What a day! What a celebration! I'm glad I was there!"

"Summer turned to fall, and then came the worst winter I have ever experienced. We were living outside and we nearly froze to death. We were ordered to sleep two men in a foxhole to help keep each other warm. At night we would throw a cover over the foxhole to keep the snow and rain off us. In the morning, we would throw the cover off

214

and shake the snow or whatever off it. Most of our meals during this time were K rations.

"We arrived at Bastogne and were soon surrounded by German soldiers. After approximately ten days we heard the American 101st Airborne come in and land. Then General Patton came with his tanks. The Germans who had been keeping us cornered now began running for their lives. At this point, in the Ardennes, we began a steady advance toward the Rhine.

"While pushing our way through Germany some buddies and I found shelter in a vacant house. We were hungry and tired and needed to be cautious because there could be German soldiers close by. We looked out the back door and saw some chickens. We had gone a long time without a hot meal so we decided to have a chicken dinner. I was raised on a farm and I knew how to catch a chicken and quickly wring its neck without the chicken making any noise. I hadn't lost my touch, and we had a chicken dinner that day. The men that were with me cut up a beautiful grand piano that was in the house and that was the wood we used to build the fire to cook the chicken. I still feel guilty about the destruction of that piano.

"On our trek through Germany we were in a German town and saw a hotel. As we walked by the hotel we had the irresistible urge to take a bath and sleep in a clean bed, so we opted to stay there. The German proprietors never told on us.

"My job was to help clear the way for incoming infantry. I worked on building bridges over rivers so troops and equipment could move through. Many times we would get a bridge built and the Germans would destroy it. We had a lot of trouble keeping the bridges over the Rhine intact. Progress was slow in that regard. My job was also to go into towns that had been bombed and clear away the rubble so the infantry could get through. It always made me feel very sad to be working on a power-shovel or a bulldozer and come across bodies of women and children.

"I must say, I really admired General Eisenhower because he seemed to be a man who cared about his soldiers. His leadership helped us win the war. I have a funny story to tell about the General. I was kneeling on the ground working on a piece of equipment and I had my pipe in my mouth. I heard a jeep behind me and I glanced around and there was General Eisenhower in the jeep with several men. I immediately jumped to my feet and saluted him. But I forgot I still had my pipe in my mouth.

"The General returned my salute and laughed and said, 'At ease, soldier.' He then asked me a few questions on how things were going. He could have reprimanded me about the pipe in my mouth, but he didn't. I think he was a great person and a very competent general.

"I also liked General Patton because he really knew how to get things done. When we would be in a jam and he showed up, things would start to move and we would be able to come in behind the tanks and get our job done. There were also times when we were pinned down and could not move and the air force would come in and clear the way for us. Good cooperation!

"I guess I never got over the lack of value that Hitler placed on human life. I saw Buchenwald, one of the concentration camps, and I saw the stacks of human bones and I saw a conveyor belt covered with bones. I could not forgive a leader like Hitler and his followers for doing something like that. Nor can I forget my friends who died on the Omaha beach. I still see pictures in my mind of my friends lying there on the sand. War leaves a lot of memories behind, some that I wish I could forget.

"About this time the army sent me to the Riviera for two weeks for some much needed R & R. The plush resort where I stayed was unbelievable with a magnificent view of the Mediterranean Sea. The food was delicious, especially after a steady diet of K rations. Having hot water for showers and a clean bed to sleep in helped me feel civilized again. But after two weeks the army had other plans for me.

"When Germany surrendered, my orders came that I was to be transferred to the Pacific Theater to fight there. I was tired and I did not want to be in any more battles. I was on a troop ship, ready to leave from a French seaport, when the announcement was made that the atomic bombs had been dropped on Japan and the war was over. My orders were then changed to 'honorably discharged.' I had experienced over four years of hell and I was ready to go home.

"You have probably heard that the Russians acted as if 'they' had won the war all by themselves because they reached Berlin first. I wonder what they thought the Americans and the British had been doing all that time. Oh well, most people in this country know better."

John then asked me, "How would your life be today if Hitler had not been stopped?"

216

# Arthur Miller, Airborne Radar Technician

"I said goodbye to Gloria, my wife, in San Antonio, and hurried to catch my bus out to Kelly Field, because I knew that I did not dare be AWOL on this important day. I was lucky to have been able to be home that last night, because this was the day I would start my journey overseas. I had absolutely no idea where I was going—the military doesn't tell you that until you have arrived.

"It was ten o'clock in the morning, we had been assigned to a particular military troop train, in a specific car, which had swing-down bunks on each side of the car. Nothing was comfortable, just very basic, and no cushions. The train was packed to capacity. The top three bunks were folded up and we all sat on the lowest bunk. When the train got out of the yards, we all noticed that it was heading east. We all began speculating that we must be headed for the European Theater. I had heard some pretty terrible stories about the fighting in Europe, so I must admit I was a little apprehensive.

"The troop train went to Denver and then we were parked on a spur overnight. Food was catered in, which consisted of a sandwich, fruit, and drink. We were packed into the railroad car like sardines and there was only one crude, and very inadequate, latrine in each car. We were not permitted to leave the train for any reason.

"Early the next morning, we left Denver and headed north to Montana and then headed west. The only way we knew where we were was by looking out the windows and reading signs. We found out later that while we were parked in the Denver railroad yards, our orders had been changed. We arrived in Seattle, Washington, and were taken to Ft. Lawton. Several of us grabbed towels and headed for the showers, as we felt dirty after all that time on the train. To our surprise, the showers were not what we had expected, because they were all cold water and it was late in October.

"At 10:00 P.M., we were put on trucks and taken to marine docks where we were assigned to certain ships. At this time, our weapons were all taken from us. I wondered what this meant.

"On the troop ship, I was on the first level below topside. The bunks were four high and I knew I wanted the third one. Seasickness soon set in and lasted three days. I did not eat during this time. On the fourth day I went down to the mess hall and the smell of the food made me sick again. On the fifth day, a friend felt sorry for me and went to the PX and brought me a candy bar. (Yes, they had a PX on the troop ship.) On the sixth day, I was able to go to the mess hall and get a tray of food. People had to eat at stand-up tables that had a ridge around the tabletop to keep trays from falling off due to the movement of the ship. It was an uneasy meal because so many people were seasick and you stood across from each other, at this narrow table, and you worried about them filling your tray. The faces of the people were all shades of gray, yellow and green, from seasickness, just like me, and there were lots of places on the floor where people had vomited. It was not pleasant in the mess hall, but I knew I had to try to get something to eat, and hopefully it would stay down.

"After a week at sea, the troop ship stopped within sight of land. We did not know where we were. We were stopped for a whole day. Just waiting. The next day two tugs came out to meet us and they opened an underwater gate for the ship to go in to the harbor. The underwater gate was to keep enemy submarines out of the harbor.

"When we disembarked we realized that we were in Honolulu, Oahu. Good old terra firma under my feet felt great! It was also great to take deep breaths of the wonderful fresh air, especially after being below decks on that troop ship! Everything was well planned and we were assigned to get on certain buses. As we were driven through Honolulu, we passed rows and rows of crates filled with military equipment that lined the streets. We continued on, and passed between many pineapple and sugar cane fields. The day of my arrival in Hawaii was the day that Marshal Law was lifted.

"The buses unloaded us in front of a two-story brick barracks at Wheeler Field. We just walked down an aisle and if there was an empty cot, we took it. There were 100 Civil War army cots in the room. The facilities were very clean with tiled permanent latrines. Later on a friend and I found a small room off a screened porch on the second floor and we moved there to get a semblance of quiet and peace in this barracks that was full of noisy and boisterous men.

"Shortly after our arrival, we were called to the orderly room and we were given our assignment and told where the mess hall was. I was told that my friend and I would be in charge of the radar workshop and he and I were taken to the workshop. The workshop was located in a one-story double house, and there was an MP on duty with a German shepherd dog, twenty-four hours a day. The MPs always stood between the two front doors of the house. There were approximately twenty guys working at the radar shop, and I was to maintain records and assign work to the guys.

"Our work consisted of modifying the radar that had been installed on the PBYs that were made in Canada and replace it with American equipment. There would also be other planes that would come in and would need repair on their radar equipment. Bombers that had over 100 missions or more were retired from service, and we were to salvage all useable radar and communication equipment before the planes were destroyed. Mechanics and other technicians also salvaged equipment like we did. The salvaged equipment was stored in a large hanger. Nothing useable was ever thrown away.

"I felt very fortunate to have this assignment because the weather was always good, the food was good, and our commanding officers were congenial and easy to work with. Knowing how indefinite the military assignments can be, I knew that I could not count on being in such a pleasant place forever.

"I was asked to select some of the radar guys to help me build an electrical power line. We used German POWs to do the heavy work such as digging the holes and setting the poles. These power lines were going into an area that had never had power before. The MPs that were assigned to us also guarded the German POWs as they worked on the power lines. There was no danger of the Germans escaping, they liked it in Hawaii. Who wouldn't?

"I don't remember how I found out that my brother, Walter, who was in the U.S. Navy, was stationed on the same island, close to Hickam Field. We made connections and spent one Sunday together taking pictures of the beautiful Hawaiian flowers and just catching up on each other's assignments. He took me to the submarine where he was stationed and showed me his bunk that was next to a torpedo. It was really good to see him—a touch of home, and the hope that someday we would both get back to Ohio. We made plans to spend another Sunday together within a couple weeks, but that was not to be.

"I was given ten days of R & R time, so I went over to the island of Hawaii, to look at the volcanoes, all the beautiful scenery, and the fields and fields of volcanic cinders. It was all very different than what a person would see back in Ohio. The military had built small wooden cottages near the volcanoes, and there was steam coming out of the ground all around them. The military people could stay there at no charge when on R & R. There were buses that would take the military people to the different scenic spots, also at no charge. My thoughts were that these accommodations for the military people were a great way of boosting their morale. It certainly had a positive affect on me.

"My R & R time was not quite up, but a bad storm came up and I was feeling that I needed to get back. There were three guys that worked in the radar shop with me and we headed for the airport. I told them I knew some of the pilots and I would see if we could hitch a ride back to Oahu. There just happened to be one I knew at the Hilo Airport and he took us all back to Wheeler Field.

"As I got out of the plane, a guy came running up to me and said for me to hurry and report to the orderly room, as I was shipping out that night. I was told to get my gear packed, and of course, I did not know where I was going.

"I left Hickam Field at 2:00 A.M., along with six strangers, for a 'destination unknown.' Remember that military planes did not have cushioned seats, only hard benches along each side, and it was not a comfortable ride. After approximately eight hours, the pilot said to us, as he made a nice landing on a small airstrip on a tiny island in the South Pacific, 'Well, guys, you are now at Kwajalein. Good luck!'

"My first response was, 'Where the hell is Kwajalein? I've never heard of it!'

"I discovered that Kwajalein is in the Marshall Islands group. It is three miles long and two miles wide. The navy had a base at the east end of the island and the air force was at the west end. There was a small metal building that was the terminal and also the PX. The mechanics were in a Quonset hut and there was a storage hangar and our radar shop was in a separate little building. There was no vegetation of any kind on the island, except for one shell-shocked tree, broken off about six feet above ground. Since I was raised on a farm, I looked for some good rich dirt, but there wasn't any, only coral sand everywhere on the island.

"The United States Marines took control of Kwajalein on February 14, 1944 after a fierce battle with the Japanese. When the island was secured all the natives were removed to a nearby island to live. They were brought in every day, on a voluntary basis, and the native men helped with odd jobs around the island, and the women did cleaning. The military paid the natives for their work and they seemed to like the arrangement. Close to our radar shop were two mass gravesites, with approximately 4,000 Japanese buried in the one and 3,000 in the other. There was a fence around the area and a sign indicated the number of Japanese in each site and the date of the battle in which they lost their lives.

"The C.O. informed me that I was in charge of the radar shack. We had five technicians including myself. We worked on all airborne equipment that had been removed and sent to us for repair. The mechanics would install the radar equipment after we repaired it. We had approximately two planes per day that would need some work from us. We would also get about two planes per day that would be taking the injured back to Hawaii or the States. Once several planes arrived that were carrying nurses to Hawaii. They had evidently been traumatized by something and they showed signs of severe mental stress. It was sad to see this.

"Talk about a coincidence, I happened to be down by the runway and the chaplain who married my wife and me in Florida was getting off the plane. He apparently was just passing through and did not hang around for any long-term assignment on this Godforsaken island.

"We had a non-com club with some rickety tables and chairs, where people could play cards. We could get our ration of two cans per day of warm beer. All available water was distilled, orange in color, and so it was better to drink pop or coffee. The distiller on the island was in very poor working condition. The food was pretty bad, with lots of canned chicken and frozen bully beef (horsemeat) which came from Australia. We had little tiny bananas, lots of powdered eggs, Spam and baked beans. The bread was made with wormy flour, so everyone would hold their slice of bread up to the light and pick out the largest worms and bugs before eating it.

"The temperature never got below ninety degrees, it was always hot and humid and mildew was a big problem. With water all around us it would have been nice to go swimming except for the abundance of Portuguese Man-of-War and jellyfish in the waters.

"After the atomic bombs were dropped, and the Japanese surrendered, the air traffic through Kwajalein began to diminish. Most of the planes were now carrying the wounded back to the States. Although I had the points to get discharged, when I saw the wounded and battle-stressed military people on the planes there was no way I would have tried to take a seat away from them.

"One day in August two B-29s landed in Kwajalein and were immediately surrounded by MPs. They departed before the day was up. Of course, this sparked a lot of questions from the people at the base. We were informed that the one plane was the *Enola Gay* that carried the atomic bomb *Little Boy* to Hiroshima, and the other plane was *Bock's Car* that carried the atomic bomb *Fat Man* to Nagasaki. We were not permitted to get close to the planes to get a better look.

"Intense boredom was setting in after the atomic bombs had been dropped and my men and I needed to keep busy. We built a washing machine out of a steel tub, and made the agitator out of prop-pitch motors. We needed rain water, so we took four-foot and five-foot pipe, split it lengthwise, and hung it on the radar shop to act as spouting. We then hoped for rain so we would not have to use the orange water that was available to us from the distiller.

"It was now getting extremely quiet at the base. The Red Cross people with their handouts and treats were gone. The PX was no longer in operation. Fewer and fewer planes came in. The mail delivery was not being delivered as it had been before. We had read everything available on the island. The food was worse and the flour even wormier. We played card games to pass the time. More people were leaving, but my crew and I had not heard anything about when we would be leaving. And so we waited—and we waited."

# Nolan C. Core, Coast Guard, Harrowing Experience at Sea

My name is Nolan Core and I was born on a farm on January 22, 1921, in Allen County, close to the small town of Columbus Grove, Ohio. I was the oldest in a family of five boys. There were no girls in the family, but I had a girl cousin who was like a sister to me. I attended Monroe Center School, which was a one-room country school with grades one through eight, and I graduated from Columbus Grove High School.

In August 1942, when I was twenty-one years old, I knew I was about to be drafted into the army and I knew for certain that I didn't want to be wading around in the mud for the army, as I had had enough of that on the farm. I was thinking about the Navy, and my preference was for smaller boats rather than the larger boats, so I enlisted in the Coast Guard and I served for three years, one month, and twelve days. My parents were understanding and supportive of my decision to join the Coast Guard. My father had served in World War I and he and my mother both understood that certain things develop in the world that have to be taken care of.

In times of war, the Coast Guard is considered to be part of the Navy, so a lot of the training I received was with Navy personnel and sometimes there would be a little friction there because the Navy people thought they were better than the Coast Guard people. I received my boot training in Buffalo, New York and then I was sent to Erie, Pennsylvania for rifle and marksmanship training. We were instructed about fighting in close quarters with fixed bayonets and we were told that after you thrust the bayonet into a person you shoot the gun so that the recoil of the gun helps to pull the bayonet out as quickly as possible. That was to help in case the bayonet had gotten stuck in a bone. I was then sent to Port Clinton and I was taught the handling of small boats and craft and also received survival and rescue training. I thought it was interesting that the Coast Guard lifeboats are different than the ones on other ships. The Coast Guard lifeboats are totally sealed and are buttoned down from the inside. At Buffalo and Port

Clinton we had a lot of marching to do, which was probably a form of discipline. I wore out a pair of shoes every two weeks during that time.

I took an aptitude test and received a high score and was sent to New York to Hemphill Diesel Engine School for training on diesel motors, gasoline motors and diesel-electric systems. Diesel-electric was just coming in for propulsion systems for smaller boats. From there I was sent to Grove City, Pennsylvania for training on main propulsion motors, which were the big motors that the government was using on the Liberty ships. You can't imagine—one engine would weigh up to sixty tons. From there I was sent to Harvey, Illinois, to the Buda Diesel Engine Plant and I was assigned to work there.

The government had plans for me to use all this knowledge on a Liberty Ship. I had been assigned to a particular ship and I went to watch it being built. I saw them lay the keel and I didn't like the looks of it. They were tubs! I put in for a transfer. I never thought I would get it, but I did. I worked for the captain of the port, and I was assigned to work on security detail, port security, and fire detail. They sent me to Duluth, Minnesota, to show them techniques and use of fire equipment.

I hate to tell you, but this was one of my worst moments. I was working as a guard at a warehouse and there was a civilian working there whose brother was in the Marines fighting in the islands of the Pacific Theater. This civilian was also a guard at the warehouse and he resented me being in the military in a relatively safe job while his brother was away in a dangerous position. The guy would frequently make a point of looking for me and he would try to provoke me and would call me insulting and obscene names. Well, I had had enough and I hauled off and hit him twice alongside of his head. He reported the incident and since it is against the law for a serviceman to be aggressive toward a civilian I received a reprimand and was transferred to Alaska.

When I got to Alaska I had to build gun emplacements, dig drainage ditches, things like that. I told them that I didn't think I was sent there to dig ditches. They told me to bear with them and I would be assigned to something else.

Eventually I was assigned to a patrol group and there were ten ships in the group. I was assigned to one of the boats as a machinist, or "motor mac." There were five ships assigned to Ketchikan, Alaska, and they would go out for a week, and then be back in port for a week. The patrol boats were approximately fifty feet long and fourteen feet wide and were equipped with various ordnance and nautical depth charges (ash cans) to be used against submerged submarines. The patrol boats looked a lot like a PT boat and we usually had a crew of ten people on board: a skipper, several yeomen, a cook, several seamen, and myself. While in port we had to take care of repairs on our ship, and sometimes replace an engine, and always have everything ready to go.

At this time Alaska was a territory and the U.S. Marshals were the law. If something went wrong, we would take the marshals to wherever the problem was. The terrain at Ketchikan was mountainous and not conducive to building an air base, the only planes that could land there were amphibian planes. The government built an air base on the island of Annette, located about forty to fifty miles out in the middle of nowhere. The island generated its own electricity, and they were noted for the beautiful boats that were built there. Fishing was good in the area and there was a fish cannery there. Most of the military planes would stop at the air base on the island to refuel or take care of whatever repairs were needed.

When we were out on patrol we were primarily looking for Japanese subs, or Japanese vessels of any kind. There was speculation that the Japanese were going to try to shell America's west coast, and cities like Seattle were to be the targets. We had ash cans on our ships and if we detected a sub, we could use them, but I always thought if we rolled one off the stern we would probably blow up our own ship.

When the patrol ships would come into port, the guys would sit around and drink and brag about what they had seen or done. One time one of our patrol boats came into port, flying high, with a broom on its conning tower. Their guys were bragging that they had dropped their ash cans and they knew they had gotten a Japanese sub, because of the debris that had surfaced on the water. We never believed them.

On the weekends that we were in port, we were always subject to extra duties. One day we got a call to fill our water tanks, get in a supply of food, fill the gas tanks and be ready to go at 0800 the next morning. We were to take on sixteen U.S. soldiers and take them to the air base at Metiakatia, on Annette Island. I don't know if they were going further north or back to the States, or where. We started out and once we were away from the islands and out in the open water, it got rough. I mean we were really bouncing! Remember we've got these sixteen soldiers on board and about twelve of them were seasick, so seasick that they wished they could die. They were lying all over the boat, they had the dry heaves, and nothing would come up anymore. There were only four of them that were still standing.

On our boat we had what you call a dual cooling system. We had a heat exchanger and we pumped water right out of the sea that cooled the water for the motors so that they didn't mineralize from the salt. Our boat bounced around so hard that it came right up out of the water and right down the middle, where the keel is, we had a pump on each side of the keel. That was where we drew the water in, never thinking that we would get an air lock. There was air in our lines! One of the motors started sputtering. I raised up the hatch and saw that our engine room was flooding—water was in there—and it was deep. Then the other motor started sputtering. I tried to see if I could reach the engine room with my suction hose, but it wouldn't reach.

I was running short of my normal crew of ten and only had seven with me this trip. We're dead in the water and we were in a fix! The sergeant in charge of the sixteen soldiers came up to me and asked, "What can we do?" I tell you, he was a man! We both understood that we were fighting for our lives here. The skipper also understood the seriousness of our situation and he was busy sending out the international distress call of "May Day, May Day."

I told the sergeant, "We have two things we have to do, we have to plug the hole in the side of the boat and get the water out of the engine room, so we can keep the boat upright in the water." An over-heated engine had burned a twelve-inch hole in the side of the boat and the water was pouring in.

I told the sergeant that there was a fire pump on the ship but we would have to carry it up over the top of the boat, bring it down on the bow, then lash it down, then would have to attach the suction hose to it. I thought I could then reach the engine room and pump the water out. I told the sergeant that we would need four men to carry the pump.

The sergeant said, "Let's go!" He, two of his men, and I carried the pump. I don't know how we carried it because it was very heavy, but we did it. And I don't know how we did it without losing someone overboard. I put that suction hose down in the engine room, fired up the pump, and she took off like a jewel. I am so glad that I always checked that fire pump every other day just to make certain it was working okay in case of an emergency. I never thought I would be using it for a situation like that.

In the meantime, our crew selected their best man for another almost impossible job. They chose a man on our crew who was from Ketchikan and had previously worked on a fishing boat before joining the Coast Guard. He knew the sea and he understood how cold the water was. They tied a rope around him and dropped him in the water and then lowered a mattress to him to begin stuffing it in the hole in the side of the boat. Of course, the sea was still rough and the boat was going up and down and he had to do his work when the hole in the boat was above the water. No easy job! Once he had the hole stuffed, the crew on deck passed a piece of plywood and a hammer and nails to him. And again, while the boat was moving up and down he nailed the plywood over the hole. A terrific accomplishment!

A PBY plane flew over and then disappeared. A little later I looked on the horizon and I saw a column of smoke. It was a ship that was approaching at full speed toward us. It came up on our leeward side and used lifeboat hooks to hook onto our ship. The captain asked us, "Where do you want to go?" We told him that we had been heading for Metiakatia. And he asked us, "Do you want to ride with us?" And he threw us a "Jacob's Ladder" and the seaman who had patched the hole in our boat and who was soaking wet and cold, and I went aboard the rescue ship.

Our boat was put in dry dock, the hole was properly patched, the oil was changed, and we were ready to leave. Just then the Army sergeant came up and shook my hand and said, "It has been nice knowing you." I responded, "It has been nice knowing you, too." The unsaid words between us were of gratitude for being able to work together and keep that boat afloat in those critical hours at sea just several days before. I'm certain neither of us will ever forget that experience, but we never exchanged names and addresses and have had no contact since then.

You know, when you go through training and you go through a war, it makes you hard. It's like you have a chip on your shoulder. I noticed it when I went to work after I got out of the Coast Guard. It's no wonder they have a training program to turn you back into a civilian again before they discharge you. I didn't feel that I needed that—I just wanted to go home.

The Coast Guard filled an important need for our country in World War II, as well as today, and for that I'm very proud to have served in the United States Coast Guard.

# Part Eight
# European War Ends

# Allies Closing In on Germany, Roosevelt Dies

## Benito Mussolini Fails Again

Hitler sent military support to help his friend Mussolini save his country from the advancing Allied troops. In the spring of 1945, the Allied forces overcame the German and Italian armies in Northern Italy and the German troops were retreating. Mussolini, fearing for his life, decided to flee to Switzerland, taking his mistress Clara Petacci with him. The Italian Underground found them on the shores of Lake Como, and quickly conducted a brief trial before shooting them. Their bodies were taken back to Milan and were hung by their heels in front of a garage. Mussolini was the founder of Fascism and had been dictator in Italy for twenty-one years. Like other dictators, he rose to power by his use of violence, force and treachery, and he met his own death in the same manner.

## Hitler Refuses to Listen to His Advisors

Hitler had ordered German troops and equipment out of Poland and had them sent to the Ardennes. They arrived too late to change the outcome of the Ardennes Campaign. The Soviets now had the Germans greatly outnumbered and the Soviets had three armies, with one army headed toward Danzig, another army encircling Warsaw, and the third moving toward the border of Germany. The Soviets quickly overwhelmed the Germans in Poland, and their armies were greatly feared because of their barbaric treatment of prisoners and civilians.

Again Hitler refused to listen to his military advisors and to realistically assess the seriousness of his situation. He had failed in his plans for the Ardennes offensive and now he began using the fear people had of the Soviets to try to get the English and the Americans to back off from the "unconditional surrender" terms. But the unstoppable Russian troops kept marching steadily toward the German border. There was a segment of Russian troops that was just thirty miles from Berlin, and there was no doubt that the Russians wanted to get to Berlin first.

## Big Three Meet at Yalta

On February 4, 1945, Roosevelt, Churchill and Stalin met at Yalta. There was always an element of distrust between the Anglo-American leaders and Stalin that needed to be dealt with when the "big three" leaders conferred. Roosevelt told Stalin at Yalta that as soon as the fighting ceased in Europe, American troops would be going to the Pacific to fight. Eisenhower had told Roosevelt that he was not going to try to get to Berlin first because he considered Berlin a political prize, not a military prize, and he felt going on to Berlin would cost too many American lives. Roosevelt upheld Eisenhower's decision in this matter. Churchill, although disappointed with this decision, agreed that the Anglo-American forces would go no farther than the Elbe River. The Soviet armies stopped and remained at the Oder River until April.

## Allies Cross the Rhine into Germany

As the Allies were pushing the Germans back toward Germany, the Germans were destroying the bridges as they retreated. They had done this to all the bridges except one, the railroad bridge at Remagen. The Germans had tried to destroy that bridge but were unsuccessful. This was the opening that the Allies had been hoping for, and soon Allied troops were crossing the Rhine into Germany. It wasn't long until the Allies had more than sixty bridges built and Allied troops were pouring across the Rhine and getting ready to strike at the heart of Germany.

## Roosevelt's Declining Health and Death

President Roosevelt had been elected to a fourth term as president, in November 1944, receiving 432 electoral votes, as compared to the 99 that his opponent, Tom Dewey, received. Throughout Roosevelt's campaign and during the winter months Roosevelt had suffered from frequent colds and was losing weight. At the Yalta Conference, in February 1945, many people noticed that President Roosevelt did not look well. When Roosevelt reported to Congress about the conditions set forth in the Yalta Conference, he made a rare reference to his physical handicap by saying, "I hope that you will pardon me for this unusual posture of sitting down . . . it makes it a lot easier for me not to have to carry about ten pounds of steel around the bottom of my legs."

On Thursday, April 12, 1945, at 4:35 P.M., President Roosevelt died of a massive cerebral hemorrhage. He was sitting in front of a fireplace in the Little White House, at Warm Springs, Georgia, and was posing for an artist at the time he was stricken. His death occurred on the eighty-third day of his fourth term as President. No other president has served more than two terms.

The people in the United States and all around the world were saddened to hear of Roosevelt's death. They held Roosevelt in high esteem because they felt his innovative programs helped the people at the time of the Great Depression, and they also admired his leadership abilities that had helped bring the war to what looked like a coming victory for the Allies. Winston Churchill was deeply saddened by his friend's death. These two leaders of the Anglo-American forces trusted each other, had worked together on strategic planning, had agonized over their defeats, and rejoiced over their victories, and commiserated over the element of mutual mistrust of the Soviets that they could not dispel. Allied troops were now practically at Hitler's doorstep and close to being on Japan's shores, but now, Roosevelt would not get to experience the joy of "unconditional surrender" upon which he had insisted.

## Harry S. Truman, from Independence, Missouri, Becomes President

At first the American soldiers and sailors around the world refused to believe that their commander-in-chief was dead, and they wondered, "Who is Harry Truman?" But two hours and thirty-four minutes after the official announcement was made about the president's death, Vice President Harry S. Truman took the oath of office and became the thirty-third president of the United States. The swearing-in ceremony only lasted one minute. Truman picked up the large Bible on the Cabinet conference table, held it in his left hand and after repeating the oath bent down and kissed the Bible. President Truman, the ex-haber-dasher from Independence, Missouri, immediately announced that he had requested all of Roosevelt's Cabinet members and other appointments to remain in place. He assured the people that he would try to continue as Roosevelt would have wanted.

Roosevelt's funeral was to take place on Saturday, at 4:00 P.M., in the East Room of the executive mansion. It was decided that his body would not lie in state and only approximately 200 people would be invited to attend the funeral services. On Sunday, his body was to be interred at Hyde Park, New York. The American people were reminded that we were a country at war, and the usual ceremonial procedures honoring a dead president had to be foregone at this time.

Little did the people know that Roosevelt had not taken his vice-president into his confidence about many of the planned strategies of the war, the non-published agreements with various leaders, and the complicated diplomacy of working with Churchill, Stalin and other leaders. Truman needed to hit the ground running because the war wasn't going to pause and wait for him to catch up.

Roosevelt had maintained a strong guiding force in the decision-making process as it applied to military issues in World War II. Although he and Churchill were friends, they did not always agree. Roosevelt's "unconditional surrender" is a case in point. President Truman was now faced with decisions regarding the war as it entered into its important final phase. The question of the Anglo-American troops not going all the way to Berlin needed to be addressed, as well as the question of how to work with Stalin, whose military tactics now appeared to be a threat to the free world.

# Willis F. (Bill) Early,
## Shot Down Over Berlin, Captured,
## Relates POW Experiences

### Introduction

Willis (Bill), Franklin Early was born on April 30, 1921, and was raised on his family's farm in Allen County. He had three brothers and one sister. They all were expected to help their parents with the farm work. Bill's family belonged to the Pleasant View Church of the Brethren. After Bill graduated from Lima Central High School, he enrolled in the Brethren College, at North Manchester, Indiana.

Bill was a handsome young man with dark brown hair, brown eyes, and skin that seemed to have a perpetual tan. He was very energetic, he exuded confidence and strength and he gave the impression that he had great plans for his future. He was very sociable and he made certain that everyone was having a good time when there was a gathering of friends.

At college, Bill met Betty Jane Schul and immediately fell in love with her. She was very petite, a natural blond and extremely pretty. They made a striking couple. World War II started, and Bill knew that the draft board would soon be looking for him. He and Betty decided that they would wait until the war was over to get married. He enlisted in the Army Air Corps Reserve, in the Manchester College Cadet Program.

Like many other couples in wartime, they changed their minds about waiting, and they were married on May 1, 1943, in Hernando, Mississippi, hoping they would have a little time together before Bill would be sent overseas. Bill was in flight training and received his wings and commission at Ft. Sumner, New Mexico. Betty went with Bill on his stateside assignments in Tennessee, California, New Mexico and Nebraska.

When Bill and Betty realized that she was pregnant, and Bill also realized he was nearing the time to leave for overseas, he told Betty that she should stay with his parents. Bill knew that they would be good to her and would take good care of her and the baby when it arrived.

Bill was in Nebraska and could not get home when Betty went into labor. His father took her to the hospital and stayed with her. When her labor pains became worse he knelt beside her bed and said, "Betty, just grab my hands and squeeze as hard as you can. I helped Bill's mother through this five times and I certainly can help Bill's wife get through it."

Betty gave birth to a sweet baby girl, named Sandra Kay, who has been called "Cookie" ever since. The Red Cross was able to get Bill an emergency leave to come home for just a few days. At least he was able to see his baby daughter before he returned to the base and almost immediately, on November 2, 1944, was shipped overseas and began flying missions out of the air base at Manchester, England.

(Seven years after WWII was over, Bill wrote the following account of what happened on his thirteenth mission and the subsequent time he was a POW.)

## And They Call This Democracy—*The Land of the Free*

### Willis F. (Bill) Early

Seven long years ago on a beautiful, clear, winter day in February, we were flying our B-17 on a bombing mission over Berlin. Yes, the target was Berlin—the toughest target in the European Theater. For two consecutive days, we had been briefed to bomb Berlin, and each time the mission was scrubbed (canceled) due to bad weather. True, courageous airmen are scared on every mission, but the thought of Berlin struck terror in our hearts.

When we were briefed for our mission early on the morning of February 3, 1945, we were intensely afraid that the target would be Berlin again. This time we knew that it would not be scrubbed, because the weather was cold and clear as a bell. Sure enough, the colonel opened the meeting with the announcement, "Gentlemen, your target for today is Berlin—the traffic center of Berlin." Yes, even peace-loving, Christian Americans are guilty of planning to kill civilians, barbaric as it may seem. Our target for February 3rd was to bomb the traffic center of Berlin at the time of day when there would be the most possible foot traffic and auto traffic on the sidewalks and streets. The purpose, presumably, was to raise the morale of our allies, the Russians, who were then fighting east of Berlin on the Oder River. By bombing the German civilians we were to confirm to the Russians that we were supporting their efforts by weakening the Germans' desire to resist.

As we were preparing our flying equipment for the mission, the pilot, Bernie (I was flying co-pilot), seemed to have a premonition of tonight's luck. He came over to me and said, "Bill, this is going to be a tough one. I think that we had better wear our G.I. shoes on this mission (normally we wore electrical heated shoes inside our flying boots) because we stand a good chance of having to walk back." This made sense to me, as I put on G.I. boots even though I knew my feet were going to be awfully cold at 25,000 feet where the temperature was forty degrees below zero centigrade.

After carefully checking over our ship, we fondly bade farewell to Mac, our crew chief, and proceeded to warm up the plane. We taxied out to the end of the runway, and nobody said a word for we were all busy with our thoughts and prayers. When it came our time to take off, we mechanically headed the nose down the runway, shoved the throttles to the firewall and headed for Berlin. Little did we know what was in store for us.

After an uneventful take-off, we climbed to the pre-determined altitude and headed for the rendezvous. Nine men diligently peered out of every window to watch for other planes, for at rendezvous, thirty-six planes converge on an imaginary point and circle it until each plane slowly works itself into its proper position in the formation.

February 3rd was an armchair general's conception of a perfect day for a bombing mission, but it was a horrible day for a combat airman with loved ones at home who wanted to see him get back alive. There wasn't a cloud in the entire sky.

We proceeded on toward Berlin—the dreaded target. No enemy fighters were in sight. The crew remained unusually quiet. I didn't bother to ask why, for I knew what they were doing just as I was doing—they were praying. Yes, when you have no other place to turn for help, your thoughts turn by instinct to a high power. At 25,000 feet, you are so high in the sky that you feel that you can almost reach up your hand and God will take hold of it and lead you through, and that was what all of us were asking God to do on this mission.

As we approached our target one or two clouds began to appear. And for a second we thought that our prayers for clouds to hide us from flak were going to be answered, but our hopes were soon shattered, for the clouds disappeared.

Nearer and nearer we approached Berlin. All of a sudden the sky ahead of us was blackened by bursts of black smoke. Our hearts sank in desperation for we knew that the black bursts were flak from the deadly accurate German 88 on a clear day. At the same instant, B-17s began to fall from the sky in a sickening, careening manner that indicated that they had been badly hit and were out of control. The chances of their crew members parachuting to safety were slim. But the fact that worried us most was that the flak was concentrated right in the position that we had to fly through due to our position in the formation.

As the next group directly ahead (groups are spaced two minutes apart) of us went over the target, several planes experienced the same disaster as the preceding group. And again we noted the immense concentration of flak in our area and I prayed, "Dear God, please spare us. If you ever heard and heeded my prayers, please heed them now." Believe me, I was scared. I longed for a foxhole to jump into, or a tree to hide behind, but at 25,000 feet, those things are pretty scarce. Even though we longed for an escape, the discipline taught by the army and sheer courage forced us to proceed unfalteringly to what we knew was disaster, so like clay pigeons, we were led by the lead plane over the target.

While our minds were intent on flying the plane, we heard the bombardier announce over the interphone system, "Bombs away"—then it happened. The first burst of flak was a big black cloud right in front of us at our altitude and we flew right through it. The second burst was just off our left wing. Then there was a terrible sickening noise like an explosion and the plane lurched in the air. Amid this we could detect the tearing of metal, then simultaneously, three engines roared out of control. Yes, the third burst hit us squarely, for we had been zeroed in by German 88 flak guns.

As the pilot was flying the plane out of formation, I was hitting the feathering buttons for the propellers of the uncontrollable engines, but nothing happened. I throttled back the engines, but they still roared at twice their normal speed, shaking the plane violently all the while. We knew that it was only a matter of time until a propeller came off or the engines caught on fire. With the thought that we would have to abandon ship, I switched on the automatic pilot, but even it had been shot away. About that time I decided it was time to get ready to leave. I jerked off my flak suit and positioned myself between the seats, so I could make a quick get-away through the escape hatch in case of emergency. The pilot looked at me and asked, "Where are you going?" I replied, "I'm getting ready to get the h———— out of here." His reply was, "Stand back and let me get between there."

Ever since we had been first hit, we had steadily lost altitude. That was the only thing that saved us, for we were hit again and again by flak, but the flak went on through the ship and exploded above us. Two flak holes were made in our right wing, one in our left wing and one through the radio room, which severed my control cables. Gas was pouring out of the punctured wing tanks.

While I was mentally conceiving how I would abandon the ship in case of an emergency (like fire or uncontrollable altitude), I noted that the navigator and bombardier were clustered around the small escape hatch under the cockpit. Between the escape hatch and me was also the engineer, waiting for orders to abandon ship. Seeing that a quick escape was impossible under the circumstances, I ordered them all back to the gunner's section of the fuselage where the main door is located. About that time, the pilot who was keeping the ship level from between the pilot and copilot seats, informed me that his flak suit was caught, so I helped him out of his flak suit. All of this time we were heading east with the hope of getting safely behind Russian lines (forty miles east of Berlin) before it was necessary to abandon ship.

Then it happened. Number three engine burst into flames and ignited the gas streaming out of the tank. The pilot jerked off his oxygen mask and said, "Go back and bail the boys out." A look of stark terror showed on his face that indicated that he was really frightened. I immediately hastened through the bombbay and radio room, motioning as I went, for the crew to bail out. As I got to the radio room, I felt the ship go into a spiral and centrifugal force made it hard for me to maintain my balance. I knew then that the pilot must have abandoned ship by the front escape hatch. As soon as the crew saw my bail out signal, they began to bail out. The gasoline fire was swept by the slip stream the full length of the ship and the crew was bailing out through the fire. At first, centrifugal force had some of the crew momentarily pinned against the fuselage, but they soon found something to grab to pull themselves to the door. In the meantime, I was racing through the ship, grabbing whatever I could grab to prevent being overcome by centrifugal force. When I finally reached the door, nobody was going out, so I stepped up to the door ready to bail, but centrifugal force finally caught up with me and pinned me against the door frame. Just then the navigator kicked me in the pants, and I was out. I never was so glad to get out of anything or any place in my life. I breathed a sigh of relief there in space and said to myself, "Boy, I got out of there."

My mind was clear as a bell as I counted one, two, three (rather hurriedly), then I reached for the rip cord handle. I pulled it slow and steady and there it was, free in my hand. Since I was wearing a back pack, I couldn't see the chute open, but a tug soon told me that it had. I thought to myself that now my worries were over, but they had just begun.

When I looked up at my chute, I was horrified to see that it was badly torn. One panel and half of another panel were torn out of the chute. There I was at 15,000 feet with a torn parachute flapping in a forty mile-per-hour wind. I began to pray all over again, for I was scared to death that the chute would continue tearing out and I would plummet to my death, but there was nothing I could do but pray. I prayed; "Please, God keep that chute together. Please, God, you have spared me this far, please help me once more." Fortunately, God answered my prayers and the chute held together. I descended faster than my pals, but I felt that I could survive the fall if the chute held together.

After my fear regarding the chute subsided, I began to take stock of my situation. Then I noticed that two ME 109 German fighters were headed right for us. This bothered me for a moment, but they soon changed their direction and headed toward our exploding ship. I noticed that below me was a small town with two rows of trees leading out from it. About one to two miles east of us, there was a large river. I thought that that river was probably the Oder and we didn't quite make it across, but then it couldn't be, for it seemed that we were in that crippled plane for an hour and the Oder should be well behind us.

As I descended to tree-top level, the thought ran through my mind that I should get ready to land. I had never made a parachute jump before, but we had been shown movies on how to land. No sooner had the thought of landing gone through my mind when boom, I had hit—not the ground, but a cobblestone highway right between the two rows of trees. My legs doubled up and it felt like I had busted by tail-bone. I lay there dazed for a moment and finally cleared the haze from my eyes and spotted a soldier by my side. I said, "Polish?" He said, "Nix, German." I laid my head back down and said to myself, "The war is over for you, boy, the war is all over for you."

Soon the Germans had five of us captured and took us all to the small village for interrogation. The village was rear echelon military headquarters, and the river that I saw was the Oder. If we could have stayed in the plane three more minutes, we would have been safely behind Russian lines. Three of our crew members had bailed out earlier and the pilot had made a delayed opening jump and was captured separately. He had broken his leg when he landed, but was the only one seriously injured besides me with a back injury that now gives me a 10 percent disability.

After interrogation, we moved to Berlin and then to Wetzler for further interrogation.

After interrogation we were moved to a prison camp at Nuremberg, where we spent many cold nights without blankets or heat. Our food consisted of a cup of tea for breakfast, two very small boiled potatoes for lunch, and a slice of bread and a cup of saltless grass soup for supper. Everyone lost considerable weight, including me, for I lost forty pounds the first month. We all became infested with lice and fleas, but believe me, we were happy to be alive.

In the meantime, my family had been notified that I was missing in action. This could mean anything in the Army Air Force, but my wife, daughter and family held out hope that I would be found alive, and their hopes were answered about six weeks later. Their hopes were soon shattered, however, when they subsequently learned of the death of my kid brother who was killed in action.

(NOTE: The following was crossed out by Bill Early and was never rewritten so I have taken the liberty to include this section below. Submitted by Bill's widow, Betty.)

In April, we marched approximately 120 miles south to a place called Moosburg. On April 29th, we were liberated by the U.S. Third Army. A few days later the Congressional Investigating Committee visited our camp on their tour of prison camps in Germany. There I met John Vorys, Republican Congressman from Ohio, who was on the committee. Then we knew that we had not been forgotten at home.

When I arrived in the States, the first thing I did was call home. There I learned for the first time that my brother (who had been my roommate in college and was very close to me) had been killed in action. This was quite a blow to me. After a sixty days rest and recuperation leave and the capitulation of the Japanese, I——

(Bill never finished the last sentence.)

         ✿      ✿      ✿

Bill appeared to be reluctant to discuss details pertaining to his time as a prisoner of war, but gradually he began to tell Betty about the deplorable conditions within the POW camps where he was kept prisoner. The following information was supplied by Bill's widow.

"When Bill was sent overseas, I knew that he would be flying a B-17 bomber. I surmised that his missions would be over Germany. On his thirteenth mission his plane was shot down. The entire crew parachuted out and landed safely on the ground. The pilot landed in a tree and broke his leg, but he was alive. Bill made a hard landing on a cobblestone street, which resulted in injuries to his spine. As soon as the crew touched the ground they were captured by some armed teenage boys and taken to a POW camp.

"The Red Cross sent someone out to the farm to tell us that Bill was 'missing in action.' That could mean anything. We worried, we prayed, but we did not give up hope. Six weeks later, Phil Holstein, one of the owners of the Lima Leader Store, called and said he knew Bill was alive and in a POW camp. I don't know how he knew, but it was good to know Bill was alive. Later Bill was permitted to send three postcards to us, which were like a piece of heavy paper or thin cardboard. The only thing he was permitted to write on it was his POW number—no message.

"Life in the POW camp at Nuremberg was not easy. Later I learned that the prisoners were taken out and forced to march unceasingly day after day, for no reason at all. Some of the prisoners dropped from exhaustion and the guards just let them lay by the side of the road and many died. The guards didn't care. By then the men were beginning to suffer from malnutrition and the continuous marching was very hard on them. I'm certain the objective of the German guards was to break the spirit of the prisoners, so that they would be easier to manage.

"As the war continued, Bill was moved to several different POW camps. Germany was beginning to suffer from lack of sufficient food for its own people so the POWs got even less food. For awhile the prisoners were fed boiled potato skins. At the end, they were fed bugs and worms boiled in water and the Germans called this stuff 'soup.' The only way the POWs could eat the disgusting stuff was to find a dark place where they could not see what they were eating. Once in a great while, a Red Cross package would get delivered to them. Bill told the story of getting a can of Spam in a Red Cross package. Someone in the group of prisoners had a razor blade and they used it to slice the Spam as thin as they could so that everyone could have a bite of it.

"American POWs were supposed to receive Red Cross packages on a regular basis. That was not the case with where Bill was. The packages were supposed to contain Spam, crackers, cheese, a chocolate bar, cigarettes, and toilet articles. Bill said that his packages contained mostly shaving cream and cigarettes. I wonder what happened to the food that the Red Cross usually sent? I always had a suspicion that the Germans took that out because they were also on the verge of starving toward the end of the war.

"Bill said that they all had to wear prison garb and luckily they did have the opportunity to take showers. Bill was glad that his G.I. shoes lasted the entire time he was a POW and that they held together through all that marching. There was no medical treatment available for the prisoners, so he did not get anything to help his back problems after he made that hard parachute landing on the cobblestone street. He was captured in February, the weather was cold, and he was not issued a blanket. None of the prisoners were given blankets.

"Knowing Bill's personality and his leadership qualities, it is not surprising that one of the German guards approached him to become a guard at the POW camp. I never heard what words Bill used to tell the German guard 'No,' but I'm certain he got his point across. Bill and the other prisoners in his section of the camp had formed a tight bond that no German guard would have been able to break.

"Eventually, the prisoners were cheered to hear the Allied bombers flying over their camp. To them it signaled hope. As the Allied bombing increased, the POWs now had to get under tables and bunks in their quarters because the bombs were falling close by. Several times their camp came close to having direct hits and there were no good places to find shelter. But the fact that the Allies were on the offensive gave them the reassurance and hope that they would soon be out of that terrible place. I can't imagine how depressing everyday life was for these men.

"Bill said that when it was quiet and the men were all in their bunks, he would picture in his mind what life would be like to be back in Ohio. He said he thought about me and how our baby would have grown and how she would look by then. He imagined that she would have his brown hair and brown eyes. She was just a few days old when he last saw her. He said he pictured in his mind us living in a house and having lots of good food on the table. Those were all those things we took for granted before the war. The harsh reality of the prison camp would then set in and he would try to get some sleep. When Bill did get home he seemed to crave salt and candy.

"On April 29, 1945, the U.S. Third Army liberated Bill and the other POWs in the camp. Bill was taken to a hospital in Paris for rehabilitation. It took two months for him to finally be released from the hospital and fly home. I know he was grossly underweight at that time, but those two months seemed like a long time for them to keep him.

"When Bill arrived in the States and called his parents he sensed that something was wrong with his mother. It was then that he found out that they had just received word that his brother, Richard, had been killed in Okinawa. We were all very concerned about Bill's mother, because she had worried and worried about Bill being shot down and a POW, and then when the news came about Richard, it was more than she could handle. We were all trying to help her hold together. Emotions ran the gamut from extreme happiness at having Bill back to the feelings of total despair of knowing that Richard would not ever be coming back. Immediately after Bill's return, he wrote the eulogy for his brother's memorial service. Richard Early is buried in the cemetery next to the Pleasant View Church of the Brethren.

"When Bill arrived back home he discovered that his daughter did not have brown hair and brown eyes like he had pictured in his mind while in the POW camp. Instead, he found a miniature replica of me with blond hair and blue eyes. Sandra Kay, now called 'Cookie,' suited her daddy just fine.

"After Bill became a civilian again, he wasted no time in getting more education, finding the kind of work he wanted to do, and then starting his own business. He didn't sit around and feel sorry for himself because of what he had been through as a prisoner of war—instead he forged ahead into his future. His spirit and energy returned.

"I'm proud to say he became a very successful businessman, dealing in the heavy road equipment business. He wanted more children and we had two more daughters and a son. He was a great father and our home life was wonderful. Along with Bill's success came a sense of wanting to help his two remaining brothers and other family members, and he offered them positions in the business. He became a member of the United Methodist Church, in Columbus, Ohio, and a number of civic organizations in the Columbus area. He contributed very generously to a mission clinic in Alabama. Bill was the epitome of the country boy who became successful, but who never forgot his roots. Many days he went to work wearing cowboy boots, jeans, and carrying his hard hat, just in case he would decide to go out in the field and see how his company's equipment was working.

"However, Bill had one more big battle to fight and that was cancer. After being sick for two years and trying numerous cancer treatments, he lost that battle and died on August 1, 1988, at the age of sixty-seven years. At Bill's funeral service, the American flag was placed at the head of Bill's casket, his hard hat was at his feet—and a son-in-law stood and sang, without accompaniment, a beautiful rendition of the hymn 'Amazing Grace.' And that was how we all said goodbye to a very special person." (*Submitted by Betty Early, widow of Bill Early*)

# Final Days of World War II in Europe

## Eisenhower's Controversial Decision

The Supreme Commander Dwight D. Eisenhower had the authority to make the decision that the Anglo-American generals and their troops would not go to Berlin, but would instead stop at the Elbe River. Eisenhower based his decision on the fact that it would probably cost 100,000 American casualties. He knew that the troops in Europe had fought hard and they were exhausted. He also knew that as soon as the war was over in Europe, many of the American soldiers in Europe would be sent to help finish the war in the Pacific. President Roosevelt had agreed with Eisenhower's decision, but Winston Churchill did not. In the meantime the Russians were moving quickly in the direction of Berlin.

## Eisenhower and Patton Visit Concentration Camp

On April 12, 1945 General Patton took Eisenhower to visit the Nazi concentration camp at Ohrduf Nord. Both men became physically ill after viewing the actual place, the remains and the gruesome evidence of the unthinkable and inhuman atrocities that had taken place there. These two men had seen the horrors of war many times, but they found it incomprehensible that the Germans could commit such heinous acts against innocent men, women and children. The visit to the death camp filled Eisenhower with overwhelming hatred for the men responsible for the deeds committed at this and the other concentration and slave labor camps throughout the Third Reich.

## Churchill Contemplates Future Decisions

April 12, 1945 was a critical time in the war when President Roosevelt died. Winston Churchill was filled with grief and wanted to attend his friend's funeral, but was persuaded to stay in London and not go to the United States because he was told that he was needed at home in England. Churchill knew that his friend Roosevelt was a shrewd domestic politician, but he also felt that he was out of his league in international politics. Specifically, he felt Roosevelt was too trusting of the Russians, and he also felt that Eisenhower was just as naïve about the true intentions of the Russians.

Churchill did not yet know that the new president, Harry Truman, had not been kept informed about the complexity of issues that would come to bear on him as the president of the United States in wartime. Churchill's knowledge about Truman was very limited, but the final blow for Churchill was reached when he discovered that Truman had announced that he planned to carry out all the orders and plans that Roosevelt had made before his death.

Churchill had the discomforting realization that when the fighting ceased in Europe, the Americans would leave and go to the Pacific and he would be left with the problems of reconstruction in Germany, the prevention of mass starvation, and a breakdown of law and order. He knew that France was in no condition to help in this matter, and he was well aware that his own country was exhausted after their long and arduous battle with the Germans. Churchill was troubled about where the strength would come from to fight the spread of communism.

## Field Marshall Montgomery Given Important Assignment

Churchill and Eisenhower soon became alarmed at the aggressive behavior of the Russian troops in Poland and their relentless press to reach Berlin. The Anglo-American plans were changed and the British Field Marshall Montgomery was given the seemingly impossible objective of taking the port cities of Bremen and Hamburg and the villages and towns in between, to prevent the Russians from declaring possession of these areas and occupying them after the war. The towns in between were Uphusen, Achim, and Verden, which were presently occupied by Germans who had refused to surrender.

The British soldiers proved they were up to the challenges of the monumental task presented to them. The Kings Own Scottish Borders (KOSB) of the 52nd Division, a formidable group, began to accomplish

247

their assigned objectives, despite being hampered by heavy rains, enemy gunfire, and SS troopers that had infiltrated their positions.

Colonel Davidson was the commanding officer of the KOSB and he began giving the orders. There was first an artillery barrage using twenty-five pounders, then he ordered the barrage to cease. There was a short period of silence, and then a long stream of yellow and red flames shot from the first crocodile's cannon (flame-throwing tank). It was aimed at the first house and all the occupants of the house were seared by the flames and quickly died. This scenario was repeated as the crocodiles moved from house to house and the reluctant German soldiers, who could have surrendered, screamed in agony as they met their death by fire.

## Montgomery's Troops Continue Advance to the Baltic

As the British proceeded on toward Bremen the villages of Dreye and Arsten were dealt with on the way. Many people now began surrendering and prisoners were being taken. Resistance was weak in most cases. It was April 26th and the 4th and 5th Wiltshire Regiments were readily accomplishing their military objectives.

On the way to Burgerpark, the Germans were dug in, heavy fighting occurred there and more casualties were suffered. The Somerset Light Infantry plus two troops of the flame-throwing crocodile tanks were the ultimate persuaders in the house-to-house fighting.

Again, the Germans could have surrendered, but they foolishly decided to make a stand. The Wiltshires wasted no time because there were many more objectives to be accomplished, so as the German soldiers ran out of their flaming houses they were mown down by machine-gun fire.

The British soldiers soon found an enormous bunker, and with fixed bayonets the infantry entered the bunker's dimly-lit corridors that were littered with debris. Inside they found about thirty drunken officers sprawled about the room and on the table were many empty bottles of French champagne. The room was in complete disarray and in a corner of the room there was a pile of dead soldiers where the drunken German officers had thrown them. All the German officers were taken prisoner.

The following morning the Wiltshire Regiment resumed its march and was ready to storm a barracks when a small group of Germans came out waving a white flag. They were the staff of the German Major General Becker. In a few more minutes General Becker emerged and he joined the now 6,000 men who had already surrendered.

When the Wiltshire Regiment reached the once proud city of Bremen they found it had been reduced to piles of rubble everywhere. As the soldiers entered the city they were greeted by an overpowering stench of ruptured gas mains and a broken sanitation system. There had been a slave labor camp at Bremen and the people had been set free. The former slaves were filthy and their clothing was nothing but rags. With their newly found freedom, they had gone on an orgy of stuffing themselves with food and schnapps taken from the Wehrmacht supplies. The slaves were completely out of control, as they danced, and looted, and murdered, and copulated among the smoldering ruins of Bremen. It was equal to a glimpse into Hades.

A patrol of the Somersets was looking for the headquarters of the Nazi Party leader for Bremen. When they found him, he had shot his wife and then killed himself. The battle for Bremen was over quickly, but the cleansing of Bremen would take much longer.

It was April 27th, 1945 and Field Marshal Montgomery had just received word that Himmler had made an offer of capitulation to the West through the Swedish Count Bernadotte. Montgomery knew that the war with Germany was practically over and that now his most important task was to get to the Baltic and form a flank facing east against incoming Russians. Montgomery was angry because he felt Eisenhower had convinced Churchill to apply pressure on him to get to the Baltic.

## Hitler's Last Days

Early in 1945, Hitler had moved from his command post in East Prussia to the bunker under the Reich Chancellery in Berlin. As he continued to receive reports of the Allies advancing into Germany on all fronts the Fuhrer's mental state was rapidly declining into total madness. He lost touch with the reality of the deteriorating conditions of his troops and the German people and the orders that he issued to his commanders made no sense. He felt betrayed by his officers because the German troops could not stop the advancing Allies. Eventually, the only people he trusted were the Goebbels family and his longtime companion, Eva Braun.

When Hitler heard of Roosevelt's death he declared it to be "the turning point for us because it was written in the stars that fortunes would change in the latter days of April." However, Hitler became infuriated to hear that the German soldiers had begun surrendering to the Anglo-American troops because they feared the advancing Soviet troops. It looked as if the Soviets would reach Berlin first and the German soldiers and the civilians were terrified.

As Hitler's madness increased, he decided that the German people were not worthy of a great leader like himself and he denounced them and ordered his officers to destroy all the remaining German industries, the utilities, and transportation systems. However, the officers did not carry out their irrational Fuhrer's orders because they knew these systems would be needed for the rebuilding of post-war Germany.

On April 28th Hitler turned the leadership of Germany over to Admiral Karl Donitz. He then wrote a diatribe of accusations to the German people and to the rest of the world, in which he also included a warning about the "evils of international Jewry." Hitler then married Eva shortly after midnight. In the meantime the Russian artillery was advancing closer and closer to the bunker.

Early on April 30th Hitler and his bride went into a room in the bunker, closed the door and shortly afterwards Eva took poison and Hitler shot himself. Three of Hitler's few remaining followers rushed into the room and were aghast at what they saw. Eva lay on a couch and the strong odor of cyanide emanated from her body. Her long blond hair was laying attractively loose about her head. Obviously, Hitler had arranged Eva to look her best in death and had meticulously arranged her hair and placed her clothing carefully over her dead body—he probably took one last look at his faithful companion—and then shot himself in the head.

The three men, Martin Bormann, SS Otto Gunsche, and SS Erich Kempka stared at the face of their dead master, which was covered with blood and whose hand still gripped the Walther PPK pistol. Eva had always hated Bormann, so when he reached down and picked up her lifeless body, Gunsche, who knew of Eva's hatred of the fat, toad-like man, took her from Bormann's arms.

The question now became one of "what shall we do with their bodies?" Hitler was dead—the Russians were almost at the door of the

Reich Chancellery, and the inhabitants of the bunker needed to hurriedly determine what to do next. Gunsch completely wrapped Eva's body in two blankets. Hitler's body was wrapped in a single blanket with his bloody head completely covered and his legs protruding. The bodies were carried up the stairs and laid side by side on a piece of flat, open sandy ground, about three meters from the door to the bunker.

There was not enough time to look for a more suitable spot, since the Russian artillery was getting closer and closer. Petrol had been brought up from the bunker and was poured over their bodies. One of the men made a torch with some rolled up paper and ignited the gruesome pyre. The men stood for a moment watching the macabre scene, they raised their arms in a final "Heil Hitler" salute, and then hurriedly returned to the temporary safety of the bunker.

Two guards were sent later to check on the bodies and they reported that Hitler and Eva were just two charcoaled, shrivelled, unrecognizable corpses. There was barely a shovelful of remains for each body to be thrown into a nearby bomb crater. The bomb crater had been used as a dumping ground for a nearby hospital to dispose of body parts and whole corpses. Hitler's and Eva's remains were thrown into this grotesque open burial pit.

Later more Soviet bombing created more craters and body parts became mixed and scattered. When the Soviets arrived at the Chancellery, they immediately began to search for Hitler and Eva. Nine days later they took a cigar box containing part of a jaw-bone and two dental bridges to the dental technician Fritz Echtmann, who had worked for Hitler's dentist, Dr. Johann Hugo Blaschke.

A careful check of the records indicated one of the bridges had been Hitler's and the other belonged to Eva and the jawbone belonged to Hitler. How ironic that all that remained of this once powerful and feared man was now contained in a single cigar box.

The situation inside the bunker had deteriorated into pure chaos and many of the workers were committing suicide. Others tried to make an escape on foot through the Russian lines. Goebbels poisoned his wife and six children and then took the poison himself.

A power struggle was now taking place with Bormann thinking he might salvage a position in post-war Germany. When that possibility seemed remote, he disappeared and his whereabouts have been a mystery ever since. Goering and Himmler were now banned from the Nazi Party by the last-minute will of Hitler, which stated that they had "brought irreparable shame on the country and the whole nation by secretly negotiating with the enemy without my knowledge and against my will."

Three days later Russian soldiers raised the Soviet flag over the chancellery and Hitler's dream of a Thousand Year Reich was finished and had lasted less than thirteen years.


## Surrenders Begin

Although the communication system in Germany had broken down, Donitz was able to contact Eisenhower and make a request that the German military would be able to surrender only to the Western Allies. Eisenhower was approached by other German commanders with the same request, and he refused all of them. Donitz finally accepted the unconditional surrender terms.

On May 7, 1945, German Field Marshal Alfred Jodl, Chief of the General Staff, appeared at SHAEF headquarters in Rheims to sign the surrender documents. High-ranking officers from the United States, Great Britain, France and the Soviet Union were there to witness the signing.

Eisenhower refused to witness the signing because his visits to the concentration camps had filled him with extreme hatred for the people who were responsible for such atrocious acts. He remained in another room and had Jodl escorted to him after the signing was finished. He did not offer any of the amenities that are customary from general to general. He icily asked Jodl if he understood what he had signed. When the German field marshal indicated he did, then Eisenhower told him he was responsible for carrying out the terms of the surrender. He then told him to make himself available to the Soviets at their pleasure, and at that point he dismissed him.

The Soviets were not pleased with the surrender at Rheims, and they conducted their own agreements to be formally ratified in Berlin, on May 8th under the protection and patronage of the Soviets. The ceremony there was to be an acknowledgment of the sacrifices that the Soviet people endured in World War II. Stalin had requested that the surrender that took place on May 7th not be announced until May 9th so that the surrender in Berlin would be completed. But as the radio stations began announcing for the German soldiers everywhere to put down their arms, the word was out, and people began celebrating. By May 10th the Russian people began to celebrate, without Stalin's permission. That evening the Soviet government joined the world in celebrating with a thirty-salvo salute from 1,000 guns stationed around the city of Moscow.

## Churchill Speaks to His Country and to the World

When the news of Germany's surrender was released in London, Churchill prepared his victory speech and he surmised that it would probably be the last speech of his wartime premiership. He was tired and he asked his Major Desmond Morton of his personal staff to hear his speech and to offer comments. When he finished he asked Desmond what he thought of it. Desmond answered him truthfully, by saying that with such a soulful performance, he needed some reference to the Almighty.

Churchill's response was, "I will soon go to the House of Commons and inform them the war with Germany is over, then I will go to the wireless and tell the people of these islands that the war with Germany is over, and then I will go to St. Margaret's Westminister and tell the Almighty God that the war with Germany is over!"

There was no humor in Churchill's broadcast that day. After re-marking that "I wish I could tell you tonight that all our toils and troubles were over. Then indeed I could end my five years' service happily, and if you thought that you had had enough of me and that I ought to be put out to grass I would take it with the best of grace," he continued—

"On the continent of Europe we have yet to make sure that the simple and honorable purposes for which we entered the war are not brushed aside or overlooked in the months following our successes, and that the words 'freedom,' 'democracy' and 'liberation' are not distorted from their true meaning as we have understood them. There would be little use in punishing the Hitlerites for their crimes if law and justice did not rule, and if totalitarian or police governments were to take the place of the German invaders. We seek nothing for ourselves. But we must make sure that those causes, which we fought for, find recognition at the peace table in facts as well as words. And above all we must labour to ensure that the World Organization which the United Nations are creating at San Francisco does not become an idle name, does not become a shield for the strong and a mockery for the weak. It is the victors who must search their hearts in their glowing hours and be worthy by their nobility of the immense forces that they wield." (Churchill's speech, May 10th)

## Power Plays—Final Words

Donitz spoke to the beaten German people that day with a doleful tone.

"Comrades . . . We have been set back for a thousand years in our history. Land that was German for a thousand years has now fallen into Russian hands. Therefore the political line we must follow is very plain. It is clear that we have to go along with the Western Powers and work with them in the occupied territories in the west, for it is only through working with them that we can have hopes of later retrieving our land from the Russians.

"The personal fate of each of us is uncertain. That, however, is unimportant. What is important is that we maintain at the highest level the comradeship amongst us that was created through the bombing attacks on our country. Only through this unity will it be possible for us to master the coming difficult times and only in this manner can we be sure that the German people will not die." (From speech made by Admiral Donitz, May 10, 1945)

It soon became clear that Admiral Donitz and Field Marshall Busch and other former high-ranking Nazis were attempting to establish a regime, a power play, and intimated that it was not truly an "unconditional surrender." These matters needed to be dispensed with immediately.

Montgomery hurried to London to meet with Churchill after the surrender, hoping to receive a clarification of the decisions on the organization and the political control of the British Zone of Occupation. He also wanted to spend some time with Major Reynolds who had looked after his son during the holidays.

The following day, General Patton arrived, and he had just received a decoration from General DeGaulle, and the next day he was to receive more honors in London, and then would be flying to the United States to a tumultuous welcome and more honors. The gregarious Patton who

254

was always quick to "shoot from the lip," was in Paris receiving his decoration, and later was at a hotel talking with friends when he stated the following: "It's all a God-damned shame. That's what it is!" Someone asked what was a shame. "I'll tell you," said Patton.

> "Day after day, some poor bloody Czech or Austrian or Hungarian, even German officers, come into my headquarters. I almost have to keep them from going down on their knees to me. With tears in their eyes they say, 'In the name of God, General, come with your Army the rest of the way into our country. Give us a chance to set up our own governments. Give us this last chance to live before it's too late—before the Russians make us slaves for ever.' That's what they tell me, and every damned one of them has offered to fight under my flag and bring their men with them. Hell, a German general offered his entire air force, the Third, to fight the Russians if necessary! I'll tell you this; the Third Army alone, with very little other help and with damned few casualties, could lick what's left of the Russians in six weeks. You mark my words. Don't ever forget them. Some day we'll have to fight them and it will take six years and cost us six million lives."

## One Last Chance—One Big Bluff

General Rooks and Robert Murphy, of the Allied Control Team, waited on the SS *Patria* for the arrival of the Grand Admiral Donitz. General Rooks was the American chief of the Allied team, and they planned a short meeting with Donitz, to assess the true nature of this once feared leader of the dreaded wolf packs of the Atlantic. Donitz arrived in his Mercedes, which had previously belonged to Hitler, and was piped aboard the SS *Patria*. He was asked to show his documentation that was to prove his legitimate claim as head of the "new German government." Donitz handed Murphy the message that Bormann had sent to him and Rooks and Murphy nodded approvingly. Donitz was given time to talk and he spent that time talking about the coming Bolshevification of Europe. Donitz left the meeting believing he had made a good impression on Rooks and Murphy. However, this was not the case with the representatives of the Allied Control Team. A second meeting with Donitz was scheduled for the following day, at Donitz's headquarters.

Rooks and his British deputy arrived at Donitz's headquarters where all the Nazi flags and Hitler busts had been removed. Again

Donitz went into a long diatribe about how things were better in the Russian Occupation Zone. Donitz then began to say he was being defamed in the press, where the emphasis was on what terrible things the Nazis did at Belsen and Dachau. He defended the actions of his submarine campaign as "hard but fair." He complained that he was being portrayed as a war criminal and he reminded Rooks and his British deputy that if he is regarded as a war criminal then he would not have any influence on the German Wehrmacht. Again Donitz thought he had made a favorable impression on Rooks and the British deputy.

Former German Defense Minister Albert Speer had accompanied Donitz on the second meeting, and Speer immediately perceived that the apparent friendliness of the Americans was not genuine. Speer soon decided that he would need to distance himself from the former grand admiral and disappear when this meeting was finished.

As Rooks and the British deputy returned to the SS *Patria*, they talked with Robert Murphy and then forwarded their recommendation to Eisenhower, which was simply stated, "DONITZ MUST GO!"

## The Final Surrenders and Arrests

Donitz continued to believe that the Allies would grant him a position of authority, but the other prominent members of the Nazi Party realized that it was all over for them. Many were finding ways to escape, either by drink, by poison, or by joining the homeless refugees. It was said by Speer, "They made great heroic speeches about fighting and dying for the Fatherland without risking their own necks, but when their own lives were at stake, they shiver and look for all kinds of excuses—and that's the kind of heroes Germany had, and it led to destruction!"

SS General Ohlendorf had protested to Heinrich Himmler, "You can't just walk out! You must make a radio speech, or send some message to the Allies that you take responsibility for what's happened. You must give the reasons!" Instead, Himmler shaved off his mustache, put a patch over one eye, and changed his name to Heinrich Hitzlinger, and then set off with several companions to try to escape.

For two weeks, Himmler wandered with his companions through the chaotic backroads. Eventually Himmler's group was arrested and was placed in 031 Civilian Interrogation Camp near Luneburg. The group's demanding behavior made Captain Tom Selvester, the commandant of the Interrogation Camp, suspicious and he ordered the men to appear before him.

Captain Selvester's attention became focused on the little man wearing the black patch over his left eye, but before he could start his interrogation the little man removed the patch and put on a pair of spectacles. The captain gasped! Suddenly he knew who was standing there before him! The little man quietly introduced himself: "Heinrich Himmler," he said.

Also, on May 22, 1945, Lt. Commander Ludde-Neurath received an unexpected telephone call from the SS *Patria*. The British interpreter was brief and to the point. He introduced himself, and abruptly said, "Tell Admiral Donitz that General Rooks would like to see him tomorrow morning at zero nine forty-five hours—*precisely!*" With that he hung up.

Ludde-Neurath walked into the Admiral's office and repeated the Allied message. Donitz was silent as he comprehended the message, and then with a faint smile on his face, said, *"Neurath,"* "Pack the bags!" He knew what the summons meant.

※　　　※　　　※

On the morning of May 23rd a French fishing boat approached one of the Channel Islands—the tiny island of Minquiers. It had been five years since they had sailed these waters and the French fishermen were happily looking forward to a record catch. Lucien Marie was the captain of *Les Trois Freres,* and he suddenly became aware that the island was inhabited. He was surprised because he had thought there was no one on the island since the Germans had gone. He announced, "It looks as if the English have taken possession." The French and English fishermen had fought over the island and its very desirable fishing ground many times in the last century.

After realizing that they were not fishing, the skipper exclaimed, "They look like Germans, and they're wearing uniforms! Let's have a look at them."

The French fishermen weighed anchor off the nearest reef and waded ashore to where a small group of soldiers waited curiously. Abruptly Captain Marie stopped and said, "The men ARE Germans, and they are ARMED!"

Puzzled by the sight of an armed enemy nearly three weeks after the surrender, the captain wondered what he should do.

The nearest German, a sergeant, raised his pistol and spoke in fairly good Norman French, "Hey you, come here. We have been forgotten by the British. Maybe nobody told them we were here. We are out of food and water and we want you to take us to England so we can surrender."

These were the last armed Germans at large west of the River Elbe that passed into Allied captivity. They joined the rest of Division Kanada, in Canada, just as it had been predicted.

✿    ✿    ✿

On May 23, 1945, at exactly nine-forty-five, the Grand Admiral's car drove up to the SS *Patria*. This time there was no grand welcome and no guard to present arms. The British infantrymen eyed them coldly and motionlessly as they crossed the wharf. On the deck above them were the news correspondents with their notebooks and the photographers with their cameras. Donitz gave his adjutant a knowing look, he knew that this meeting would be different than the others.

They were ushered into the ship's bar, which had been changed into a conference room, where they waited for five minutes until the Allied generals came in—General Rooks followed by General Foord and the Russian General Truskov. Today the Russian was no longer smiling, as he had been when he first met with Donitz in hopes of winning the Germans over.

The three generals took their seats with Rooks in the center. Donitz seated himself opposite. General Lowell Rooks began to read: "Gentlemen," he announced, "I am in receipt of instructions from Supreme Commander General Eisenhower, to call you before me this morning to tell you that he has decided, in agreement with the Soviet High Command, that today the acting German government and the German High Command, with several of its members, shall be taken into custody as prisoners of war. Thereby the acting German government is dissolved."

He stopped and looked at the admiral, but there was no reaction. Donitz's English was not good enough for him to fully comprehend the meaning. Rooks continued.

"When you leave this room an Allied officer will attach himself to you and escort you to your quarters where you will pack, have your

258

lunch and complete your affairs. You will then be escorted to the airfield at one-thirty for emplaning. You may take whatever baggage you require. That's all I have to say."

General Rooks put his paper down and let the interpreter take over. When the interpreter was finished, he looked directly at Donitz and said, "Would you like to make a statement?"

The admiral shook his head: "Comment is superfluous."

It was all over in a matter of minutes.

Meanwhile, Schwerin von Krosigk had opened his daily "cabinet" meeting in an ex-school house in Flensburg. He was ready to begin discussion on the political problems of the day when the door of the room was flung open and British soldiers rushed in. The soldiers were heavily armed with grenades and stens. "Out—and put your hands up!" they ordered. Surprised and frightened, the assembled prominent civilians and former German officers and soldiers did as they were told.

Quickly the soldiers of the Eleventh Armoured lined them up along the wall of the corridor outside. They were frisked expertly and then came the command which shocked the German dignitaries: *"Hosen' runter!"* Schwerin von Krosigh's mouth fell open. Pants down!—did they mean?

Krosigh, a former Rhodes Scholar and an aristocrat, soon found out, as a little soldier smelling of medicine tugged at his trousers. "Bitte . . . please!" But it was no use. Everywhere the Germans had to drop their trousers to their ankles, so that a sergeant, his fingers encased in a rubber glove, could search their anus for a concealed capsule of poison.

Three battalions now encircled the Flensburg meeting place, arresting anybody and everybody connected with the Donitz Regime. Hundreds of them were forced, into the square of the Murwik Barracks, where they were ordered to keep their hands on their heads. Correspondents had arrived with photographers and they felt that today was a day that history was being made.

A British sergeant arrested Albert Speer at Glucksbug, and now it was his turn to submit to the unpleasant physical. He was insulted by the embarrassing body search, but later he thought it was probably a consequence of the numerous suicides that were being reported each day.

Heinrich Himmler was in the interrogation center and was dressed in his underpants and a shirt and had an army blanket wrapped around him.

Sergeant-Major Austin told Himmler, "That's your bed, get undressed."

"That's your bed," the Sergeant repeated. "Get undressed."

Himmler did not seem to understand although Austin spoke German.

He told the interpreter, "He doesn't know who I am."

"Yes I do," Sergeant Austin said, "You're Himmler, and that's your bed! Get undressed!"

A little later Colonel Murphy of Intelligence and the military doctor, Wells, came in to carry out yet another search to ensure that Himmler had no poison hidden on his person. Suddenly Murphy noticed a small black knob sticking out between the gap in the teeth in Himmler's mouth.

"Open your mouth. Come nearer the light," the doctor ordered.

The doctor thrust two fingers in Himmler's mouth and Himmler suddenly pressed down and bit very hard! "He's done it!" Wells yelled.

Murphy and Austin jumped on Himmler and flung him onto the floor, rolled him on his stomach trying to prevent him from swallowing the poison. Wells put his hands around his throat trying to make him spit it out while Murphy shouted for a needle and cotton. The Colonel threaded the needle, and quickly stuck the metal through Himmler's tongue and pulled his tongue out of his dying mouth. Meanwhile the others were using a stomach pump on Himmler, and at the same time others were administering emetics. But it was no use, the chief of the SS was failing fast. The doctors tried everything to save him, not because they admired him, but because they wanted him to stand trial for his war crimes. Sergeant-Major Austin's recorded message for the BBC the following day, simply stated, "Himmler died today and when he died, we threw a blanket over him and left him."

(Note: Two days later, Sgt. Major Austin buried Himmler. Himmler's body was wrapped in army blankets and covered with camouflage netting that was secured with telephone wire. Today, Austin is the only man who knows where the ex-chicken farmer who had ravaged half of Europe, is buried.)

Admiral Donitz remained silent when he heard the news about other suicides of other prominent Nazis on this dark day. That day he lost his home, and all his valuable belongings. Now he and Jodl had to be subjected to the disgusting anal search.

Churchill also had an unpleasant duty to perform that afternoon. He was to hand in his resignation to the king at Buckingham Palace. He knew that the King would probably empower him to form a transitional "caretaker" government, but Churchill wondered what would happen in the coming general election?

Montgomery, the newly appointed head of the British Zone of Occupation, knew that the British people were completely fed up with the war and could never be persuaded to fight the Russians. He briefed his officials on the problems they would be facing, and he emphasized re-establishing civil control.

Donitz, Jodl, Speer and other once-feared Nazis, were driven to Flensburg airport with a forty-vehicle escort, and there they boarded an American DC-4 to be flown off to their place of imprisonment. The photographers gathered around them before they emplaned to get their last pictures before they would be imprisoned.

Did Donitz, Jodl and Speer, plus the other prominent Nazis have thoughts that turned to their future, which would probably consist of long bitter trials and long, long years of prison? All those top Nazis on the plane that night had bought into the dream of *The Thousand Year Reich*. In the quiet of the plane trip did any of them wonder what they did wrong that made the dream disintegrate into an explosive, destructive worldwide war? Did any of these men have any regrets?

The destination of their trip was the Palast Hotel, which had been turned into a prison. Here they found many of their Nazi friends that had scattered, hoping to escape a war crimes trial, incarceration in a prison, or perhaps death, but they were also captured and brought to the same prison. What a conglomeration of evil in one small area of the world!

# Duane Edgington, Fought in Africa, Italy, Germany, Helped Liberate Death Camps

Albert Duane Edgington was born on September 7, 1924 in Lima, Ohio. He was called "Duane" by his friends and classmates. Duane had two brothers, Robert and Richard and two sisters, Phyllis and Marceil. When the Japanese attacked Pearl Harbor on December 7, 1941, Duane wanted to enlist immediately, but his parents told him that he had to first graduate from high school. He followed their wishes and ended up being drafted into the United States Army Infantry on May 19, 1943. Duane's father was proud of his own military background of having served four years (1910–1914) in the U.S. Marines and then later in World War I. When Duane left for overseas his father said, "I have just one piece of advice to give you, Son, and that is to always remember to keep your head and your butt down and you'll be okay." Duane's story follows:

On May 19, 1943 I was made Acting Corporal of twenty-one new recruits who were being shipped from Lima, Ohio to the 69th Infantry Division, at Camp Shelby near Hattiesburg, Mississippi. From June to August 1943 I was attached to the 442nd Regimental Combat Team (RCT) and the 100th Battalion, the famous Japanese-American Soldiers in Training for World War II (WWII).

After finishing Basic Training, followed by Advanced Infantry Training, I then entered an indoctrination course to prepare for Ranger school, which included much physical and mental training, patrolling, and classroom work. I was assigned to Army Ranger training at the end of August. If you do well in those courses, you then advance to more rigorous training and are taught hand-to-hand combat skills, knife fighting techniques, martial arts, stealth-like movements, ambushes, handling explosives, reconnaissance, and many more skills that will be necessary to become a "Ranger." It seemed as if the training would never end and we were pushed to extreme limits. I was one of the few men from the 69th that finished a seventy-five-mile forced march with a full field pack on and carrying a machine gun and mortars.

I was sent back to the 69th Division and was promoted to Sergeant. I helped to train men of Company D in 30-caliber machine guns and 60 mm and 81 mm mortars. I was immediately put on a shipping list to go to North Africa.

I was at a camp in Newport News, Virginia, on November 23, 1943, and was getting ready to be shipped overseas. I decided to go to a movie that evening and later learned that my brother, Bob, and I were at the same camp that night, the same movie, and the same time, but we never saw each other. He was coming back from overseas and I was leaving for overseas. We had not seen each other for two years.

I left the United States on November 24, 1943, and arrived in Casablanca, Morocco, Africa, on December 4, 1943. I was assigned to the 4th Ranger Battalion, Company D, on December 5, 1943. I received the orders and was instructed to deliver them to the 4th Ranger Head-quarters (HG) in Algiers. After my training there I taught grenade firing from the 03-Springfield Rifle Grenade Launcher, as the M1 had not yet been developed for this task.

During the Italian Campaign, we Rangers (the 1st, 3rd, and 4th BN) made the landing and established a beachhead at Anzio, Italy, on January 22, 1944. Col. Darby led the Rangers here and he remained in a farmhouse on the Isolo Bella-Cisterna Road.

On January 30, 1944, I served in the 4th BN, in reserve and was sent to a position north of the 1st and 3rd BN and attempted to help them, as they had been pinned down by the new fresh German troop build-up. I had the machine gun section. The German troops were in front of Cisterna, and not behind, as we had been told.

On January 31, 1944, the 4th Rangers moved through the Musso-lini Canal and engaged the enemy. We were busy for three days and three nights with tank fire, machine-gun and mortar fire by the Germans. Very little sleeping was done. At Isola Bella, we were soon pinned down. After the third day the 45th Division Infantry came to relieve us since we were still pinned down and could not move, and we were running out of ammunition. My close friend, William (Bill) Custer was an ammunition truck driver in the 45th. There was no time for a happy reunion as we both had important and immediate tasks to accomplish.

It was as if the enemy knew the American invasion plan. The German troop build-up had been successful. We sustained heavy losses but held our position until the rest of the invasion force came ashore with infantry, tanks, etc. to help push the enemy back.

In late February or early March of 1944 on a night hike, I fell thirty feet, and thankfully a large rock kept me from falling farther. I fractured my right ankle and was sent to a 69th station hospital in Italy. I was sent back to Oran, Africa to recuperate. In March I heard that the 1st, 3rd and 4th Rangers had been disbanded.

After the stay in Oran I was sent to Bizarte and Tunis in Tunisia and was assigned to 2681 Depot Guard Co., APO 765 RM, New York, N.Y. It was in Tunis that three of us soldiers saw a little girl, about five or six years old, who was going to be sold at the slave market. Most American GIs can never tolerate seeing small children being mistreated, and I guess we were no exception, so we bought her for $50 and then turned her over to the Red Cross. We never heard what happened to her, but we could not stand by and do nothing as they were getting ready to put her up for sale and she would have been used as a slave for the rest of her life. I hope what we did helped her to have a better life than what she was originally destined to live.

When my recuperation was complete I was re-classified as 1-A in June 1944 and assigned to the 36th Infantry Division in Italy as replacement. I participated in the Rome-Arno Campaign. In August 1944 during the Southern France invasion I was sent to France to oversee an Italian company that was unloading ammunition ships.

A short time later I signed up for front-line duty and was sent to Brest, France for two weeks of infantry training. From there I made Staff Sergeant and was sent to the 12th Armored Division, 43rd Battalion, H.G. Company as reconnaissance platoon leader. In February 1945 we were sent to the Colmar Pocket in France to prevent the Germans from taking control of that area and fierce fighting took place at that location.

Our reconnoiter procedure was to drive one to one and a half miles ahead and check out the area. There were twenty-one men in my platoon, five jeeps, and one half-track. In my jeep I had a radio man, the driver, and me, plus a machine gun. On a reconnoiter I would be busy checking the terrain, reading or sketching maps and we were always on the lookout for the enemy.

Our recon platoon led General Patton's Third Army almost to Bastogne, Belgium and from there we went to Trier, Germany, crossed the Mosell River and continued on to Worms, and crossed the Rhine River close to Worms. We were the first division to enter Germany.

The following battles, Erback, Wurzburg, Schweinfurt were all big battles. No wonder, with all my moving around, my parents received a telegram from the government stating that I was missing in action, but I was never missing. However, I know that telegram caused my parents to worry.

On April 20, 1945, we turned south to Nurmberg and on to Dinkelsbuhl. It was here that my jeep, number thirteen, was shot to pieces by enemy machine-gun fire. My radioman was wounded in the hand, and I told him I thought it was just a scratch but to go back and have it checked. I then looked down at my leg and saw that I had two bullet holes in my pants leg. I felt around, there was no blood, the bullets had only gone through the cloth. This was another close call and those of us in jeep number thirteen were very lucky that day, even though the jeep was "fatally" damaged.

(*When I saw those bullet holes in my pants leg it made me think of how I wanted to come back from the war all in one piece, because I had this wonderful girlfriend back in Ohio. Marilyn was a nurse, and the sweetest person I had ever met. She would have accepted me no matter how I returned from the war—she was like that. I figured that we could have a wonderful life together—if I made it back.*)

We got a new jeep and continued leading the 12th Armored Division Task Force to Dilligen, Germany where we were fortunate to take a bridge intact that spanned the Danube River. This helped to hasten the end of the war because it permitted the Allies to gain immediate and easy access further in to Germany. My Ranger training came in to good use at a critical time when I helped cut the wires to six 500-pound bombs that the Germans planned to use to destroy the bridge.

It is now late in April 1945, the war is still raging, and the 12th Armored Division—part of the Seventh Army—went to the west and south parts of Germany to find and liberate concentration camps. I was an advanced scout—Platoon Staff Sergeant in the Reconnaissance Platoon, Hdq. Co, 43rd Battalion, 12th Armored Division. At first I had no idea that these camps that we were about to enter were more than a prison. *They were actually camps of persecution and death!*

We found eleven death camps and proceeded to help liberate them. Some of the camps were at Augsburg, Darmstadt, Dachau, Landsberg, Wurzburg, Weilheim, and Murnau. High fences that were topped with barbed wire surrounded the camps and the camps were heavily guarded. The German guards that we had to contend with were well trained and ruthless. In some cases when we entered the camp the guards ran away when they saw us coming. In other cases they were ready to fight us and we had to quickly do away with them.

Mostly tanks broke through the gates to enter the camps, but in one camp I was able to open the gate with my jeep. The nauseous odor of death hit us as soon as we entered the camp. Once inside the camp, our jobs became very gruesome as we began to search the buildings and liberate the people that were still alive. We saw live people that looked like walking skeletons. They had been forced to sleep in tiers of three to four feet with just enough room to allow them to crawl in. There were outdoor toilets for the prisoners to use in the daytime, but at night they had to crawl into those tiny bunks and were locked in until morning. There was not enough room for the number of prisoners so they were very crowded in the bunks and sometimes forced to sleep on top of each other. If they had to relieve themselves, they had to do it right there in the crowded bunks. We also discovered many dead people in the camps, and their bodies had not yet been disposed of.

On April 29th we liberated two death camps, Augsburg and Dachau. Dachau was one of the first concentration camps the Nazis built in 1933 and it was an extermination camp for Jews. When we liberated the Dachau camp there were about 35,000-plus prisoners there. One part of the camp was like a large science lab, and we found out later that they had professional scientists in charge who conducted grisly experiments on people. I saw a glass enclosure and was told that an experiment of oxygen depletion was done there. A prisoner would be put into the glass enclosure and air would be gradually drawn out a little at a time. This was to see how little air the person could/could not survive on.

I saw the ovens at Dachau and I'm thinking there were ten ovens used at 2000 degrees and these ovens were in use twenty-four hours a day. They did not know what to do with all the ashes, so the ashes were mixed with oil and regular road building materials and were used to build roads. More people were put to death at the Dachau death camp than at any of the other death camps. Many brutal medical experiments were performed there on the prisoners and most of the people died as a result. Later some of the prisoners talked with us and told us what had been going on at this horrible place. One prisoner wanted me to give him my gun so that he could go kill German guards. Of course, he did not get a gun from any of us, but we could understand why he wanted to do that.

We left Dachau and continued on to the Landsberg death camp where we found approximately 1,000 dead Polish people. Our soldiers made the townspeople come to the camp and bury the dead. There were many dead prisoners in all the camps. Landsberg is where Hitler had been a prisoner before he became Chancellor, and there were plates on the door naming the prisoners that had been in that room. Hitler's name was there and I took it off the door and put it in my pocket. Later it disappeared and I do not know what happened to it.

In the town of Dinkelsbuhl we came upon a house where German officers were playing cards. A piano was sitting nearby with one side pulled away from the wall. I looked around the piano and saw a lieutenant colonel changing clothes. He had a German Luger aimed at me. I told him, "Go ahead and shoot, but you won't get out of here alive." He turned the butt of the gun around and handed it to me. We took him and all the other German soldiers in the house prisoner. I kept the Luger for a while but later gave it to a new American soldier.

We went south to Weilheim and Murnau, two more death camps. Six of us in two jeeps brought in 500 German prisoners who wanted to surrender. They knew the war was about over and that Germany was defeated and they wanted to surrender to the American soldiers and not the Russian soldiers.

I took four jeeps and twelve men and went to Innsbruck, Austria. A man was running from a dugout and was trying to get away from us. I shot him in the buttocks and stopped him. We told him to remove his pants so we could see his wound and discovered that our man was actually a young girl about thirteen years old. She was taken to a frontline hospital. This was my last major engagement. Here we found out we were fighting against twelve to fourteen year old boys and girls that had been taught to kill just like the men soldiers. The armistice was signed while I was in Innsbruck and this was the end of the war in the European Theater.

We were sent back to Dinkelsbuhl, Germany to help set up the Army of Occupation. I was given a one week of Battlefield Fatigue Leave in Nice, France. In August 1945 I was transferred to the First Armored Division because I did not have to go to Japan because I had already served in Italy and Germany.

I'm pleased to say that in my 18 months of combat, I only lost five men in battle, and that was because they had bunched together and one 88 shell got all of them. I served as a Staff Sergeant in the war and earned the following medals:

Army Good Conduct Medal
American Campaign Medal
Victory Medal WWII
French Croix de Guerre
Combat Infantry Badge
4th BN Patch
4 Overseas Bars
Expert Shooting Badge with
    bars: Rifle, Pistol, Carbine,
    Automatic Rifle, Bayonet,
    Grenade, Machine Gun,
    Mortar

American Defense Service
Europe-Africa-Middle East
WWII Occupation Medal Army
Victory in Europe Commemorative
Presidential Unit Citation
Ruptured Duck
5 Bronze Stars (Silver Star)

I went to Shrivenham American University, at Shrivenham, England, to study intermediate accounting and management from September to December. On December 22, 1945 I boarded a Liberty ship, The USS *George Washington*, at Southhampton, England to come home. I could have sailed on the *Queen Mary*, but I thought I would arrive home faster on the Liberty ship. I was wrong—the *Queen Mary* passed us. We encountered a violent storm which pushed us back fifteen miles in two days. During the storm, a propeller shaft broke. Later on, they allowed me to watch them weld it back together. After this I had an attack of appendicitis and they radioed the *Queen Mary* to stand by. The *Queen Mary* had a surgeon on board, but the pain subsided and I stayed on the Liberty Ship. I landed at New York City on January 6, 1946. I called home from the Billy Rose Horseshoe Bar and Nightclub. This was the first time I was allowed to call home in thirty-three months.

I was sent to Indiantown Gap, Pennsylvania, and was discharged on January 15, 1946 and arrived at the Pennsylvania Station, on East Wayne Street, in Lima, Ohio. My parents and my sister, Phyllis, met me at the station and took me home to Clum Road, Lima, Ohio.

When we got to the house I told my father I wanted to borrow the family car. He told me I couldn't have it because of gas rationing. I told him I was going to take it anyway because I wanted to go see Marilyn, my girlfriend. I had thought about her a lot while I was gone and I couldn't wait to see her. When my father realized why I wanted the car he gladly permitted me to take it. A few weeks after returning home I asked Marilyn to marry me. We were married on June 9th, 1946. We have two sons and one daughter, seven grandchildren, and one great-grandchild.

In March 1946 I was employed by the Ohio Power Company (AEP), and I worked there for forty years. After I retired I worked as an instructor for the D. L. Steiner Engineering and Technical Services, on the techniques of working with high voltage.

When I think back to my WWII experiences, and in particular the liberation of the death camps, it rekindles the feelings of anger and bitterness I felt for the Nazis and the SS troops responsible for committing such heinous acts. With my own eyes I saw the results of the Holocaust! You don't forget something like that! As I stood in the center of each of those death camps, I could not help but feel an overwhelming sense of revulsion and absolute hatred toward the people responsible for creating such a hell on earth for all those innocent men, women and children who were tortured and died there.

When people ask me how I feel about World War II, my answer is, "There was no other alternative! There had to be a war because there was no other way to stop Germany and Japan and their ruthless takeover of other countries and their total disregard for human life. I'm glad I did my part to help put an end to the carnage!"

# Victory in Europe—VE Day
## (Official Date—May 8, 1945)

The Allies planned to have an official announcement of the "unconditional surrender" in Europe which was to be announced simultaneously by Truman, Churchill, and Stalin, but actually Germany made the first announcement on May 7, 1945. To complicate matters further, the Associated Press, by some means, managed to scoop the other news services, and they announced the details of the surrenders before the "Big Three" could carry out their plans of a simultaneous announcement. The Associated Press appeared to have all their facts accurately reported, but nevertheless they were reprimanded for their breach of protocol. To further complicate matters, the Soviets had their own reasons for delaying another day before joining a Big Three announcement.

Once the word was out, official or not, the people began celebrating. The celebrations in New York City took on the look of Times Square on New Year's Eve. Enthusiastic, jubilant people, some with tears coursing down their faces, were walking around blowing horns and whistles, and sometimes forming spur-of-the-moment parades down the middle of a street. However, there were a greater number of people in New York that stayed home or went to their churches to pray. They were thankful that the war in Europe was over, but they were painfully aware that the war in the Pacific Theater was far from over.

Most of the small towns and villages received the news quietly. When they heard the church bells ringing, they knew what it meant and they were ever so thankful to have that part of the war finished. Lima received the news, both the unofficial, and the official, with a business-as-usual attitude. There were small clusters of people on the downtown sidewalks talking excitedly about the surrenders, but after a short while they dispersed. The defense plants continued to work on their war contracts, and the stores remained open, except the liquor stores. Church bells were ringing in all sections of the city announcing that the anticipated surrenders had happened and that the churches were open for the people to come and offer prayers of thankfulness for the ending of hostilities in Europe.

The war in Europe had lasted 2,076 days, (five years, eight months, and six days) and was considered to be the bloodiest conflict and the most costly in human lives and the most extensive destruction of property that Europe had ever experienced.

When Japan heard of the surrender of the Axis powers, they announced that they had never expected help from their Axis partners and they would go on to victory without any help from the Third Reich. Simultaneous with Japan's announcement the newspapers were carrying the details of intense fighting on Okinawa in the Pacific Theater with a total number of Japanese casualties in this battle reaching 36,535, and America was experiencing 1,000 casualties per day.

Within the last few weeks of the war in Europe the Allies began discovering the concentration camps and the slave labor camps that the Nazis had used to work and to kill millions of men, women and children. There are people who discount the stories of these camps and they say that the Holocaust never happened. These doubters need to talk with the American soldiers who opened the gates of these hellholes and found the few remaining survivors, living in filthy conditions, sick and starving. These American soldiers had been quickly organized to rush food, medical help, and other necessities to fill the basic needs of these unfortunate tormented human beings.

Inside these camps were mountainous piles of skeletons, various and sundry human bones and the crematorium furnaces that were silent testaments of the atrocities that took place in these direful death camps. The people that doubt the existence of these infamous camps should talk with the American soldiers that liberated the survivors from the most heinous captivity imaginable. The liberators cannot erase from their minds the horrific conditions that they saw and it made them realize how important it was to stop the maniacal Hitler and his anti-Semitic beliefs. Heinrich Himmler, Hitler's SS leader, and Joseph Goebbels, Hitler's Propaganda Minister, willingly carried out the necessary orders for the extermination of approximately six million Jews, including one million innocent children, and also one million Gypsies.

Now that the war was over in the European Theater, most of the military people began receiving thirty-day or sixty-day furloughs to go home, rest and await orders. These people had fought their way from Africa, Sicily, Italy, some had landed in Normandy and fought their way through France, Belgium, and Germany. There were sailors who fought in naval battles and successfully out maneuvered the German wolf packs and there were Air Force people who fought the enemy fighter pilots and the deadly anti-aircraft firing. They were all tired and had been stressed to the limits of what they could endure, and they went home on furloughs thinking their next move would be to report to a base and receive an honorable discharge from the military branch they had served so well.

Many of these service men and women had been in the war for three years, some three and a half years, and some for four years. Imagine how they must have felt when they discovered after their furlough that they were being sent to the Pacific Theater to fight. The comments made by many of these battle-weary men and women were: "I'm tired, I don't know how much more I can endure." "I've been lucky to make it this far, but will I make it through the next enemy encounter alive?" "I don't know about the kind of island-jungle fighting in the Pacific, it was different in Europe." "I don't want to go."

But they all knew that in World War II, when they were drafted or enlisted, they were in the military for the "duration of the war"—and the war was still raging in the Pacific Theater.

Meanwhile, on May 10th, Washington announced that a point system had been agreed upon for the discharge of ground, air and service forces of enlisted men and women. A minimum of eighty-five points would be required to be eligible for discharge. The government estimated that 1,300,000 military personnel could be released in the next twelve months according to the point system. The points would be established on the basis of Service Credit, Overseas Credit, Combat Credit, and Parenthood Credit.

Service credit was established at one point for every month of army service since September 16th, 1940. More than fifteen days would be counted as a full month. Overseas credit would be based on one point for each month served overseas. Combat credit would be five points for each combat decoration earned since September 16, 1940. The parenthood credit would be twelve points for each child under eighteen, up to a limit of three children. The release of all who had attained the minimum score of eighty-five, or more, was subject to retention until replacements were secured.

Women who were in the Women's Army Corps had a temporary score of forty-four points established as their minimum. Officers, because of their additional training and heavier responsibility, would have a higher set of minimums established and would not be granted a release on the basis of military necessity. Any release could be rejected if the person possessed highly technical skills that would be needed in the war with Japan.

# English Return to the Channel Islands

The Germans arrived in 1940 at the English Channel Islands and also at all the ports from Lorient in the western French province of Brittany to the Dutch Island of Texel in the North. At Guernsey the Germans arrived with a totally unexpected and despicable show of disregard for human life when they killed the Guernsey farmers loading their tomato harvest on a ship. A few days later the Germans were on the island, setting up headquarters and using Guernsey's hospital for sick and wounded German soldiers. The islanders on Guernsey opted to stay and endure the impostors that were moving onto their island. They optimistically thought they could wait until the end of the war, never dreaming of the consequences of that decision. Little did any of these people know how long the war would last and what hardships they would be facing before the war would end.

Immediately the Germans hired local Guernsey contractors to supply them with services. They opened clubs and cinemas, and began to take control of every aspect of life on the island. It is difficult to comprehend, but even black market activities became rampant and ordinary goods that had once been plentiful now could only be purchased at an exorbitant cost, such as tea, silk stockings, soap, postage stamps, and more. Brothels sprang up, supplied with French, Belgian, Dutch, and even British girls, brought in for the pleasure of the soldiers.

In the Channel Islands, where once life was pleasant and bountiful, the years that followed were strange ones with extreme hardships and food shortages. It is difficult to explain, except it was probably a means to avoid the realities of the time, but the Guernsey islanders continued to have their games of cricket and football. Secretly they held dances behind locked doors because the German occupying authorities would not permit them to listen to British music on the BBC.

In 1942 the German Authorities published an order stating that because the VD rate had risen so rapidly, sexual relations either with the German soldiers or with civilians were strictly forbidden for the next three months. Severe punishment by the occupying authorities was to be expected in cases of noncompliance, even if no infection took place. Control of this situation was almost impossible, and the occupying authorities eventually opened brothels with only French girls. Ironically, the French girls received "heavy workers' rations" for their services, and their brothels were divided into two types, those intended for officers only, and those for the noncommissioned soldiers.

By 1944 the food situation of the islanders was serious, but that of the 30,000 occupying Germans was even worse. The occupying Germans called themselves Division Kanada, believing this assignment to be their final destination. By that time the Germans' fuel supplies had given out, and their food rations were cut to 1,125 calories a day, tuberculosis had reached epidemic proportions, and only 5 percent of the men were capable of combat.

The Channel waters could have provided seafood for the hungry people, but the authorities believed that if the English went fishing, they might try to escape to England, so they could only go fishing if they took an uniformed German soldier with them. The RAF men flying over the channel and seeing the Nazi uniform would frequently shoot at the fishermen not realizing the other occupants of the boat were mainly starving British people. Eventually, the occupying authorities issued an order that there would be no fishing in the Channel waters. By 1944 the starving German soldiers attempted an unsuccessful move to force their commanders to surrender to the British. The situation on the Channel Islands was becoming desperate.

The German occupation of Alderney differed greatly from that of her neighboring island, Guernsey. Guernsey is larger, being approximately a thirty-square-mile area with a pre-war population of approximately 47,000, as compared to Alderney's six-square-mile area and a population that was less than 1,500. On Alderney the German soldiers immediately moved into the homes of the departed people and thought they had a desirable assignment on this lovely island. And it was desirable at first. There was plenty of food and the homes were very comfortable. Prostitutes were brought in and Reg's house was turned into a brothel. The contents of Lil and Charlie's store were soon depleted.

Alderney and the other Channel Islands became a part of the German Atlantic Wall, and immediately after the arrival of the German troops they began to make fortresses out of the islands and prepare for the invasion of the British, which never happened. Excessive restrictions were placed upon the few islanders that remained and every facet of their existence was regulated, including driving, fishing, and gathering firewood. Clothing and footwear were rationed immediately and the pound was replaced by the Reichsmark.

The situation at Alderney became extremely grim as the Germans began to immediately pour concrete and build bunkers, towers, and gun placements on the nearly deserted isle. The most despicable act was to build the infamous Sylt concentration camps and fill them with slave laborers. The organization Todt brought the laborers from Eastern Europe, dragged them from their homes and turned them into slaves at the four camps, with each camp holding approximately 1,500 people.

The living conditions in the camps were extremely poor, there was insufficient food and clothing, frequent beatings, no medical help, and many people died of malnutrition, dysentery, septicemia and pneumonia. At the height of the work there were between 5,000 to 6,000 slave workers on Alderney, plus 3,500 German troops. An accurate number of slaves that died will never be determined, because some were just buried in the trenches where they had collapsed while working. If they died in their barracks their bodies were thrown onto lorries and dumped into the sea off the breakwater. The Nazis inflicted their anti-Semitic harassment on the hundreds of Jews who were brought to their slave labor camps on Alderney. It was reported that on August 15th, 1943, nearly a thousand French Jews were taken to a labor camp on Alderney. Although there was no deliberate extermination of these Jews such as took place in the "death camps," many died from exhaustion and malnutrition. There were 384 Jews buried in the camp, but nobody knows how many bodies were thrown into the sea.

In June of 1944 when the Allies invaded Normandy, the German soldiers in the Channel Islands were completely cut off from their "Fatherland" and no longer received shipments of food and other supplies. The Allied Forces were flying over and sailing around the Channel Islands and the food situation rapidly became critical. The people on the islands were basically trapped and eventually a frantic plea was sent to the Red Cross for help.

The winter of '44–'45 was extremely severe, there was no coal for heat, no electricity, and the food they were eating was minimal and lacked the vital life sustaining nutrients. At the end of 1944 the Red Cross ship *Vega* arrived with 750 tons of food. The Canadian and New Zealand Red Cross sent their POW parcels which contained coffee, tea, butter, chocolate, raisins, and canned meat. The eleventh hour arrival of the *Vega* probably saved many lives, but it was too late for a number of people. After that the *Vega* made monthly stops at the islands. (Actually the German commanders had a huge store of food hidden in some caves, but they were withholding that food thinking the German soldiers might need the food more at a later date.)

On VE Day, May 8, 1945, the islanders and even the German soldiers eagerly waited to be liberated. It took a few more days to accomplish this on all the islands. It had been a wretched and miserable ordeal from the time the enemy showed up at the dock and the Luftwaffe strafed and killed those forty-four civilian farmers on Guernsey in June 1940 and then began landing on the islands several days later. The occupation lasted four years, ten months, and seven days. The audacious German soldiers came onto the islands in hordes, swaggering pompously, and exuding bravado from every pore. They met no military resistance, but they eventually became trapped along with those whom they sought to conquer.

After the liberation, eleven hundred German soldiers were made to stay on Alderney as POWs and begin to clear the rubble they had created from buildings that they had destroyed. They were also required to help the British troops clear the island of more than 30,000 land mines they had laid, plus other booby traps. They were also required to repair the houses they had damaged. It was December 1945 before any of the islanders were permitted to return. The first groups of islanders that returned were those with useful reconstruction skills.

The following was in a phone call from Reg to his brother Jim in America. Jimmy shared the following information with me:

Reg started out by saying that he and the people in this early group of returnees had been cautioned that the island would not look the same, and they had received instructions on where to get needed supplies and food and other necessities.

Reg said, "The most startling sights were the massive amounts of concrete constructions. Those of us in the early group wanted to go see our own homes right away. But everything seemed strange as I began to walk toward our house. I had begun thinking about all those people who had been crowded onto this little island. There must have been German soldiers everywhere, and all the slave laborers in those horrid, filthy camps! It is so hard to imagine because Alderney had previously been a little-known, beautiful, quiet, peaceful island that also became a secret retreat for wealthy and famous people from England and America."

Reg said, "I was walking down the road carrying my suitcase, the same suitcase I had carried when I left Alderney, and the same one that I had in London, and in Scotland. Now, I thought, here I am finally back home with this same old suitcase filled with my now badly worn clothes, and dear God, it has seemed like such a long time!"

Reg continued, "I could see our house and the outside was not looking much different, perhaps a little more weathered from the salt air. I put my suitcase down and pushed the unlocked and unhinged front door open. I walked in to an empty room, our furniture was gone, it had been burned as firewood. Immediately I could smell a terrible stench coming from somewhere, even though one of the German POWs was supposed to have cleaned the rooms. The problem was that during the occupation some Germans had defecated in the corner of one of the rooms and the walls and floor there had retained much of the odor. A white powder had been sprinkled in the offending area.

"The tables, chairs, bookcases, books, china cabinets, everything was gone, probably also burned to get heat. All the rooms were bare. There were no curtains at the windows and no rugs on the floors. The kitchen was lacking in dishes and cookware, only the cook stove remained. The hardware had been removed from all the doors and cabinets throughout the house, as the Germans had melted all the hardware on the island to make bullets."

Reg said, "I then walked through the bedroom areas upstairs. There were three bedrooms, Jessie's and my bedroom, our son (young) Jim's bedroom and our daughter Patricia's bedroom. Nothing remained in each bedroom except the bed—no bedding, no dressers or chest of drawers, none of the clothing we had left behind. I had been warned that our house had been turned into a brothel, and when I looked at my daughter's bed, and the beat-up door to her room, with no hinges, it hit me. It was as if my whole family had been raped! I felt sick—I needed some fresh air, I walked to the front door, looked to where I had left my suitcase, and it was gone. Somebody had stolen it! Why would somebody steal it—my clothing, as worn as it was, was all I had. That was the final insult to my homecoming!

"Jim, I hate to say, but I just sat down on the ground and cried. I could not stop. I did not cry the whole time when we had to hurriedly prepare to leave the island. I did not cry when Papa died in England. Here I am now—I'm back home and I'm crying. I'm glad Jessie, Jim and Pat are not here to see me break down—there is so much to do and there is no time for tears. Oh, Jim, I feel so ashamed because there are many people in the war that don't have a house to go back to. At least we have the outside of our house in place and we can start from there.

"There I was in front of our desecrated home, and suddenly my grief turned to anger and I stopped crying and I started yelling. I looked skyward—I guess I wanted God to hear me. I yelled as loud as I could, 'Those damned German pigs! Those stupid heathen German pigs! How could they do this to our home? How could they destroy our beautiful island? How could they pour all that hideous concrete on our island! And worst of all—those ghastly slave labor camps! Why, God? They defiled everything they touched!' "

Jimmy quietly listened to his brother as he poured out his grief and then as he vented his anger. Reg knew his brother was the one person on earth that he could bare his true feelings to. Jimmy knew that when the initial shock of his homecoming would be over, Reg would take charge in rebuilding his life and his home.

Jimmy then asked Reg what were his most immediate needs. It was winter and Reg answered, "We will need warm clothing, blankets and canned food."

Immediately Mother and Jimmy began sending packages filled with those requested items.

Reg's family joined him back in Alderney about a month later, and Lil and Charlie were also in that group of returnees. It was Christmastime and holiday cookies, candy and popcorn to pop were included in one of the shipments from America.

Mother laughed when she told me, "You know how the English are, they don't know what to do with corn. I guess it's more of an American food. Jessie put the popcorn in a pan on the stove and didn't realize you had to put a lid on the pan, and she said, 'Oh Jim and Madaline, it flew all over the house and we had to run around and pick it up off the floor. It was so funny!' "

Upon their return, Lil and Charlie immediately began to work on getting their store ready to reopen. Of course, their stock had been depleted and it took awhile before they could be open for business. Their living quarters were soon made habitable and they were happy to finally be back on Alderney.

Sometime during the following spring Lil called Jimmy and said she was having their father's body brought back to Alderney to be buried next to their mother. Considering all the people who had been killed in England, it did not take long to have all the identification and paperwork taken care of and soon his casket arrived. Lil immediately called Jimmy again and said she had requested that the casket be opened so that she would be certain it was their father's body in it.

Jimmy was shocked at his sister's courage to do this, but he could not refrain from asking, "Was it our father's body?"

Lil replied, "Oh yes, Jim, it was our father, and he only looked a little moldy. And remember I said that when he died he had a little sore on his right cheekbone? Well, it was still there, plainly visible, with a little crusty look on top. Now our parents will be together in their burial plot on the island. Are you pleased with what I did?"

Jimmy assured his sister that he was well pleased with the way she had handled the return of their father's body.

Approximately a year later Jimmy received a check from a bank in England, for a large sum of money. As the oldest in his family, Jimmy received the money from his father's estate according to the English birthright privilege. But Jimmy felt his brother and sister had been through extremely austere times during the war years and had suffered heavy financial losses, therefore, he divided the money evenly among them. Their friends on the island marveled at Jimmy's generosity, because at that time most people took their birthright without sharing with siblings.

# Part Nine
# Biographical Tribute to
# Two Great Leaders

# Dwight D. Eisenhower—
# A Brief Look at His Life

Dwight D. Eisenhower was born October 14, 1890, in Denison, Texas, and when he was two years old his family moved to Abilene, Kansas. His parents were David Jacob Eisenhower and Ida Elizabeth Stover Eisenhower. Dwight was their third son in a family of seven sons. His parents were of German-Swiss ancestry who came to the United States in the 1730s seeking religious freedom. They belonged to the Church of the Brethren and were opposed to war and violence of any kind.

Dwight's father was a mechanic in a creamery. When Dwight was in high school he worked nights at the creamery. The Eisenhower family lived in a modest home surrounded by three acres. Ida grew lots of fruits and vegetables and sold what her own family could not use to get extra income.

After Dwight graduated from high school he took a full-time job at the creamery. He planned to help his brother Edgar with his college expenses. A friend persuaded him to apply for an appointment to West Point Military Academy. He received the West Point appointment in 1911 and graduated in 1915, sixty-first in a class of 164. Although his parents did not approve of him entering military service, they permitted him to choose his own career.

During Dwight's first year of military duty he met Mamie Geneva Doud, the daughter of a wealthy meat packer. Dwight and Mamie were married on July 1, 1916, the same day that Dwight was promoted to first lieutenant. The Dwight Eisenhowers had two sons. The first son, named Doud Dwight Eisenhower, died of scarlet fever when he was three. The second son was named John Sheldon Doud Eisenhower, and he graduated from West Point and is a career army officer.

During World War I, Eisenhower trained tank battalions at various army bases, and he received the Distinguished Service Medal for his work in 1918 as commander of a tank training center at Camp Colt in Gettysburg, Pennsylvania. He also served as the executive director of Camp Gaillard in the Panama Canal Zone. His commander thought that there would soon be another war and he encouraged Dwight to attend the Command and General Staff School at Fort Leavenworth, Kansas. It was a very difficult course and there were many dropouts, but Dwight finished at the top of his class of 275. Two years later he graduated from the Army War College in Washington, D.C.

Eisenhower held various positions during the next few years, and in 1933 he became an aide to General Douglas MacArthur and Dwight helped establish the Philippine Air Force and the Philippine Military Academy. He learned to fly a plane and received his pilot's license. He was an executive officer at Fort Ord, near San Francisco, in 1939 when World War II began.

Eisenhower became a full colonel in March 1941, and three months latter he was made chief of staff of the Third Army with head-quarters at San Antonio, Texas. He had a brilliant record in maneuvers, which earned him a promotion to brigadier general in September 1941. His notable accomplishments and promotions in his military career brought him to the attention of General George C. Marshall, the Army chief of staff.

Five days after the attack on Pearl Harbor, Marshall appointed Eisenhower to the War Plans Division, where he worked on plans to defend the United States possessions in the Pacific. In March 1942 he became head of the Operations Division of the War Department, with the task of unifying all the forces in Europe under one commander. Three days after submitting his plan he was made the commanding general of American forces in the European Theater of Operations. He had made a spectacular rise through the military ranks and he was about to be tested with his assignments in Africa, Sicily, and Italy. The Allies were victorious on the African, Sicilian and Italian campaigns and in February 1943 Eisenhower was promoted to a full general.

In early December 1943 Roosevelt told Eisenhower that he would be in command of the invasion of Europe, called OVERLORD, which would turn out to be the largest military maneuver and invasion force that the world had ever seen. By January 1944 Eisenhower had quickly set up headquarters in London, called the Supreme Headquarters Allied Expeditionary Force (SHAEF). From this location, Eisenhower began working on his plans to bring two million American soldiers to England. From the beginning he stressed the importance of British and American unity. He told his men "This is an Allied battle . . . There will be neither praise nor blame for the British as British or the Americans as Americans."

Eisenhower felt strongly that the greatest single factor in a successful war is the effect of troop morale and he spent a considerable amount of time talking with the troops. Eisenhower had a down-home-like manner of talking with the soldiers, looking them in the eyes, putting them at ease and making them realize the importance of what they had been assigned to do.

There were several times that Winston Churchill thought Eisenhower had overstepped his authority and ignored protocol, which was very important to Churchill. Eisenhower took these rebukes good-naturedly and managed to keep an admirable rapport with the sometimes cantankerous prime minister. Eisenhower admired Churchill for his command and use of the English language and his ability to rally the English people when they were facing overwhelming odds against the Germans. These two great leaders surfaced at a time when the free world sorely needed both of them.

On June 11, 1945, King George and Queen Elizabeth of England, in a private audience, conferred on Eisenhower the Order of Merit, the only British decoration bestowed by the Crown without Cabinet approval. Eisenhower became the first and only American soldier to receive this honor.

On the morning of June 12, 1945 at Guildhall, at ten-forty-five, Air Marshall Tedder arrived at the Dorchester in the ceremonial horse-drawn open landau that would bear both men through the City of London.

The lord mayor, Sir Frank Alexander, in his colorful gold and scarlet robes and holding a 600-year-old mace, greeted the coach and accompanied Eisenhower into the cathedral-like chamber filled with the entire officialdom of England.

When the lord mayor presented Eisenhower with the jewel-encrusted sword carried by Wellington at Waterloo, Eisenhower remarked, "If I were not so sure I was among friends, I do not know if I could make this speech."

In the opinion of those who heard him that morning, his delivery was flawless. Eisenhower stood ramrod-straight, and spoke in clipped, emphatic tones and his words were noble. He expressed his gratitude for the honor and the poignancy he felt for so many lives that had been lost. He was proud of his ties to Kansas and his adopted ties to London.

He expressed the value and inspiration the American soldiers received from their association with their heroic British as brothers-in-arms. Eisenhower expressed the hope that history would show that the coalition had proved the doubters wrong and that the ideal of unity in war could extend into a peace marked by the same good-will, the same forbearance, the same objective attitude that the British and the Americans so amply demonstrated in the nearly three years of bitter campaigning.

Churchill raised his glass to Eisenhower and above the cheers outside said, "I am quite sure that the influence he will wield in the world will be one of always bringing our countries together in the much more difficult task of peace, in the same way he has brought them together in the grim and awful cataclysm of war."

The Prime Minister was weary, but glowing, then reminisced about the awesome seriousness of Eisenhower's decision of June 5, 1944. Churchill recalled his own nervousness that night, bringing laughter. Normandy had been "the mightiest decision of the war," he said. Nothing had compared with it, and "not only did he take the risk and arrive at the fence, but he cleared it in magnificent style."

Churchill guided Eisenhower to the balcony doors and then led him out by the arm. To the massive crowds stretching as far as the eye could see, the Prime Minister introduced Eisenhower as a friend, a "man who knows the power of words and can move the human heart." Churchill then stepped back and Eisenhower stepped forward, to wave and to speak to the tumultuous cheering crowd below.

He had become a citizen of the world.

## Eisenhower's Guildhall Address, June 12, 1945

The high sense of distinction I feel in receiving this great honor from the City of London is inescapably mingled with feelings of profound sadness . . .

Humility must always be the portion of any man who receives acclaim earned in blood of his followers and sacrifices of his friends.

Conceivably a commander may have been professionally superior. . . . his honors cannot hide in his memories the crosses marking the resting places of the dead. They cannot soothe the anguish of the widow or the orphan whose husband or father will not return..

. . . This feeling of humility cannot erase of course my great pride in being tendered the freedom of London. I am not a native of this land,

I come from the very heart of America . . . Abilene, Kansas, and Denison, Texas, would together equal in size, possibly one five-hundredth of a part of great London.

. . . To preserve this freedom of worship, his equality before law, his liberty to speak and act as he sees fit, subject only to provisions that he trespass not upon similar rights of others--a Londoner will fight. So will a citizen of Abilene.

When we consider these things, then the valley of the Thames draws closer to the farms of Kansas and the plains of Texas.

. . . So even as I proclaim my undying Americanism, I am bold enough and exceedingly proud to claim the basis of kinship to you of London.

. . . Five years and eight months of war . . . blitzes big and little, flying V-bombs . . . You carried on, and from your midst arose no cry for mercy, no wail of defeat. The Battle of Britain will take its place as another of your deathless traditions . . .

. . . You had been more than two years in war when Americans in numbers began swarming into your country . . . With awe our men gazed upon the empty spaces where once had stood buildings erected by the toil and sweat of peaceful folk.

. . . No man alone could have brought about this result. Had I possessed the military skill of a Marlborough, the wisdom of Solomon, the understanding of Lincoln, I still would have been helpless without the loyalty, vision, and generosity of thousands upon thousands of British and Americans.

. . . But--a fact important for both of us to remember--neither London nor Abilene, sisters under the skin, will sell her birthright for physical safety, her liberty for mere existence.

. . . If we keep our eyes on this guidepost, then no difficulties along our path of mutual cooperation can ever be insurmountable. Moreover, when this truth has permeated to the remotest hamlet and heart of all peoples, then indeed may we beat our swords into plowshares and all nations can enjoy the fruitfulness of the earth.

# Winston Leonard Spencer Churchill—
# A Brief Look at His Life

Winston Leonard Spencer Churchill was the first child of Lord and Lady Randolph Churchill, born on November 30, 1874, at the Blenheim Palace. Winston's parents were very active in the social life of London and they often found themselves in debt, but this did not negatively affect their social life. Winston was mostly left to the care of a nanny, Elizabeth Ann Everest. It was the nanny who filled the emotional needs of Winston and his younger brother Jack. Otherwise, Winston's life was fairly normal for someone with his background.

Winston was a child of delicate health and was susceptible to colds, and one time he had a severe bout of pneumonia and nearly died. He was also a mischievous child and was involved in many childhood pranks. He attended public school at Harrow-on-the-Hill where Dr. Welldon was the headmaster.

Dr. Welldon soon discovered that Winston had a remarkable memory, and he made certain Winston was assigned to three excellent instructors who taught him the essentials of the structure of a British sentence, mathematics, and army classes. Winston's interest also turned to history and classical studies. Being a free thinker and having a penchant for making mischief, Winston managed to get "swished" many times. After one swishing he told the "swisher," "Some day I shall be a greater man than you." This retort earned him two more swishes.

Winston improved greatly in his studies and was sent to Sandhurst. Regardless of Winston's academic achievements, his father, Lord Randolph, continually berated him and sadly his parents rarely visited him at school.

Winston's father ruined his own political career through out-of-control speeches and eventually resigned his job. He had been a bright promise for the Tory party and had been an inspiring orator but began to suffer a mental and physical breakdown. Sadly, Lady Randolph learned that her husband was dying of advanced syphilis, and Lord Churchill died on January 24th, 1895. Regrettably, Winston knew that his mother had sought the affections of lovers elsewhere even before the death of his father.

Winston, who had longed for his father to show more interest in him and had waited for signs of closeness and caring, was greatly upset over the death of his father and began to read every word his father had uttered in his speeches, and vigorously defended him.

Winston did well at Sandhurst in all the military subjects, such as tactics, fortifications, musketry, riding and military administration. His mother began to show more interest in his success, and she began using her many social contacts to further his career. With Winston being the older son, and knowing his birthright, he found himself needing to work closely with his mother on financial matters. Many times he and his mother were required to sell some of their land properties and downscale their spending.

Shortly after Randolph's death, "old nanny," Mrs. Elizabeth Everest, became terminally ill. When Winston discovered this, he rushed to her side, and hired the best doctor and nurses to care for her. Winston made all the funeral arrangements and purchased a headstone in Jack's and his names. For many years, a portrait of his substitute mother, the dear Mrs. Everest, hung in his office.

Winston had many military experiences, and the expeditions and travel in far away places proved enlightening to him. However, his military career was not his primary objective—his first objective was politics. Knowing that his father had not helped him to pursue this objective, he knew that he would need to cut his own swath. He had become a voracious reader of the classics and history, but he felt he lacked the polish that could come from further education at a prestigious university.

While serving in India, Winston had taken up the sport of polo, and one of his final acts in India was to play in and win the Indian Inter-regimental Polo Tournament.

Also while in India, Winston worked as a journalist, a war correspondent, and sent anonymous articles back to England detailing and criticizing the acts of his superiors. He kept the "kettle boiling" using harsh words about certain campaigns and the politics that contained hidden agendas. During this time he was having his mother keep watch if there was to be an opening in Parliament. Although he had a minor speech impediment he made rousing speeches and was well received, but his first attempt to be elected failed.

Winston wanted to devote his full time to politics, but he was often on the verge of bankruptcy, so he used his skills in writing and doing lecture tours to earn a fairly large sum of money. He gave the money to a former banker friend of his father, who invested it wisely and it substantively increased in value, which provided Winston with much needed financial stability. His mother continued to be a financial embarrassment to him, but she was now settled into a second marriage to a man who was only six days older than Winston.

Churchill was elected to Parliament just two months before his twenty-sixth birthday. Amazingly at this young age he had been a soldier, adventurer, a hero, a war correspondent, an author, and now he was a member of Parliament. Sometimes he would find his finances dropping, and he would rely on his pen to save him from poverty and it would keep his future in politics secure. His oratorical skills by now were very polished and his use of language was carefully designed to impress people and to persuade them. He was an expert at using a colorful analogy, an impressive phrase, and could construct beautiful rolling sentences. He could absolutely electrify his audiences, he had honed these skills, and used rhetoric that his competition could not equal.

The British citizens marveled at the audacity of this boyish-looking man, who took his seat in Parliament in February 1901. There was nothing oustanding in Winston's looks, he was small in stature, lacked muscle tone and had the beginning of a slight paunch, but his eyes exuded an impish gleam that would reveal his passion as he pursued his topics. He was an elected Conservative, but his very first speech in Parliament was Liberal in tone and aggressively attacked the conservative viewpoints. Churchill began his career in Parliament, seeking the limelight, and not afraid to be controversial. Churchill's style was brilliant, powerful, insensitive, imaginative, shocking, thought provoking. People said, "The first time you meet him you see all his faults, and the rest of your life you spend in discovering his virtues."

Churchill met a number of beautiful young women but he was not adept at small talk and neither the women nor Churchill were impressed with each other and none led to romance, until he met Clementine Hozier. Clementine's aunt invited Churchill to a party she was having. Clementine did not wish to attend and neither did Churchill, as both were expecting to be thoroughly bored. But they both attended and found each other to be very interesting. Churchill pursued her for five months before proposing. Churchill told her, "There are no words to convey to you the feelings of love and joy by which my being is possessed." Clementine and Churchill were married at 2 P.M. on Saturday, September 12, 1908, at St. Margaret's Church. Churchill was thirty-three years old and Clementine was twenty-four.

After a honeymoon in Italy, the couple lived at his flat on Bolton Street and in 1909 they moved to a house on Eccleston Square. Their family grew with Diane born in 1909, Randolph in 1911, Sarah in 1914, Marigold in 1918 (died in 1921), and Mary born in 1922. Winston and Clementine had a warm and loving relationship and delighted in calling each other pet names. Their children were also all called by pet names and their upbringing was in a caring and affectionate atmosphere, which was a marked difference from Churchill's life with his parents. Churchill was not a philanderer, neither before his marriage nor after—their marriage was a union for life.

Churchill was appointed to a seat in the Cabinet in April 1908. There were many people trying to discern just what sort of man and politician he was. Their assessments ran the gamut from measured brillance to shallow-minded, self-centered, possessing inexhaustible energy, a political adventurer, unpredictable, and that he enjoyed a good fight. One thing everyone agreed on, and that was "he was the most interesting and intriguing man in British politics."

Churchill, the son of a duke, knew little of the life of the common people, but in the next few years, he became deeply involved in major reforms, the labor movement, and the Irish question. He became a catalyst for much needed social legislation in Britain.

Churchill's positions in politics were always tenuous because he "crossed the floor" twice. He could be counted on to be tenacious in what he believed and his temperament continually kept him in trouble. He was considered by many people to be abrasive and that he talked too much and did not listen enough.

In 1911 Churchill was appointed Lord of the Admiralty. His awareness of Germany's build up of its military and naval forces was viewed as a premonition of World War I. Churchill reorganized the navy, modernized Britain's fleet, and developed anti-submarine tactics. When Britain entered World War I on August 4, 1914 their fleet was ready. Because Churchill had urged an attack on the Dardanelles, which turned into a disaster, he received blame and he felt that his political career was finished. He joined the British army fighting in France and he served as a major in the 2nd Grenadier Guards, and later he was promoted to lieutenant colonel and was in command of a battalion of the Royal Scots Fusiliers. He performed in the military like he performed in politics—with total commitment and with every ounce of strength he had. In 1917 he was appointed to Minister of Munitions and was instrumental in the development of army tanks.

Sometime during the summer of 1915 Churchill began to paint and it was the only thing he did in silence. He was completely absorbed in his painting. At first this very bold man was afraid to put his brush on the canvas, but a gifted painter told him boldness and audacity were essential for an artist—and he certainly possessed those qualities. Opinions vary on how good he was, but painting absorbed him for the rest of his life.

In 1917, America entered the war and Churchill correctly announced to Parliament that together Great Britain and the United States could bring the war to a victorious conclusion. And together they did.

Winston appeared to be oblivious to the strong feelings of hostility that he aroused in the political world, but his career could be destroyed at one moment and renewed the next. After World War I in 1919, he was named War Secretary and in 1921 he was named Colonial Secretary.

Winston's mother at age sixty-four married for the third time to Montague Phippen Porch, who was three years younger than Winston. In June 1921, Lady Randolph had a leg amputated above the knee, complications set in, gangrene developed, and she hemorrhaged and died. Winston wrote, "I miss her support . . . and the wine of life was in her veins. Sorrows and storms were conquered by her nature and on the whole it was a life of sunshine."

Two months later the Churchills' youngest daughter Marigold Francis (pet named "Duckadilly") died at two years and nine months of septicemia. The Churchills were extremely distraught by their loss and shortly after that their other children became very ill with influenza. Clementine, still grieving, collapsed from exhaustion and worry in caring for the other children. Winston took Clementine to Cannes to recuperate and there she realized that she was again pregnant. She was delighted with the thought of having another child after Marigold's death. Their fifth child, Mary, was born on September 15, 1922.

In 1922, he lost his election to return to Parliament due to an emergency appendectomy that prevented him from campaigning at a critical time. In 1924 he rejoined the Conservative Party and returned to Parliament. He was named Chancellor of the Exchequer, which was an office his father had once held. During the next few years Churchill wrote the four-volume *World Crisis*, a brilliant record of World War I. He wrote a six-volume study of his famous ancestor in *Marlborough, His Life and Times*. Churchill, always alert to what was happening in the world, tried to tell his nation and the world about the dangers of the build-up of Nazi Germany. He was accused of being a warmonger.

After Germany invaded Poland on the first of September 1939, England and France declared war on Germany on September 3rd. Prime Minister Neville Chamberlain immediately appointed Churchill as First Lord of the Admiralty. The British fleet was notified with the encouraging simple message, "Winston is Back."

In April 1940 Chamberlain's government fell and King George VI asked Churchill to form a new government, and Churchill became Prime Minister. He was sixty-six years old when he was asked to guide his country through the throes of a second world war.

Churchill later remarked that, *"I felt as if I were walking with destiny and that all my past life had been but a preparation for this hour and for this trial."* Churchill said about having to take over the leadership of his beloved Britain at such a desperate hour, *"I have nothing to offer but blood, toil, tears, and sweat."*

Britain stood alone, and it seemed certain to many people that soon there would be a German invasion of their land, just like Germany had invaded the other countries in their march to conquer most of Europe. Churchill went before the House of Commons and gave his inspiring *"Finest Hour"* speech. The German Luftwaffe attempted to bomb England into submission, but Churchill encouraged the British people to brace themselves and to hold fast. He was a highly visible leader, he was tireless as he visited victims of the air raids, he toured the coastal defense areas, and walked defiantly on the streets as the bombs were falling. Everywhere he went he gave his "V for victory" salute and he was an inspiration to the British people in their darkest hour.

Churchill and President Roosevelt began a long series of communications, 1,700 messages in all, and nine meetings. These two popular leaders developed a friendship and trust that helped them to cooperatively plan the military strategies that brought World War II to its conclusion. In the dark days just after the United States had suffered severe losses by the Japanese attack at Pearl Harbor, Churchill came to America and addressed the United States Congress on December 26, 1941. He touched all Americans with his speech and his assurance that " . . . in the days to come the British and American peoples will . . . walk together side by side in majesty, in justice, and in peace."

It is believed that Churchill and Roosevelt had a mutual admiration for each other's ability to lead and communicate with their people although they differed on several issues. Roosevelt never concurred on Britain's colonial policies, and he trusted Stalin and Churchill did not.

The "Big Three," Churchill, Roosevelt and Stalin, met in Yalta, in February 1945. The purpose of the meeting was to discuss how a defeated Germany would be occupied, as it was already obvious that Germany was going to be defeated. Roosevelt did not look well at this meeting and he died two months after the conference, and Harry Truman became president. After Germany surrendered on May 7, 1945, the three leaders, Churchill, Truman and Stalin, met in Potsdam, Germany, to discuss the administration of Germany. Churchill's presence at this meeting was interrupted by having to immediately return to England because he had lost his position of Prime Minister. There had been an election in Britain, and the Conservative Party had been soundly defeated by the Labor Party. Many people were blaming the Conservatives, who had been in office since before the war, for failure to prepare Britain for World War II.

Churchill returned to England and took his place, now, as leader of the opposition in the House of Commons. He urged Parliament to plan for national defense and he talked about the dangers of communism and warned that an "Iron Curtain" had descended across the continent. He was again accused of warmongering.

Churchill kept busy with writing, lecturing, painting, and, of course, politics. He also kept busy at his country estate of Chartwell Manor with his cattle and racehorses. The Conservatives returned to power and Churchill again became Prime Minister. He was now seventy-seven years old, but he worked vigorously on matters of foreign affairs and British and American unity.

In April 1953 Churchill was knighted by Queen Elizabeth. He was made Knight of the Order of the Garter, Britain's highest order of knighthood. In June 1953 Sir Winston suffered a severe stroke that paralyzed his left side, but he made a speedy and remarkable recovery. Late in 1953 he won the Nobel Prize for Literature. He was honored for " . . . his mastery of historical and biographical presentation and for his brilliant oratory . . . "

On November 30th, 1954, Churchill celebrated his eightieth birthday and many gifts and congratulations were received from all over the world. Churchill, obviously touched when told of how he had inspired Britain during World War II, replied, *"It was the nation and the race dwelling all round the globe that had the 'lion's heart'—I just had the luck to be called upon to give the 'roar'."*

He continued to take his seat in the House of Commons, but his body was now bent with age and his voice was silent, where it had once rung out eloquently.

On the thirtieth of November 1964, Churchill's ninetieth birthday, he again received thousands of greetings, and that evening he dined on his favorite foods with family and friends. It had been a perfect day and it ended with his guests toasting to his good health.

On January 10, 1965, he suffered a severe stroke and the strength in his body slowly ebbed away. In a semi-conscious state, he uttered his last coherent sentence, "I'm so bored with it all." He died at eight o'clock in the morning on January 24, 1965.

On January 30, 1965, the funeral cortege of Sir Winston Churchill left Westminster Hall for St. Paul's Cathedral. Big Ben chimed and then was silent the remainder of the day. A ninety-gun salute began in St. James Park, firing one shot for each year of Churchill's life. Eight guardsmen carried the coffin, which was covered with the Union Jack, upon which rested a black cushion with his insignia of the Order of the Garter. The coffin was placed on and secured to a gray gun carriage with an honor guard paying him tribute. The bands of the Royal Air Force and Her Majesty's Foot Guards played Handel's "Death March" as the procession moved forward. Clementine rode in the Queen's town coach and their son Randolph walked behind the gun carriage. Huge crowds lined the streets that the procession was to take—some people had been standing there since the night before.

Dignitaries from one hundred and eleven countries were in the 3,500 people assembled at St. Paul's. Twelve pallbearers carried the coffin through the nave to the catafalque. Churchill's favorite hymns were sung during the service: "Mine Eyes Have Seen the Glory of the

Coming of the Lord," and "Fight the Good Fight with All Thy Might" and "O God, Our Help in Ages Past." Churchill's coffin was taken to the Bladen Churchyard and he was buried next to his parents and his brother, Jack. The churchyard is within sight of Blenheim Palace where Churchill was born ninety years before.

# Part Ten
## A Traumatic and Dramatic Close to War in the Pacific Theater

# Pivotal Events in the
# Pacific Theater—1945

## The Battle for Luzon

Japan showed no sign of surrendering even though the Americans now had bases that were within the distance for America to mount air attacks on their homeland. Old planes, dwindling supplies of aircraft fuel, and young, poorly trained pilots became effective weapons that the Japanese military used against America's navy. Older boys and young men had been convinced that it was an honor to die for their emperor. With the programmed "death and glory" beliefs imprinted in their psyche, they each went through the kamikaze ceremony with the white ceremonial scarf draped around his neck and his samurai sword placed at his side. They each drank a last cup of sake and then proudly walked to their plane and flew away on a one-way trip, with orders to destroy American ships. As the war progressed, larger and larger waves of kamikaze attacks took a heavy toll on America's navy.

There existed a small number of governmental officials in Japan that thought it was time to end the war, but the very powerful Japanese military faction, specifically Hideki Tojo, wanted to fight till death, regardless of how great Japan's losses would be. Emperor Hirohito continued to remain silent.

On January 8, 1945, the Americans launched an invasion on a massive scale on the west coast of Luzon. Warships had arrived first in the Lingayen Gulf and had suffered tremendous damage by hordes of kamikazes, which flew in under the radar detection. When the kamikazes had depleted their own numbers, one thousand American ships were in the Lingayen Gulf ready to support the landing of ground troops. General Walter Krueger's Sixth Army, with I Corps on his left and XIV Corps on his right moved in with 50,000 troops on the first day and with 125,000 troops landing in the next several days. General MacArthur was in charge of the overall operation and again he waded ashore the last few yards making another great publicity shot. His first message to the people of the world was, "The decisive battle for the liberation of the Philippines and control of the Southwest Pacific is at hand."

The Japanese General Yamashita Tomoyuki, was in charge of 275,000 men ready to defend the island. He divided his troops into three groups. The Shobo group was sent to the mountains on north Luzon, the Kembu group was sent to defend the Clark air bases in the southwest which the Japanese had captured from the Americans in December 1941.The Shimbu group was sent to defend positions east of Manila. By February 3rd, several of the American forces reached the outskirts of Manila and General MacArthur hastened to announce that Manila was about to be liberated.

Yamashita did not really want to defend Manila because he did not think it had any military value, but Manila's city naval commander decided to fight. The battle for Manila was fought block by block, with extremely heavy human casualties and a monumental destruction of property. The Japanese soldiers went into a killing frenzy and were responsible for the merciless killing of 100,000 noncombatant Filipino civilians. The carnage stopped on March 3rd, and Manila was then in the hands of the Americans.

MacArthur was displeased with the progress being made by General Walter Krueger's troops and he ordered several division commanders to circumvent Krueger. I Corps had to contend with a series of bloody battles in the north against Yamashita's main troops. Instead of sending General Robert Eichelberger to assist I Corps in the north, MacArthur sent Eichelberger to invade the southern islands without authorization from the Joint Chiefs of Staff. Actually, the Shobo group, the largest group, occupied the mountains in north Luzon and they held out to the end of the war.

The recapture of the Philippines and the Clark Air Fields, plus the harbor facilities at Manila, could possibly become a staging area for the planned invasion. As MacArthur had orchestrated the American forces in the Philippines, he became the "great liberator," but military strategists are equally divided in their thoughts about a number of the decisions he made. There were 8,000 Americans killed on Luzon and 200,000 Japanese killed.

## Iwo Jima

The battle for Iwo Jima began before the battle for Luzon was finished. Iwo Jima was another tiny Pacific island located in the northwestern Pacific area that had great strategic military value. The island is five miles long and about two and one half miles wide at its widest point, and is shaped somewhat like South America. Iwo Jima means "sulfur island" and the soil on the island is made of gray volcanic ash. Mount Suribachi is a volcano located at the southern tip of the island and it is 546 feet up to the cone of the volcano. The Japanese had used Iwo Jima as an air base for their fighter planes to attack U.S. bombers.

The American commanders knew the importance of removing the Japanese from Iwo Jima and they anticipated fierce resistance to remove them from their extensive fortifications. The Japanese had 20,000 of their best troops garrisoned on the island. The marines had asked for ten days of intensive naval and aerial bombardment before they would go in, but they received only three days of naval and aerial assistance. The navy gave as their reason that they wanted to use their carriers for raids against the Japanese home islands. It is felt that the marines suffered unnecessarily from this decision.

Iwo Jima D-Day was delayed from January 20th to February 19th which gave the Japanese that much more time to prepare for the invasion. The Third, Fourth, and Fifth U.S. Marine Divisions began landing on the 19th and soon discovered that they had greatly underestimated the ferocity of the Japanese soldiers and their advantage of better defensive positions. Ash and cinders covered the steeply sloping beaches and made it difficult to quickly move the men and their military equipment off the beaches. The Japanese poured massive fire on the approaching American landing craft and the men that were ashore. The Japanese overwhelmed the men on the beaches and turned Iwo Jima into a virtual hell on earth.

The Fifth Marines drove across the narrow part of the island, while the Fourth drove to the island's southernmost airfield. On February 20th the marines continued to progress inland and the 28th Infantry Regiment of the Fifth Marines began assaulting Mt. Suribachi. After tortuous crawling up the sides of the mountain and fighting for every inch of ground, on February 24th a group of men placed a tiny flag on its peak. It was a great morale-building accomplishment and the marines cheered and the ships offshore sounded their horns, bells, and whistles.

There are a few people who have tried to put a negative tone on this event by saying it was staged for publicity. Many more people have realized the call to bravery and the enormity of the sacrifices that were made there on Mt. Suribachi. They regard the event as a symbol of the fighting American spirit in the hearts of the marines that persevered when the enemy resistance was especially savage and brutal.

Actually, Joe Rosenthal was the brave newsman carrying his heavy camera and accompanying the marines as they were advancing and attacking the Japanese on Mount Suribachi. He immediately sensed the significance of the planting of the flag and he took the picture. About a half-hour later, a larger flag was taken from the ensign of a nearby beached landing ship, Tank 779, and it replaced the little flag.

Rosenthal won a Pulitzer Prize for his picture of the second flag being put in place. There is a bronze memorial in Arlington, Virginia, and that picture appears in many history books and on numerous postcards. How fortunate for the American people that this historic moment was captured in pictures and later in bronze for future generations to appreciate and be inspired by the legacy that the WWII generation gave to mankind.

The Third Marines, with three more divisions on the day Suribachi was captured, moved toward the Japanese lines. The Japanese were fighting from caves and concealed fortifications and the American marines had a very tough fight on their hands. There were only 200 Japanese remaining from their garrison of 20,000. The American marines lost 7,000 men and 20,000 were wounded.

When the island was secured, the Seabees, the Navy's construction crews, immediately moved in and began repairing the airfields. A crippled B-29 landed on the airfield before the fighting had ceased. Before the war was over, 2,400 B-29 landings took place on Iwo Jima and the lives of many pilots and crew members were saved when they were able to make emergency landings there.

It is interesting to note that the marines were using Navajo Indian code talkers on voice radio to direct the military operation on Iwo Jima. Six Navajo code talkers sent 800 messages without error during the first forty-eight hours of the landing and the organization of their shore positions. Major Howard Conner of the 5th Marine Division said they would have never taken Iwo Jima without the help of the code talkers.

It wasn't long after the U.S. flag had been raised on top of Suribachi, that "Tokyo Rose" came on the Japanese radio station NHK, a Japanese-English radio service, and in her sweet voice and perfect English, informed her listeners, " . . . soon that American flag on Suribachi will be thrown into the sea." Tokyo Rose, whose real name was Mrs. Iva Ikuko Togori D'Aquino, was a Nisei, and thirty-eight years old at the time. She was visiting in Japan when the war broke out and had been hired as a disc jockey for the Japanese propaganda campaign. She played songs that were popular in America and the GIs would listen to her music but hated her for her propaganda-tainted comments.

## Okinawa

The Americans intended to use Okinawa as another staging area for the invasion of Japan. The island is located approximately 350 miles from Japan's southernmost home island. It is sixty-seven miles long and ranges from two to eighteen miles wide. The origin of Okinawa is volcanic and coral, and the island has a jagged coastline with many harbors and bays, and there are 200 miles of sandy beaches. The terrain is rugged in the northern part and has an elevation up to 1,650 feet. The climate is hot and humid, the rainfall ranges from fifty to 120 inches a year and there are an average of forty-five destructive typhoons each year.

The Japanese defenses on Okinawa were located in the southern part of the island where it is mountainous. There were more than 100,000 soldiers on Okinawa under the command of General Ushijima Mitsuru. He had his troops build three strong defensive lines against an expected invasion of American troops, and he had made up his mind to not challenge them as they first arrived on the beaches. His plan was that the kamikazis would be able to destroy the American supporting naval ships and render them useless, and then he could come with his troops and annihilate the stranded ground forces.

Shortly before the Americans planned to invade Okinawa, Admiral Mitscher's Task Force 38 began conducting carrier attacks on Japanese airfields to destroy their planes and divert military personnel away from the Okinawa campaign. During this process, there was increased kamikaze activity, which seriously damaged four American carriers.

The Japanese sent their best and the world's largest battleship, the Imperial Japanese Majesty's *Yamato,* escorted by a cruiser and eight destroyers and sailing under the flag of Vice Admiral Ito Seichi. Seichi's objective was to sail to Okinawa, sink American ships that were already there, then beach the *Yamato* and use it as a giant fortress, complete with extensive supplies of weaponry and including eighteen-inch guns to wreak further havoc in the beach area.

American submarines alerted Spruance of the incoming fleet and he ordered Mitscher to attack. The Americans did not know that the

*Yamato* was actually on a suicide mission and did not have enough fuel to return to Japan, however her magazines were full of ammunition to fulfill the other part of her mission.

As soon as the submarines spotted the great ship her fate was determined. Mitscher's carrier planes, nearly 300 in number, were relentless in their attacks on the Japanese prize ship and its escort vessels. The great *Yamato*, the cruiser and four of her escort vessels went down, but four of the escort vessels received only minor damage and they were able to escape and return to Japan. In this battle the American carrier, *Hancock*, was attacked by a horde of kamikazes and sunk, killing eighty-four Americans and destroying nine planes.

In late March, a fleet of 1200 ships arrived under the protection of the Fifth Fleet. The invasion began on April 1st and lasted until late in July. The newly created Tenth Army was a mixed force of veteran army and marine divisions commanded by General Simon B. Buckner. The first line of defense, along the Kakazu Ridge, slowed the Americans progress to a halt. There were attacks and counterattacks on both sides.

On April 18th, General Buckner renewed the offensive but it also came to a halt at the second line of defense, at the town of Shuri. That line held for a month, and again both sides suffered many casualties. Okinawa became the scene of many bloody battles.

The navy and marine commanders were upset with Buckner and blamed the stalemate on him. Admiral Nimitz was upset over the number of American ships that were being sunk and he made a visit to Okinawa to personally see the situation. He told General Buckner to speed it up or he would be replaced.

The pace had been agonizingly slow as the Americans fought the Japanese on three different well-prepared and entrenched defensive lines. General Buckner had led his troops through the first two successful attacks but was killed by a Japanese shell at the beginning of the third big push. He was not there to claim the honor of the "liberator."

On June 17th, American units, headed by flame throwing tanks, overran the last of the Japanese positions. On June 22nd Okinawa was declared secure.

General Ushijima, on the morning of his defeat, comitted ritual suicide by disemboweling himself with his ceremonial samurai sword and then severing an artery in his neck. He had lost 70,000 troops and 80,000 civilians to the Americans.

The battle for Okinawa was costly for the Americans. The American ground forces suffered 8,000 dead and 30,000 wounded, and the navy suffered 10,000 casualties. The Americans questioned, "Why did the Japanese continue to fight when they knew it was a losing cause?" The concern in everyone's mind was that the Japanese spirit remained strong and the American military predicted that they would defend their homeland with equal resolve, if there was to be an invasion. Why did Hirohito wait until Okinawa fell before speaking and urging his Prime Minister Suzuki to seek a solution to cease the fighting?

At the close of the battle the Seabees again moved in quickly and built military installations on the island.

## Roosevelt—Truman—Potsdam

The ailing President Roosevelt had died on April 12th, of a cerebral hemorrhage, at the age of sixty-three. Upon the death of a U.S. president, the Constitution of the United States clearly provides for a smooth transition of power to the vice president. In this case it was Harry S. Truman, a sixty-year-old, physically fit man who had been vice-president for only four months. He immediately appeared up to the job as president when he was confronted with critical decisions regarding World War II. His weak point might have been lack of knowledge about foreign affairs, but his secretary of state, Edward R. Stettinius, Jr., proved very helpful in the area of diplomacy. Truman had always distrusted Stalin and was quick to take a tougher approach with him.

The last of the great wartime conferences was to be held in Potsdam, west of Berlin, in a newly occupied and prostrate Germany. The conference was code named "Terminal" and was due to open on July 16, 1945, but was delayed a day because of the late arrival of Stalin.

While waiting for Stalin's arrival, Truman was taken on a tour of the ruins in Berlin. When Truman arrived back at the Palace Cecilienhof, where the conference was being held, he received a coded message that revealed to him information about the $2 billion scientific program code-named "Manhattan." The message stated that there had been a successful test in Alamogordo, New Mexico.

The Big Three members were now Harry Truman, Joseph Stalin, and Clement Attlee (who, during the middle of the conference, succeeded Winston Churchill). The objectives of the meeting were (1) to determine occupation zones, (2) determine reparations, (3) establish administrations for enemy territories, and (4) arrange for peace treaties. Also the members of the Potsdam Conference drafted an ultimatum to be given to Japan, Russia was granted control of Europe east of the Elbe River, and Russia agreed to declare war on Japan three months after the date of Germany's surrender.

## Scientists and the Bomb

Germany's persecution of the Jews resulted in the famous scientist Professor Albert Einstein going into exile in the United States, along with other German scientists. Einstein had warned President Roosevelt in October 1939 and in April 1940 that the Germans were working on developing an atomic bomb. Increased Nazi violence against the Jews had forced nearly all of Germany's best scientists to flee the country and thereby Germany had unknowingly determined, in advance, that they would lose the race to build the bomb.

The scientists in Japan, Britain and America considered uranium to be the promising element in the search for nuclear energy. Japan's main interest was using nuclear energy to power ships. There were uranium deposits in northern Korea and Japan began to investigate possibilities of nuclear energy and their leading nuclear physicist, Nishina Yoshio built the first cyclotron and was ordered to develop an atomic bomb in April 1941.

The Japanese built a large mysterious nuclear installation at Hungnam in Korea. The Russians dismantled it and removed it after the war and it is not known how they used it. In 1943 Japan did not think that Germany or the United States would have a bomb within ten years, so they turned their efforts to perfecting radar, which they had neglected.

It takes a large amount of ore to produce a tiny quantity of uranium, and the search for ore became very important. Precious stores of the ore had mysteriously disappeared and some had been stolen to keep Germany from acquiring it when they were aggressively conquering other countries. Britain and the United States decided to share their research and materials with the emphasis to do research to develop an American bomb. Top British scientists in nuclear power research were sent to the United States to assist in the project.

Brigadier General Leslie R. Groves led the military part of the Manhattan Project and Dr. J. Robert Oppenheimer took the lead in the scientific part of the project. The research lab for Manhattan was based at Los Alamos, New Mexico.

The Americans at the Potsdam Conference had realized that the Japanese would not surrender unless the Allies guaranteed that they could keep their imperial system. The Allies were committed to the previously established "unconditional surrender" terms that they had demanded in the surrender of Germany, and they felt the same terms should apply to Japan. The Allies realized that public opinion viewed Hirohito as a war criminal of the same caliber as Hitler and Mussolini. The Allies were determined to stay the course.

America had a "stockpile" of two bombs. Oppenheimer opposed a demonstration of the bomb so that its power would be revealed to the Japanese people without any significant damage to the people of Japan. He could not think of a foolproof way to demonstrate the bomb because the scientists at Los Alamos did not know for certain what would happen when the bomb would be triggered. Oppenheimer stated that he estimated that one bomb on a city would be no greater than a big B-29 incendiary raid which was already being inflicted on Japanese cities at that time.

Truman listened to all sides of the issue on whether America should or should not use the bomb. Truman made the decision around June 1, 1945, based on the following: If Japan did not surrender—(1) drop the bomb on a Japanese industrial target such as a factory surrounded by workers' houses; (2) do it without warning; (3) do it as soon as possible; (4) do not let the Russians in on the secret in advance (because they had shown no interest in nuclear power).

The Americans wanted to avoid an invasion of Japan. Truman's main objective at Potsdam was to hold the Russians to their promise to join the war against Japan. He knew that the Japanese had an enormous fear of the Russians and perhaps if Russia declared war on them, they would quickly surrender.

In the meantime the United States Army, Navy, and Air Force were preparing for an invasion of Japan. After Germany's surrender, vast numbers of American servicemen were being told they would be going to the Pacific Theater to participate in the invasion. Many of these men were now mentally and physically exhausted and they felt as if they had seen enough of the horrors of war. They had experienced many close calls with death and knew that they were very fortunate to still be alive, but many were now beginning to think that their luck might be running out. Those who had enlisted and those who had been drafted also knew that when they entered the military service in World War II they were committed for the "duration of the war" and the war was not yet over.

The war started for the United States December 7, 1941 and it was now mid-1945 and more than three and a half years later, the military personnel that had fought in Africa, Italy, France and Germany, were being prepared to fight in the Pacific Theater. The battle-hardened veterans of the European Theater did not look forward to the jungle fighting, island hopping, and a big invasion of Japan which would be their plight in an assignment in the Pacific Theater. Their destiny was in the hands of the generals, the admirals, and the U.S. president.

## The *Indianapolis*

The thirteen-year-old heavy cruiser *Indianapolis* arrived unescorted at Tinian, in the Marianas, on July 26, 1945. The purpose of her stop there was to deliver the detonation device for the first atomic bomb. She then left for Leyte to join Task Force 95 and train for the invasion of Japan. The United States Navy had carelessly felt that the Japanese Navy was no longer a threat, and the *Indianapolis* again traveled unescorted. She became the victim of a Japanese submarine attack and was the last American warship to be sunk in World War II. Only 316 of her crew of 1,199 were rescued after being in the water eighty-four hours. Distress radio signals failed to get the attention of people that could have sent rescuers to the scene in a timely manner and many more sailors could have been saved. The navy personnel at Leyte failed to notice when the ship did not arrive on schedule. Many people blame the navy for being very careless in this situation.

## America Sends Messages to the Japanese People

On July 26th, the Americans made a radio broadcast to the Japanese people, and American bombers distributed pamphlets over the Japanese cities, all of which carried the same message to the people in their own language. The Japanese people were promised "prompt and utter destruction" unless they renounced their military leaders, gave up their war criminals, withdrew from the areas that they had seized by military conquest since 1895, and surrendered unconditionally. They were asked to commit to a peaceful and responsible government based on self-determination by the Japanese people.

## Prime Minister Fails to Communicate

On July 30th, the Prime Minister Admiral Suzuki appeared at a press conference, obviously disorganized and confused, wanting to respond in a manner he thought would buy time for the Japanese to seek mediation from the Soviets. He wanted to speak in the manner that the cabinet and the emperor would wish him to speak. The Japanese language is confusing, and he thought he was saying their government would not comment *yet*. But,the American translation turned out to be *"there would be no comment at all."* The Americans felt that they were being dismissed with contempt. Whereupon the opportunity for establishing dialogue prior to surrender was missed due to the misinterpretation of small simple words, such as "all" and "yet," that carried astronomical consequences! The Japanese language can be a trap containing ambivalence and the most astute language interpreter could easily get caught in its snare. Thus, the war moved closer to a disastrous climax.

## Atomic Bomb Dropped on Hiroshima

Colonel Paul W. Tibbets was a commanding officer in the United States Army Air Force and was thirty years old at the time of this important mission. He had named his B-29 bomber plane *Enola Gay* in honor of his mother. Tibbets was in charge of a secret mission and had hand picked his crew of Captain Robert Lewis as pilot and Major Thomas Ferebee as bombardier. The cargo in the bomb bay was a dull, gunmetal black cylinder, ten feet six inches long and twenty-nine inches in diameter and weighed ninety-seven hundred pounds, and was ludicrously named *Little Boy*.

There were seven B-29s and their crews involved in this very important mission. Colonel Tibbets was delayed in starting because General LeMay had decided that this was going to be an important historical mission and had arranged for motion pictures and still shots to be taken before departure. Three weather planes preceded the *Enola Gay* and another plane followed that would be on stand-by at Iwo Jima.

The overloaded plane took off very carefully from the air base at Tinian at 2:45 A.M. on Monday, August 6, 1945. Once the plane was airborne and at an altitude of five thousand feet and headed for Iwo Jima, two weaponeers completed the assembly of the bomb. At Iwo Jima two more B-29s rendezvoused with the *Enola Gay* and the three planes flew north-northeast. The two accompanying planes carried official observers, scientists, and photographers.

One of the weather planes reported that the skies were clear over Hiroshima, so Tibbets chose that city as his target. Hiroshima was a big industrial city with war munitions plants, it was a communication center, a military training center, had multiple airfields and hidden hangars for 5,000 aircraft to be used as kamikaze planes during the expected invasion. Tibbets and his crew knew nothing of what was at Hiroshima, they only knew it had been chosen by someone in higher authority as a possible target for this mission.

Ferebee was in the Perspex nose of the plane, with his Norden bombsight; the plane was into its final approach and he was now in control of the plane. He had chosen his target and had it in his sights, and he pressed the button. It was 8:15 A.M., Hiroshima time. The bomb took forty-three seconds to fall from an altitude of thirty-one thousand feet and was programmed to detonate at nineteen hundred feet above the ground.

In a split second Hiroshima was gone, blown away, vaporized, dematerialized and so were seventy-eight thousand people. Thousands more died of radiation illness later. Hiroshima was without communication with the rest of the world.

Tokyo began to receive word that something terrible had happened in Hiroshima and sent officials out to discover what the problem might be. When the officers returned to report, they were in a state of shock as they tried to explain the enormity of the devastation they had just witnessed. The ruling government, hopelessly divided, now became immobilized by the disaster and unable to make any decisions, at a time when rational decisions were most needed.

## Russia Declares War on Japan

On August 8th, the Soviet Union declared war on Japan, just as they had promised to do. By August 9th the Red Army had marched into Manchuria. The Japanese tried to stop the Soviets' progress and kamikaze planes were used to attack the Russian trucks and tanks as they quickly penetrated Manchuria.

## Atomic Bomb Dropped on Nagasaki

On August 9, 1945, a B-29 named *Bock's Car* took off from Tinian's airfield with a bomb named *Fat Man*. The bomb was made of plutonium instead of uranium that had been used in *Little Boy*. The target was Kokura. Major Sweeney, the pilot of the B-29 that was carrying the second atomic bomb, took off from Tinian at 3:00 A.M., and began heading for Japan. The Major only had several hours of sleep in the last seventy-two hours and he was getting sleepy. He turned the controls of the plane over to his co-pilot and crawled into the pilot's compartment and was soon sleeping soundly. The co-pilot and the flight engineer were fully awake, and the other members of his crew were asleep, as there was nothing for them to do at that time.

They were about three hours out when warning lights began to flash indicating that there was something wrong with the plutonium bomb. The two bomb technicians immediately began to check everything on the bomb and were doing their best to fight off panic. They soon discovered a switch-over error in the bomb's wiring system, which had activated the warning lights. No one had notified the bomb experts onboard that the switch had been irregular. This was no time to have anything be "irregular!" After checking and double-checking they discerned that everything was okay and they continued on their way. They all knew there was little room for error on this mission.

Sweeney woke up at 7:00, feeling somewhat refreshed, took back the controls and he began climbing to an altitude of 31,000 feet. Just before 9:00, Sweeney's plane received a message from the weather plane over Kokura, the primary target, that the skies were clear. The second weather plane over Nagasaki reported there was a slight haze but the clouds appeared to be dissipating. Sweeney was upset, because

311

he was to rendezvous with two instrument planes at this altitude and one of the planes had not appeared. He could not wait.

Specifically the target in Kokura was to be an arsenal. Captain Kermit Beahan was the bombardier and he recognized the location of the arsenal, but just as Sweeney flew toward the arsenal with the bomb bay doors open, clouds drifted across the target area. Sweeney tried three times to make the bombing run, but the clouds continued to hide the target. He then headed the plane toward Nagasaki. By 11:00 A.M. the plane was over Nagasaki, and clouds had blown in, and the city was seventy-percent invisible. He had been told that he had to make a visual drop and not a radar drop. Major Sweeney knew of nothing else to do, and decided to make a radar drop when the bombardier called out that he had a clear spot in the clouds and he could clearly see a Mitsubishi Arms Plant. The bombardier took control of the plane and dropped the bomb. Although the bomb did not drop where it had been planned, it probably did more damage where it did drop. Everything within a radius of a half-mile in all directions was pulverized. Nothing lived within the circle and three Mitsubishi war plants were destroyed. People were vaporized and even steel beams were turned to liquid and became a twisted mass of metal.

*Fat Man* was set to explode on impact. The effect was contained somewhat because of the rugged terrain around Nagasaki. Twenty-four thousand people were killed instantly and thousands more died later. Thus, the atomic age began with violence and death and an eerie and uncertain feeling was cast upon the future of the world.

## Japanese Council Deadlocked

The Japanese council met in the bomb shelter beneath the palace and they remained hopelessly divided down the middle. They were at an impasse, emotionally paralyzed and unable to realistically view their situation. General Anami Korechika, the war minister, and the military and naval chiefs of staff, Umezu and Toyoda, were against accepting the conditions of Potsdam, and the foreign and navy ministers were ready to accept the conditions set forth at Potsdam. The only person who could break the deadlock was Hirohito and it had to be by direct action. A second meeting was held that same night in the hot, airless bomb shelter under the palace, and again there were the same people

312

creating the deadlock. Then Prime Minister Suzuki did the unthinkable. Never before had a prime minister asked for the "Voice of the Crane." He asked and begged the emperor to intervene and break the deadlock.

Finally, their imperial leader, viewed by his people as a holy man, who had lived a secluded life in a palace, removed from his people and had appeared to be oblivious to the havoc and misery his country had created, decided to speak. "The time has come to endure the unendurable."

The Emperor spoke clearly and told the ministers he did not believe them when they had told him they were well prepared to fight off the invasion. He had sent representatives to view the military installations and armaments and their statements were not based on the actual situation. He pointed out one falsehood after another that they had made to him. He told them he was faced with the decision to save the Japanese nation. He said there was only one course open to them—Japan must accept the declarations of Potsdam. He said it was not important what happened to him, but the nation must be preserved. He then stood up and walked out of the bomb shelter. It was one hour before dawn on August 10th.

On August 10th, Japan's Foreign Ministry notified their ambassadors in Sweden and Switzerland to notify the Big Four that they were ready to accept the terms of the declaration issued at Potsdam. As yet, the imperial announcement had not been made to the Japanese people.

## Allies Distribute Message to Confused Japanese People

The Allies again distributed an airdrop to the confused Japanese people, which stated, " . . . from the moment of surrender the authority of the Emperor and the Japanese Government to rule the state shall be subject to the Supreme Commander of the Allied Powers, who will take such steps as he deems proper to effectuate the surrender terms."

## The Emperor Speaks to His People

On August 14, 1945, the last imperial conference of the war took place in the hot and humid shelter, with Hirohito present. All those present wore uniforms or morning coats. The emperor was wearing an

313

army uniform and was looking very tired. Again he had to listen to the arguments of his ministers and officers. He finally told them, "It is all over, and the next morning I will go on the radio and tell the people."

There were long arguments between the military and civilian advisors about the wording of the emperor's speech. An unsuccessful coup was mounted and an effort to steal the recording of the emperor's speech was thwarted. Hirohito cut the recording at his palace with the help of the radio station NHK technicians, because as the divine ruler of Japan he could not make a live broadcast. At noon on August 15, the recording was played to the bewildered and confused Japanese people, who never before had heard their emperor's voice. His voice was high pitched, there was a lot of static on their radios, and he spoke in a dialect that only the most educated Japanese people would understand.

"To our good and loyal subjects: . . . We have decided to effect a settlement of the present situation by resorting to an extraordinary measure.

"We have ordered our Government to communicate to the governments of the United States, Great Britain, China and the Soviet Union that our Empire accepts the provisions of their joint declaration.

" . . . Indeed, We declared war on America and Britain out of Our sincere desire to ensure Japan's self-preservation and the stabilization of East Asia, it being far from Our thought either to infringe upon the sovereignty of other nations or to embark upon territorial aggrandizement. . . . The war situation has developed not necessarily to Japan's advantage, while the general trends of the world have all turned against her interest. . . . The enemy has begun to employ a new and most cruel bomb, the power of which to do damage is indeed incalculable . . . how are We to save the millions of Our subjects; or to atone Ourselves before the hallowed spirits of Our Imperial Ancestors? This is the reason why We have ordered the acceptance of the provisions of the joint declaration of the powers.

"We cannot but express the deepest sense of regret to Our Allied nations of East Asia, who have consistently cooperated with the Empire toward the emancipation of East Asia. . . . However, it is according to the dictate of time and fate that We have resolved to pave the way for a grand peace for all the generations to come by enduring the unendurable and suffering what is insufferable.

"Let the entire nation continue as one family from generation to generation, ever firm in its faith of the imperishableness of its divine land, and mindful of its heavy burden of responsibilities, and the long road before it . . . "

Imperial Seal Affixed
THE 14TH DAY OF THE 8TH MONTH OF THE 26TH YEAR OF
SHOWA.

The emperor's message was full of understatements, vagueness, and ambiguity. It clearly demonstrated that Japan did not intend to admit to their wartime deeds and failures, and neither did the emperor use any words that meant defeat or surrender. The tone of his message was not submissive and showed a refusal to face the reality of the situation in Japan.

General Anami was one of the first to commit *seppuku,* by taking a dagger and disemboweling himself and then severing a neck artery. Many of the generals, admirals, and military people close to Hirohito began committing suicide. The people who had planned a last minute coup used their samurai swords or pistols to kill themselves. The members of the government resigned and the emperor's younger brother Prince Higashikuni, replaced Suzuki.

## Truman Orders Fighting to Continue

Truman said that the Americans would keep pounding Japan until he saw legitimate signs of surrender on the part of the Japanese. Admiral Halsey's fleet began a series of attacks against the airfields, planes, ports and ships. He discovered that the Japanese had cleverly camouflaged planes and fuel tanks in preparation for the invasion. British and American pilots were busy hitting airfields, planes, rail lines, industry, transportation and shipping.

Hirohito told his ministers and council they would keep receiving Allied strikes until the surrender took place. In Tokyo there were young army officers that were demanding from their superiors that the war must continue. They were concerned about what would happen to them after the surrender because Potsdam clearly stated that there would be no more Japanese army. The Japanese generals were forced to summon help to keep the young army officers quiet so as not to disrupt the peace negotiations.

The Soviets continued to move aggressively into Manchuria. The American generals did not want to have to share joint occupation duties with the Russians in Japan like they were having to do in Europe. They needed to get things settled quickly with Japan.

## Secret Preparations

Meanwhile, Captain Parsons was getting ready to assemble two more plutonium bombs, with the one to be used as a third strike on August 12th, and one to be used on a fourth strike on August 16th. Most people, including the Japanese, did not know that the Americans could put together more bombs that quickly.

## Soviets Make Demands

Also, during this time, on August 11th, the Soviet forces were 125 miles past the border and were driving onto the Mutanchiang Plain. The Japanese were trying to stop them with regular weapons and kamikazes but were not able to, and the Soviet military machine kept moving on. In Moscow the Soviet foreign minister, Molotov, was having heated debates with the American Ambassador Harriman about the coming occupation of Japan. The Russians wanted two commanders in the occupying force and they should be one of them. They were suggesting Soviet General Alexander Vasilevski.

Harriman explained that the Americans had been at war in the Pacific keeping the Japanese busy from attacking the Russians while they were busy fighting the Germans. Now they had been in this war for two days and they wanted equal power in the occupation.

Stalin made Molotov back down on these requests, but they still wanted to have input on who would be the supreme commander. Truman held his ground and did not intend to have a repetition of what happened in Europe. Truman also wanted to keep the pressure on with continual bombings so that the Japanese would be more amenable to the conditions of Potsdam. He was adamant that the Japanese could keep the Emperor but the Emperor and all military and government officers would be subject to the supreme commander and the occupying forces. The supreme commander was not yet named.

## Japanese Newspapers Reflect Less Militaristic Influence

During this time period, the Tokyo newspapers were now giving their people more information about the war, and were making obvious statements to be ready for drastic changes and difficulties and to rise to the challenges to protect their empire. Gone were the references of the past to "fighting to the death." A new word was being used, "polity," which possibly indicated a change in government. But there were also statements from the military about the war with the Soviet Union that had just begun and that would call for more sacrifices. One can only imagine the quandary that the Japanese people felt in trying to understand what was really happening in and to their country.

## Public Announcement of Surrender Terms

On August 12, 1945 an official note was passed through diplomatic channels and broadcast over Voice of America that listed the terms of surrender: (1) that the Emperor would be subject to the Supreme Commander of the Allied Powers from the moment of surrender, (2) that the Emperor would authorize the government to sign the surrender documents, (3) command all armed forces to lay down their arms, (4) surrender all prisoners of war and interned civilians, and provide a safe place where they can be immediately picked up by the Allies, (5) that the Japanese people would be able to freely choose the form of government, republic or monarchy, (6) and that Allied occupation forces would continue until the Potsdam Declarations have been achieved.

The message contained more than the Japanese could quickly respond to. Again the foreign minister and the prime minister argued and vacillated and the militarists pushed to continue fighting. In Washington the powers were waiting for a response from Japan. In and around Japan the war continued.

## Waiting—Waiting—Waiting

It was August 12th, and the Americans did not know what was happening in Tokyo. Truman announced that General MacArthur would be the Supreme Commander. The skies were quiet as Halsey's planes and the Admiral waited out a typhoon. Truman had alerted the military to suspend all activity and that there were to be no B-29 flights as he was awaiting word from the Japanese.

The fact that military action had ceased for awhile gave the Japanese militarists reason and courage to continue with their hard-line position. The war between the Japanese and Russians was heating up. Halsey was aboard his flagship, the *Missouri*, and was making plans in case there was a notification of a Japanese surrender. He was ordered to have three battalions of marines and possibly five more battalions ready to be the first of the occupation forces to go in. He needed the location of prisoner of war camps and rescue missions were organized to get to work as soon as the surrender word came.

The word of acceptance by the Japanese did not come. Nimitz ordered Halsey to proceed to Tokyo Bay "with caution." Halsey ordered strikes for the next morning. At 4:00 A.M. on August 13th, the Third Fleet's air task force hit Japanese targets.

## Internal Problems Prevent Concurrence

Intrigue followed more intrigue as the hard liners wanted to continue with the war and attempted to coerce other members of the military group, the ministers, the family of the emperor, anyone who could prevent the surrender from happening. Meanwhile, in Washington their patience was wearing very thin. Washington received word that the Japanese had serious internal problems and could not agree on the surrender terms. And they waited some more and the hours ticked by. There were advisors to the president that suggested that the U.S. drop another atomic bomb.

The Japanese military actually thought that they could take control of Japan, that they could conduct a coup d'etat, dispense with the present cabinet, and establish a military oligarchy. The fear of possible assassinations was beginning to grip certain officials, and palace guards were ordered not to let anyone pass no matter how high their rank.

## August 14, 1945

The American military leaders, knowing that the Japanese military factions wanted to continue the war, decided to continue bombing Japan, hoping that would apply enough pressure to break the stalemate. Truman knew that for years the Japanese people had not been kept informed, and so he ordered another drop of leaflets with information about the proposed surrender. Seven B-29s dropped five million leaflets and that was thought to have had a positive psychological affect on the Japanese citizens.

Admiral Halsey's Task Force was taking on fuel and was put on alert to stay close to Japan. British ships joined Halsey's Task Force. There were to be air strikes the following morning. He sent several ships back to Iwo Jima to pick up Japanese translators and interpreters that would be needed during surrender and occupation times.

Hirohito called a meeting in the bomb shelter under the palace. He attempted to explain to those present that the Potsdam Declarations would not destroy the Japanese imperial system. He said it was his wish to stop the war and spare the people any more suffering. "I wish you all to act with that intention." To the astonishment of the people gathered there, it was not the Voice of the Sacred Crane, but it was a directive from the Son of Heaven, directing his subjects on the course to take. The last twenty-four to forty-eight hours before the surrender saw many suicides in Japan among the hard-line militarists.

On the afternoon of August 14th, Foreign Minister Togo's office sent translations in several languages announcing the acceptance of the American terms of surrender. The message was sent to Switzerland, where the Swiss government was to forward the word to the Allies. The news was released simultaneously to General MacArthur, Admiral Nimitz, and the Japanese government so that all fighting would cease. The news was immediately released to the press and radio. As the news spread, people began to gather in the streets of cities, towns, and villages all across America and they began to experience the joy of victory.

## The Formal Surrender of Japan

The Japanese had surrendered on August 15th, 1945, but the 'formal' surrender took place on Admiral Halsey's flagship, the USS *Missouri*, on September 2, 1945 in Tokyo Bay. General Douglas MacArthur, as the Supreme Commander, was in charge of the surrender procedures, which were marked by solemnity and strict adherence to protocol. A large number of Allied warships filled the harbor. Every Allied general and admiral who had played a part in the war in the Pacific had been invited to this auspicious occasion.

The emperor and his new prime minister did not attend the ceremony. The nine men in the Japanese delegation had been ferried from Yokohama to the *Missouri* and were the last to arrive. The members of the Japanese military wore their drab military uniforms without sidearms and the civilians wore ill-fitting pinstriped pants and tailcoats with cutaway collars. One can only imagine the thoughts of the members of the Japanese delegation as they walked up the starboard gangway and saw the mass of sailors sitting, perching, and hanging from every conceivable place on the super structure of that magnificent battleship. They were all hoping to get a glimpse of the historic event that was about to happen.

The surrender documents had been neatly placed on a nondescript mess table that had been brought on deck. Everything was in readiness for signatures. Behind the table were Admirals Nimitz and Halsey, who stepped aside to make a place of honor for the two famous, emaciated lieutenant generals, A.E. Percival of Singapore and Jonathan M. Wainwright of the Philippines. These two generals had been flown in from a hospital where they had been receiving treatment after being liberated from a Japanese concentration camp.

General MacArthur arrived four minutes late and a hush fell over the decks of the ship as he walked up to the microphone. He gave instructions on who would be signing and the order of the signing. There was confusion on the part of the Japanese as to where to sign, which was probably attributed to lack of fluency with the English language.

The Supreme Commander, MacArthur, was the last to sign, after which he made a short speech: "It is my earnest hope—indeed the hope of all mankind—that from this solemn occasion a better world shall emerge out of the blood and carnage of the past, a world founded upon faith and understanding, a world dedicated to the dignity of man and the fulfillment of his most cherished wish for freedom, tolerance and justice."

The signatures on the documents were completed and the documents collected and then MacArthur returned to the microphone to say, "These proceedings are closed."

As the Japanese were being piped off the ship the first wave of two thousand planes flew overhead. The thunderous noise made by the aircraft overhead was like placing a giant exclamation point at the end of a war that contained unimaginable statistics of death and destruction. The people on the deck were now busy congratulating each other.

MacArthur returned again to the microphone and said, "Today the guns are silent" (he then reviewed the tragedy of war and the need to build a peaceful world), and he concluded with . . . "and so, my fellow countrymen, today I report to you that your sons and daughters have served you well and faithfully . . . They are homeward bound—take care of them."

# Part Eleven
# Military People Return

# V-J Day and the Day After

## V-J Day in Lima, Ohio—August 14, 1945

I was working at my desk in the office when I began to hear the factory whistle blowing and I heard people yelling. I surmised that word must have been received that the Japanese had surrendered because we had been expecting it for several days. Our boss, Mr. Moore, came through the outer office door and yelled, "The war is over! It is finally all over! The people are going crazy out there!" he said as he pointed to the factory door.

The workers were whooping and yelling and basically all work had stopped even though most of them were still at their workstations. Mr. Moore sent everyone in our office home, and luckily I found a ride with someone I knew, because I couldn't find the driver in our carpool. When I walked to the parking lot to catch my ride I could hear church bells ringing and factory whistles blowing all over town. I was staying at my aunts' house at the edge of town and the driver had to take a round-about way to avoid the confusion in downtown Lima and he dropped me off at the end of our street. When I walked into the house my two aunts were already there because their bosses at work had told everyone to go home.

Aunt Annie and Aunt Minnie said they were too tired to walk to town, but Annie said, "Glory Ann, you must go to town and join the celebration—it's history—and then you can come back and tell us all about it. We'll fix some dinner and if you are late we will keep something warm for you."

I changed into a pair of shoes with low heels that were more suitable for walking and started my trek toward downtown Lima. It was approximately 4:30 in the afternoon on what had been a beautiful summer day. I wasn't certain how much walking I would be doing, so when I saw the Findlay Road bus I decided to ride the remainder of the way to town. The bus driver said they were calling all the buses in after they finished their present run because many of the streets were now impassable due to people blocking traffic. We were able to get as far as the corner of Main and North Streets when the driver told all of us on the bus that he could not go any further.

When I got off the bus I could see and hear that pure pandemonium had taken over the downtown business district of Lima. The strangest sights were the long crepe-paper streamers and toilet-tissue streamers that were waving gently in the breeze and were attached somewhere in the open windows of the apartments over the stores on Main Street. During the war years, toilet tissue was not rationed but the stores were always running out of it. As I saw the hundreds of streamers of toilet tissue waving out the windows, I wondered to myself, *How many rolls of that very scarce product had those people hoarded?* The sidewalks and the streets were crowded with people. Clouds of confetti and small pieces of white paper were being thrown out the windows onto the rejoicing revelers passing below.

There were throngs of people blowing horns, ringing bells, blowing whistles, beating on tin cans and acting really crazy. People were running up to total strangers and giving them hugs and kisses. People were yelling, "Our boys will soon be home!" "No more fighting! It's over!" "We are the best because we have the bomb!" "No more killing!" "Don't mess with the USA because we have the A-bomb!"

Complete strangers were embracing and kissing, and some had been drinking. There were people carrying open bottles and they were offering to share with other people. Everyone was smiling. There were policemen standing around watching the noisy festivities and they too were smiling. Nobody really needed the police—it was all orderly chaos, if there is such a thing.

Newsboys were running through the crowds yelling, "Extra! Extra! Read all about the surrender!" They were selling special editions of the *Lima News* for four cents. I hurried and bought a newspaper, thinking their supply might run out and I knew my aunts would want to read it.

I don't know why, but I stood there on Main Street and I suddenly felt very much alone among all those jubilant folks all around me and I began to cry. All I could think of was that horrible bomb—thousands of people died—lots of people just like us were dead because of that insidious bomb. I thought, *What's wrong with these people? Don't they know that soon our enemies in other countries will discover our secrets on how to build that horrible deadly "thing" and then they can vaporize us just like our bomb vaporized all those people in Japan?* I thought about my husband and I was happy to think that he would soon be

326

coming home, but I could not join the merrymaking and the dancing in the street and neither could I understand why I was reacting that way. I could not shake the feeling of dread that had taken hold of me.

As the word spread around town that there was a big celebration going on in downtown Lima, more and more people began arriving and the number of celebrants was rapidly multiplying. I decided not to stay any longer because I could not stop crying and who wants a killjoy around at a time like that. I turned and began to walk the two miles back to my aunts' house. The church bells were still ringing and inviting people to come in and pray, and as I made my way home and with my inability to stop crying I decided not to stop in at a church. Perhaps that was a mistake, but it was now dusk and there were very few street-lights along the last mile of my lonely walk. I finally reached our street, which was actually like a long dirt country lane covered with a thin layer of crushed stone. As I walked up the hill to get to the house I slipped on some loose stones and fell, ruining my stockings. During the war, women's dress hosiery was always in short supply at the department stores and I tried to tell myself that this little mishap didn't matter, even though I now only had one pair of good silk stockings left.

When I walked into the kitchen my aunts were eagerly waiting to hear what was going on downtown. Thankfully I had stopped crying by then. They put a plate of warm food in front of me and poured some hot coffee for me and then asked for details. I told them about the toilet paper streamers, the confetti, the hugging and kissing and dancing in the streets and how happy everybody was. I didn't tell them about my trepidation about the bomb. I knew they only wanted to hear happy news, so that was what I gave them.

After I finished eating we all went into the living room and listened for awhile to the radio newscasts, which were mostly about the surrender and the destruction and deaths caused by the two atomic bombs. There were reports from different cities about how the people in America were celebrating and Lima seemed to fit the general pattern of what was going on from coast to coast.

I soon realized that I was utterly exhausted and excused myself and went upstairs to my bedroom. I quickly wrote a short letter to Art telling him about the surrender celebration in Lima. I told him that surely it wouldn't be long now before he would get to come home. I carefully checked his APO number on the envelope I had just addressed and placed the letter in my purse to mail the next day. It seemed like a miracle to me that those APO numbers were able to find the American military people that were scattered all over the world during World War II. Delivery wasn't speedy, but most of those letters were eventually delivered or returned to the sender.

I crawled into bed, puzzled by my heavy feelings of sadness, and finally I fell asleep.

## The Day After

President Truman issued a proclamation that Wednesday and Thursday, August 15th and 16th, would be considered holidays for all war workers. In downtown Lima all places of business were closed except the theaters.

The Office of Price Administration, the OPA, headed by Chester Bowles, announced that rationing for gasoline, canned vegetables and fruits, fuel oil and stoves was being lifted immediately. At the present time, fats, oil, meats, butter, sugar, shoes, and rubber footwear and tires would remain on the ration list.

The demobilization of the army would begin with a cut in the number of men being drafted and only men under twenty-six years of age would be called. There would be 5 to 5½ million men to be released from the United States military forces within the next twelve to eighteen months.

The Reconversion Director in Washington announced that all military contracts will be terminated immediately, and this affected my job with the United States Corps of Engineers. There were warnings of increases in unemployment, but that was to be expected until the factories could be converted to peacetime production. I decided that I would start hunting for another job immediately before the unemployment situation in Lima would become critical. Everyone in our office felt the same way and we had one last luncheon together, said our farewells, and everyone then took off in different directions to get on with their life in peacetime. Luckily I immediately found a job working in the office at the Superior Coach Company, that made ambulances and funeral coaches.

# The Waiting

"The war was over in August 1945, and now the months were dragging on—September, October, November, December, January, and February. It was as if the military had forgotten us. My crew and I tried to find things to keep us busy and to prevent depression from setting in. The island was nothing but sand, no trees to sit under, and there was never a let up from the heat and the humidity. Swimming was impossible because of nasty critters in the water. All these things made the waiting seem twice as long. But, finally in February the procedure started for my radar crew and me to get off the island.

"In the middle of February, with one day's notice, a troop ship came from Wake Island and anchored in the lagoon, in the center of the crater. We were taken out to the ship in a Liberty boat. We had to climb a rope net, sometimes called a Jacob's Ladder, that was thrown over the side to get on board. It was no easy job to get on board that troop ship, between carrying my barracks bag by the closure rope in one hand, trying to get higher and higher up on the net with the other hand, and meanwhile the ship is moving up and down in the wake. Also, when men are climbing at the same time, it makes the net keep moving. It is harder than it looks, but we all had the same problems and the same incentive, and my crew and I made it! We all wanted desperately to get home!

"One propeller shaft was bent on our troop ship. We were told that the ship had been in Manila Bay and had been hit by a Japanese torpedo. The ship went thump! thump! thump!—all the way to Hawaii. The passengers didn't mind, like me, we were all going home. At least we were on a ship and it was heading in the right direction—the good old U.S.A.! I didn't even get seasick on the way home.

"It was the middle of February 1946 when I got on board that troop ship, but it took until March 9th for me to arrive at Camp Atterbury, in Indiana, to get my discharge papers. I had been in the Asiatic Theater for a total of twenty months. I hitched a ride on a military plane that took me to Detroit, Michigan, where my wife was waiting for me.

"In reflecting back to when I started in the Army Reserves in radar training in September 1942, until my discharge in March of 1946, I realize that it was a chunk of time out of my life. I knew I was lucky because I did not see combat, but I would like to think that those of us who had technical skills made an important contribution toward helping the United States win the war. I did what I was asked to do to the best of my ability and I did it willingly. Later generations need to remember that America was threatened, and we had no choice but to fight. I sincerely believe that America and our way of life is worth fighting for. I'm proud to be an American!"

—Art Miller

# Homecoming

Mother and Jimmy had taken me to the airport to meet the plane that was bringing Art to Detroit. When the plane landed there were only a few people that disembarked, and there was one very skinny man in khaki who stood for a moment looking around, and then he saw me and began to run toward me. It didn't take him long to wrap those strong arms of his around me and plant a big kiss on my lips. Mother and Jimmy then greeted him and said they had rented a hotel room for us, rather than take us back to their house. They thought we might like to be alone this first night back together. Art picked up his barracks bag and we got into Jimmy's car. As we rode through the streets of Detroit, we all had many questions for Art.

When we arrived at the hotel, Jimmy said, "The room is paid for as a homecoming gift," as he slipped three twenty-dollar bills into Art's pocket. He said, "Maybe this will buy you a few good meals, you look as if you could use it."

Mother said, "I'm cooking dinner for all of us tomorrow and Jimmy will pick you two up at the hotel at 11:00 o'clock and take you out to our house, so be ready."

We told Mother and Jimmy goodbye and went into the hotel.

We found our room and we just paused there and looked at each other. It seemed as if it had been forever since we had said goodbye in San Antonio. There was so much catching up to do. After a few tender kisses, we went downstairs to the dining room and Art ordered a steak dinner with all the trimmings. He told me about how terrible the food had been on the island, especially the last several months there. When the waitress brought a plate of bread and butter to the table, Art unconsciously picked up the bread and held it up to the light.

I asked him, "What are you doing?"

He answered, "I'm sorry, I forgot. On the island the flour was buggy and wormy, and we always picked the largest bugs and worms out of the bread before we ate it. I guess I won't have to do that anymore. You know, I'm beginning to feel a little more civilized now."

Later on I asked Art, "What happened to your teeth? Why are your teeth all brownish looking?"

He then explained about the terrible distiller they had on the island and how everyone's teeth looked like that after being there for awhile. He remarked that the glass of water on the table tasted so good and that he didn't know how much he had missed a good drink of water while he was on the island.

About eleven o'clock the next day Jimmy picked us up and we went to their house, and Mother had a wonderful roast beef dinner, with mashed potatoes, Yorkshire pudding, gravy, green beans, a tossed salad, pumpernickel bread, and homemade lemon meringue pie. Mother was a great cook and she really outdid herself with this meal. This was the beginning of going to visit a lot of relatives and everyone fixing a big dinner for us. This was their way of welcoming Art back home after the war.

Later that afternoon, when Art's parents met our train, they were overjoyed to have their son safely back home. His brother was already home, and they were very thankful that they didn't lose their sons to the war. Of course, Art's mother had a big dinner planned when we reached their farm house. Again, Art forgot what he was doing and held his slice of bread up to the light.

His mother asked him, "Arthur, what are you doing? Is there something wrong with the bread?"

When Art told her the flour story, she made a face and said, "Well, I would have never served anything like that to people who sat down at my table!"

We thought it had taken a long time for Art to get home, but as we checked around with our friends, we discovered there were others that had not yet made it back. Our friend Jim Byerly was actively working at an Advanced Base Ship Dock—#1 (ABSD-1) that was anchored off the Island of Samar in the Philippines. Jim was an officer in the U.S. Navy, and was in charge of specific duties at this floating dry dock for the maintenance of ships. He returned to civilian life in May of 1946. The return of each of the friends from overseas military duty sparked another round of "welcome home" parties.

It is interesting to note that when the old friends gathered together there was no talk of their war experiences. Instead the talk was about using the GI Bill to further their education, finding a job, starting a business, finding a house or an apartment, putting together the necessary items for a livable home. There were shortages to contend with, because the American factories were struggling to produce enough cars, washers, refrigerators, and kitchen ranges to meet the demands of the returning service men. Many times the talk at these parties turned to which store to put your name on a list and wait for your turn to come up for one of these scarce items. Of course, many times the talk turned to babies, as many of our returning veteran friends began to make their contributions to the Baby Boom generation.

*Oh, wonderful, wonderful peacetime—at last! There was now a future for us and we could begin to establish our own goals and work steadily toward them each dawning day. Our destiny could now be determined by the decisions we made—not the military. Our successes, and our failures, now rested squarely on our own shoulders and we were ready for the challenges.*

# Epilogue

I speak not of that in which their remains are laid, but in that in which their glory survives, and is proclaimed always and on every fitting occasion both in word and deed. For the whole earth is the sepulcher of famous men; not only are they commemorated by the columns and inscriptions in their own country, but in foreign lands there dwells also an unwritten memorial of them, graven not on stone but in the hearts of men. (From Funeral Speech of Pericles during 4th century B.C.)

# Addendum:
# For Those Who Wonder About Hirohito

Hirohito was born in 1901, and when he was seventy days old he was taken from his mother, as it was tradition to take an heir to the throne and have him reared by outsiders. Hirohito was given to a series of wet nurses in the house of retired Count Kawamura. The count had consulted an English governess and her three basic rules for rearing a child were for inducing a spirit of independence, developing a sympathetic heart, and feelings of gratitude. The very traditional count was seventy years old at the time, and he was determined to instill in his young charge a dauntless spirit in order for him to withstand all hardships and to remove all traces of egotism and arrogance.

Count Kawamura treated Hirohito tenderly and seemed to understand the developmental stage of his young charge, but the count died shortly before Hirohito reached his fourth birthday. Hirohito was returned to his father's Akasaka Palace, but not to live closely with his parents. Instead, he lived in a separate house, attended a special imperial kindergarten along with other princely children of his own age, and was surrounded by chamberlains and courtiers, and here he received excellent teachers and developed a lifelong interest in marine biology. One of Hirohito's favorite teachers was Mrs. Takako Suzuki, the wife of a naval officer who many years later became Hirohito's last prime minister.

Hirohito had a brother, Prince Chichibu, who was a year younger, and they shared a room that was in a separate area. They were permitted to see their mother once a week and their father much less. Chichibu did well athletically and showed natural leadership abilities. However, Hirohito was not permitted to be with other children very often because he was being trained to be the future emperor and the living God. He was clumsy, he had poor posture due to a curved spine, walked with a shuffle and was weaker and less aggressive than most children his age. Although he had a severe case of myopia and needed glasses, he was not permitted to wear them for a long time because emperors did not wear glasses.

It was not long before another brother arrived, and he was also better athletically and physically. Probably a bit of sibling rivalry developed among the three brothers, but servants and teachers intervened and hovered protectively over the boy who would someday be their emperor.

Hirohito's father was not a good example for Hirohito because of his neglect of his family and his promiscuous behavior. Neither of the two men in Hirohito's life, his father and his grandfather, who could have been influential in a paternal positive way, assumed the role of exemplary personality traits and behavior. Instead, his grandfather Emperor Meiji enjoyed a life of vintage wine, beautiful women, and sleeping on a Western-style bed, as opposed to the traditional Japanese tatami floor mat. Twelve ladies in waiting (concubines) waited each night for the drop of the Emperor's royal handkerchief at the feet of one of them, which was the signal to follow the emperor to his private quarters where only a few page boys were ever permitted to enter.

Drunkenness was considered acceptable in Japanese society and the emperor's drunken behavior was not looked upon with disdain. The Crown Prince Yoshihito took his son Hirohito, at the age of five years, and forced him to drink sake and respond to numerous toasts until the young boy, who had been trained to be obedient, collapsed into an unconscious state. These experiences in his youth caused Hirohito to refuse to drink alcohol, and to live a life style that was monogamous and puritanical.

Hirohito was tutored by General Nogi, who became like a surrogate father, and under his influence Hirohito became an excellent swimmer, a sumo wrestler, a golfer, and endured extensive physical training, plus he entered into a program of an expanded range of studies. The change in Hirohito under General Nogi's tutelage was showing in Hirohito's self-confidence, improved strength and physical bearing, plus he developed an appreciation of plain living and hard work. When Hirohito was twelve, Emperor Meiji died of cancer, and General Nogi, as a faithful follower of his emperor, committed *sepuku* by disembowelment with a sharp sword, and his wife cut her throat with a dagger. Under Nogi's influence, Hirohito had begun to despise his father's life style, and his father was now the Emperor, and he was officially the crown prince.

Hirohito's younger brothers now had to treat him with greater respect because someday he would be a "living god." Also, now the crown prince had a new supervisor, who was Admiral Heikachiro Togo, but Hirohito never developed admiration for Togo because he never lived up to the high standards that Nogi had instilled in him.

While Japan, under Emperor Taisho, was parleying for positions of power and maneuverability with other countries, it became obvious that his behavior was becoming eccentric, unstable and unfit to rule, and it was not safe to let him appear in public. Hirohito was fifteen at the time and his tutors always tried to present events to him in a favorable light. However, Japan was now being viewed by the world as a bullying and predatory nation, rather than the image of the "gallant small nation" in the past.

Emperor Taisho's condition steadily worsened, and was thought at first to have been caused by an undetected stroke, but later it was thought to have been the aftereffects from meningitis which he had in his childhood. Empress Sadako began increasing her powers, and so did the *genro*, a group of elder statesmen, or advisors to the emperor.

The empress was an informed, modern-thinking woman, and she realized that Hirohito would probably become the emperor soon because of his father's failing condition, and she felt that he should have a choice in who he would marry. Her marriage had been arranged and she had not seen Taisho before the wedding day. Hirohito's mother, the court, and the *genro* made a list of the charming and pretty girls from leading families in Japan and invited them to tea at the palace. Hirohito would observe them unseen, behind an arras, a tapestry wall hanging.

Hirohito chose Nagako, who was not a beautiful girl. She was short, slightly plump, fourteen years old, and had a flawless lineage that had been reduced to near poverty. Nagako was a very bright daughter of Prince Kuni, of the Fushimi house, which had a history of family members who had intermarried with emperors for centuries.

The empress was very pleased with her son's choice, but the elderly *genro* Yamagata began to plot secretly to have the betrothal annulled. His plot was based on the fact that there was evidence of color blindness noted in Nagako's ancestors. (Secretly, he wanted someone from his own family to marry Hirohito.) Medical scientists were consulted for confirmation, with conflicting results. Intrigue followed intrigue, the leader of the underworld organization became involved, and also the press. There were parades and demonstrations shouting, "Death to Yamagata." Prince Kuni said that if Yamagata were successful in foiling the marriage, he would kill his daughter and then commit *sepuku* on himself. Nakamura of the Imperial Household was sent to the emperor and empress to ask, "What are your majesty's wishes?" The emperor said, "I hear that science is fallible." And with that, the empress impatiently motioned him to leave.

Nagako had been set up in a separate part of her father's house and was subjected to physical examinations, was tutored in the subjects of English, French, international relations, history, and was carefully groomed by her tutors and her father on the duties of being an empress. During the betrothal time, Hirohito and Nagako saw each other only nine times before they were married.

Hirohito left on an extended visit to England, France, Belgium, the Netherlands and Rome and he was granted an audience with Pope Benedict XV. In Europe he was exposed to royalty being much more relaxed and informal in their daily activities and their contacts with people. He studied the history of these countries first hand and he experienced the joy and appreciation of the arts in the various countries. He particularly enjoyed the experiences he had with the royal families in Europe. He greatly admired the Prince of Wales, the way he dressed, and the fact that the Duke and Duchess only used their castle for formal occasions and preferred living without servants in a nearby cottage.

When Hirohito returned to Japan he was extremely pleased that he was treated as a promising, liberal-minded future monarch. But soon after his return he was faced with a number of very serious events. General Yamagata, the *genro* who had opposed his choice for a bride, died and Hirohito decided not to replace him, which left Prince Saionji as the only remaining *genro*. Political violence asserted its ugly head with the stabbing death of Emperor Taisho's Prime Minister, Takashi Hara. Economic problems began with unemployment in the cities, an agricultural crisis, a break down of family values, and employer-worker relations. Socialism and Marxism were spreading in Japan although forbidden by law. Japan was entering the jazz age with flappers, but there were also numerous "secret societies," whose premise was that Japan's divine emperor, by his right of divine origin, should rule not only Japan but also all people of the earth.

Hirohito had been influenced by the freer societies he had visited in Europe and began to show a new spirit, the likes of which he had seen on his trip. His clothing, his tastes in dining, his visits to nightclubs, and races, were evidence of his new mood. He planned to be the first monogamous emperor in the history of Japan. He sent all the ladies-in-waiting away, except those who attended his mother. He decided not to wear the traditional kimonos, except for religious ceremonies and after bathing.

The Japanese people are extremely superstitious about the calendar date of September 1st, just as Americans are superstitious about Friday the 13th. On September 1, 1923, Japan experienced the worst earthquake in its history. The readings went off the Richter scale and there were many casualties and enormous damage in Tokyo, Yokohama and the Kanto area. A resulting tidal wave also contributed to monumental losses of life and property. It is believed in Japanese folklore that the earthquake damage to the coast was the work of giant catfish that lived in the bottom of the sea and the catfish were angered and aroused by the misbehavior of the Japanese people. This was the reason that Japan did not request aid from other countries, and in fact, they did not want other countries to know about their devastating earthquake because that would reveal their "misbehavior."

On December 27, 1923, a pro-communist man named Namba shot at Hirohito as he was riding in his carriage. Hirohito was not hurt, and Namba was executed.

On January 26, 1924, Hirohito and Nagako were married after being betrothed for five years. The day was named a national holiday, and all over Japan the people celebrated the wedding of Hirohito and Nagako. Hirohito rode alone in a closed carriage and he wore a lieutenant colonel's uniform. His bride-to-be rode in another closed carriage to the imperial palace. After arriving at the palace they both had to change into the heavy ceremonial clothing, which took considerable time. Nagako wore a kimono of scarlet and lilac, and Hirohito wore an orange robe and skirt, with a black lacquered hat. He carried a scepter and he had to first address the spirits of his ancestors in a court language, which is used only for rites, informing them of his decision to marry Nagako. The marriage rites were exchanged in a secluded imperial family shrine with only immediate family and several Shinto priests present.

There was no honeymoon for the couple, they spent their first night at the palace, and the following day they went to Numazu, to see Hirohito's father, Emperor Taisho, who was too ill to attend the wedding. Loyal subjects in Japan eagerly waited to hear news of Nagako's pregnancy, which did not happen until 1925. The baby was a girl, which disappointed the people because only a son could ensure the continuity of the imperial dynasty. The chamberlains and Prince Saionji felt that the next time Hirohito would be luckier and get a son. If not, they hinted, but not in Hirohito's presence, they could bring in a royal concubine.

Hirohito sadly remembered the vices of his grandfather and father, and was determined to become the exact opposite and was observed to be an affectionate husband, and a man of extreme orderliness. Nagako fit into life at the palace with ease.

Emperor Taisho died on December 18, 1926 but the news of his death was not made public until December 25th. He had been in seclusion for five years, and the public expressed very little grief over his passing. Hirohito had already assumed all the power and duties of the emperor, but only lacked the title.

The title of emperor carried with it the myth that it had originated in 660 B.C. when the Emperor Jimmu first appears in the history of Japan. Jimmu was a direct descendent of the sun goddess Amaterasu, and she was related to a series of other gods and goddesses, who gave birth to such things as oceans, light, heat and matter, and who had life spans of five hundred years or more. Eventually these became the dogma for Hirohito's grandfather, Emperor Meiji, and his authority. Meiji's authority was based on Shintoism. The holy relics were the copper mirror, the sword, and the necklace and had been passed down from prehistoric times. The copper mirror had been used to tempt Amaterasu out of her cave and save the world from darkness; the sword had been extricated from a dragon's tail; the necklace was crudely made of stones. The mirror was kept in the Japanese shrine of Ise, and emperors went there twice a year to commune with their ancestors. The other relics were kept at the palace family shrine. The Japanese were taught to believe that their gods of the past lived crude and bawdy lives, but as the years passed they gradually became humans and became the rulers of Japan.

Hirohito's schooling in the sciences, especially his instruction in marine biology and Darwinism, attributed to his refusal to take these teachings seriously. Saionji, who was a hedonist, pointed out to Hirohito that he understood his thinking. He also agreed that the myths were probably not based on fact, but on nonsense. He continued to point out that the value of not depriving the people of their faith, when this faith made them unquestionably obedient to the emperor and his wishes

342

would greatly simplify his task of ruling the people. Hirohito immediately understood this lesson.

The 1889 constitution stated that from Meiji on: (1) that every emperor would be an absolute ruler, (2) that the Japanese empire would be reigned over and governed by a line of Emperors unbroken for ages eternal, (3) that the emperor was sacred and inviolable, combining in Himself the rights and the exercise of sovereignty, and (4) that he would have supreme command of the armed forces.

The *Japan Yearbook* states: (1) the emperor cannot be removed from the throne for any reason, (2) he is not to be held responsible for over-stepping the limitations of law in the exercise of his sovereignty; (3) that all responsibility must be assumed by the ministers of state; and (4) that no criticism can be directed against the Emperor, but only against the instruments of his sovereignty; (5) laws are not to be applied to the Emperor as a principle, especially criminal laws, for no court of law can try the emperor; (6) and that the emperor is not subject to any law.

The reasoning was that by letting others make the decisions the emperor would remain untouched by human errors. The emperor was supposed to put his seal on government decrees, but the cabinet made the day-to-day decisions. The Privy Council acted as an advisory body. The Diet's powers were nebulous and not clearly defined. The two people with the most power were not elected officials and they were not imperial, they were the army and navy chiefs of staff, and they had more power than the prime minister.

The emperor was not out of the loop on governmental affairs, as some people thought, because he had the right to veto. His seal was needed on all documents of importance. Hirohito worked industriously at his job, he was very methodical and read thoroughly anything that came across his desk that needed his seal of approval. He knew at all times everything that was going on in the Privy Council, the Supreme War Command, the cabinet and the army and navy. The emperor relied on the Imperial Household Minister, the Lord Privy Seal, the chief aide-de-camp and the grand chamberlain to gather information for him.

Hirohito approved of his country's attacks on China. Under the direction of Unit 731, China was one of the first countries in which chemical and bacteriological experiments were used on a large scale on Chinese prisoners of war. Japanese Veterans of Unit 731, long years after the war, proudly proclaimed that their unit was set up by imperial

343

decree. War crimes tribunals consider that one of the most atrocious crimes that can be perpetrated on human beings is the forced use of chemical and disease-laden carriers of various means and those people who decreed such acts are to be held accountable.

Japan felt that she had been highly insulted when the United States Supreme Court, in 1921, put a ban on Japanese becoming U.S. citizens. The military people in Japan were beginning to predict, even then, that they were destined to fight the United States sometime in the future.

We now know that Hirohito was well aware of the year-long planning that went into the surprise attack on Pearl Harbor. Hirohito kept a close watch on all budget expenditures and nothing of the magnitude of the Pearl Harbor attack would have escaped him.

On April 17, 1942, the Dowager Empress Sadako summoned Kido, the confidential secretary to the Lord confidential secretary, to ask him pertinent questions about the surprise attack on Pearl Harbor and reports she had heard about "brute force." After Kido's visit the relations between her and her son, Hirohito, became very strained during the early part of the war. When Kido remarked about this to Hirohito, the emperor turned his head away and began talking about mushrooms.

If we fast-forward to the date of September 27, 1945, the atomic bombs had been dropped and the surrender had taken place, and this was the day that Hirohito would first meet with General Douglas MacArthur, the Supreme Commander of the Allied Forces in the Pacific. The old imperial Mercedes limousine (nicknamed by the occupation forces as the "cement mixer") traveled through the streets of an obviously war damaged Tokyo, with a motorcade of five cars carrying police, bodyguards and personal assistants to the Emperor. There were two motorcycles leading the procession. Hirohito, looking dapper and small, sat in the limousine, in his shabby clothing and top hat. He was nervous about the coming meeting with the Supreme Commander and had no idea of how he would be treated. As he walked into the reception area he was greeted by a strong handshake from General Bonner Fellers, an aide to MacArthur, who ignored, or just plainly did not know the fact that no one was to touch the Emperor's body.

MacArthur's staff had expected Hirohito to arrive alone or possibly with one other person, but instead he brought nine people with him. His hands were shaking because he didn't know if possibly he would be arrested or insulted. MacArthur walked toward him and Hirohito immediately bowed very low as a servant would bow. MacArthur said,

"You are very, very welcome, sir." As MacArthur vigorously shook the Emperor's hand, the difference in the size of these two important men was very pronounced.

Hirohito was determined not to show how nervous he was, but he did refuse to use the interpreter that MacArthur offered, instead requested his own that he had brought with him. MacArthur offered him a cigarette and seeing that his hands were shaking, he lit it for him. Of course, MacArthur smoked his usual corncob pipe.

MacArthur told Hirohito about a previous visit to Japan, when he was aide-de-camp to his father, General Arthur MacArthur. Hirohito's grandfather, Emperor Meiji, had said that they had a serious cholera epidemic and the soldiers were refusing to take their anti-cholera pills. MacArthur said, "My father had a piece of advice for your grandfather. He suggested that inside each box of pills there should be a notice that says, 'The Emperor requests that each soldier take one capsule every four hours.' My father's advice was followed and the cholera epidemic ceased."

From then on Hirohito relaxed a little and the meeting became less formal. MacArthur praised Hirohito for ending the war. Hirohito responded, "The peace party did not prevail until the bombing of Hiroshima created a situation which could be dramatized."

MacArthur then asked, "How was it that an emperor powerful enough to end the war had been unable to prevent it?"

Hirohito said, "I felt my heart breaking," and he then added how he had reflected on the consequences of the war on the British royal family and concluded by saying, "who had treated me with great kindness when I visited them as Crown Prince. But the idea of gainsaying my advisers in those days never occurred to me. Besides, it would have done no good. I would have been put in an insane asylum or even assassinated."

MacArthur came back with the statement, "A monarch must be brave enough to run such risks."

Hirohito revealed himself to be stubborn and came back with, "It was not clear to me that our course was unjustified. Even now I am not sure how historians will allocate the responsibility for the war."

Hirohito then told MacArthur that he came before him "to offer myself to the judgment of the powers you represent as the one to bear the sole responsibility for every political and military decision made and action taken by my people in the conduct of the war."

Although Hirohito offered himself as a scapegoat and said he would take the blame for all of his wartime advisors, he already knew that MacArthur was against trying him as a war criminal, and that he would not be asked to abdicate.

Hirohito renounced his "godliness" three months after that first meeting he had with MacArthur. His carefully worded announcement read as follows: "The bondage between us and you, the people, is constantly tied with mutual trust, love and respect. It is not brought about by mere mythology and legends. It is never founded on a chimerical conception which ascribes the Emperor as a living deity, and, moreover, the Japanese as superior to all other races of people, hence destined to rule the world."

By whatever means, Hirohito was a survivor. The dichotomy of his reign is marked by a multitude of contradictions of facts, and his entanglement in his belief system from his early training and later education often prohibited him from rational decision making. Hirohito's ability to not respond when questioned on sensitive issues, but to turn his head and change the subject, provided him with an avenue of escape from the truth. The lack of action on Hirohito's part to save the lives of his people that were being sacrificed in his name was inhuman and disgraceful.

Despite the mounting evidence that proved that Hirohito was actively involved in Japan's military conquests in Asia, the planning of the Pearl Harbor Attack, the use of bacteriological and chemical warfare in China, and the dropping of plague infected rats in China, he escaped any sort of penalty.

Hirohito survived to become the longest living monarch. During the World War II years Hirohito was thought of in the eyes of American citizens as a tyrant, and was classified along with Hitler and Mussolini. Many Americans were bewildered in later years to see Hirohito come to the United States and receive positive receptions and press because the scars on the Pacific Theater veterans in World War II were still tender. By the time of Hirohito's death he had become highly respected as Japan's constitutional monarch and was honored by many foreign countries.

Hirohito was operated on for stomach cancer and later died on January 7, 1989, from an inoperable tumor on his pancreas.

In conclusion many questions come to mind about the duplicity of many of Hirohito's statements and responses to direct questions concerning World War II. There was a complete lack of recognition on his part of the role that Japan played in the aggression in China, other areas in Asia, and the Pacific. The only people that appeared to warrant an apology from Hirohito were the members of England's royal family, who had acted as hosts to him when he visited in England when he was a young man. Was Hirohito unbelievably naïve, or did he deliberately perpetrate a ruse that kept him from assuming any blame for Japan's role in World War II?

# Bibliography

Baldwin, Hanson W. *The Crucial Years: 1939–1941 The World at War*; Harper & Row, New York, Copyright 1976.

Baldwin, Hanson W. *Battles Lost and Won—Great Campaigns of World War II*; Harper & Row, New York, Copyright 1976.

Behr, Edward. *Hirohito: Behind the Myth*; Villard Books, a division of Random House, New York, Copyright 1989.

Berenbaum, Michael. *The World Must Know;* Little, Brown & Company, Boston, Copyright 1993.

Bernstein, Alison R., *Indians and WWII;* The University of Oklahoma Press, Norman Publishing Division of the University, Copyright 1991.

Blake, Robert and Louis, William Roger, editors. (Chapters each have separate author) *Churchill—A Major New Assessment of His Life in Peace and War;* W. W. Norton & Company, New York, New York, Copyright 1993.

Bradley, James with Powers, Ron. *Flags of Our Fathers;* Ruhl, Bantam Books, New York, Copyright May 2000.

Byers, Ann. *The Holocaust Overview*; Enslow Publishers, Inc., Springfield, N. J., Copyright 1998.

Clayton, James, D. and Wells, Anne Sharp, *From Pearl Harbor to V-J Day*; The American Ways Series, Copyright 1995.

Collier, Richard. *Eagle Day: The Battle of Britain August 6–September 15 1940*; E. P. Dutton & Co., Inc., Copyright 1966.

Costello, John. *The Pacific War*; Rawson, Wade Publishers, Inc., New York, 1981.

Eisenhower, David. *Eisenhower at War 1943–1945;* Wings Books, distributed by Outbook Book Co., Inc., a Random House Company, New York, Copyright 1991.

Feis, Herbert. *Japan Subdued: The Atomic Bomb and the End of the War in the Pacific;* Princeton University Press, London, Oxford University Press, Copyright 1961.

Foster, Col. Frank and Borts, Lawrence. 5th Edition, *A Complete Guide to All United States Military Medals, 1939 to Present;* MOA Press (Medals of America Press), Copyright 2000.

Goldstein, Donald M., Dillon, Katherine V. and Wenger, J. Michael. *D-Day Normandy;* Maxwell Macmillan Co., Brassey's (US), Copyright 1994.

Hammel, Eric. *Guadalcanal Starvation Island.* Crown Publishers, Inc., New York, Copyright 1987.

Hitler, Adolf. *Mein Kampf.* Preface, Quotations pp 53, 123, 148, 177, 191, 232, 950, 968, Excerpts from Speeches.

Hoyt, Edwin P. *The GI's War: The Story of American Soldiers In Europe In World War II.* McGraw-Hill Book Company, New York, Copyright 1988.

Hoyt, Edwin P. *How They Won The War In The Pacific.* Weybright and Talley, New York, Copyright 1970.

Hoyt, Edwin P. *Closing The Circle War In The Pacific: 1945.* Van Nostrand Reinhold Company, New York, Copyright 1982.

Jackson, Robert. *Dunkirk, The British Evacuation. 1940;* St. Martin's Press, New York, Copyright 1976.

Jackson, Robert. *England—1940.* St. Martin Press, New York, Copyright 1976.

James, D. Clayton and Wells, Anne Sharp. *From Pearl Harbor to V-J Day: The American Armed Forces in World War II.* Ivan R. Dee, Inc. Copyright 1995.

Kahn, David. *Seizing the Enigma, The Race to Break The German U-Boat Codes.* Houghton-Mifflin, Copyright, 1991.

Klemmer, Harvey. *National Geographic* Vol. LXXXV, Number One, January 1944, P, National Geographic Society, Washington, D.C.

Lynton, Mark. *Accidental Journey.* The Overlook Press, New York, Copyright 1995.

MacVane, John. *On The Air In World War II.* William Morrow and Company, Inc., New York, Copyright 1979.

Maddox, Robert James. *The United States and World War II.* Westview Press, Oxford, Copyright 1992.

Michie, Allan, A. *The Invasion of Europe—The Story Behind D-Day.* Dodd Mead & Company, New York, Copyright 1964.

Phillips, Robert F. *To Save Bastogne.* Stin and Day, Inc., New York, Copyright 1983.

Rose, Norman. *Churchill—The Unruly Giant.* The Free Press, Division of Simon & Schuster, Inc., New York, Copyright 1994.

Searles, John M. USNR (Ret), *Tales of Tulagi.* Vantage Press, Copyright 1992.

Sears, Stephen W. *The Battle of the Bulge.* American Heritage Publishing Co., Inc., New York, Copyright 1969.

Takaki, Ronald. *Hiroshima: Why America Dropped The Atomic Bomb.* Little, Brown and Company, New York, Copyright 1995.

Thompson, Robert Smith. *A Time For War.* Prentice Hall Press, 15 Columbus Circle, New York, NY, Copyright 1991.

van der Vat, Dun. *The Pacific Campaign.* Simon & Schuster, New York, Copyright 1991.

Whiting, Charles. *The End of the War—Europe; April 15–May 23, 1945.* Ballantine Books, A Division of Random House, Inc. New York, Copyright 1973.

*World Book Encyclopedia.* A-Vol. 1, Field Enterprises Educational Corp., Copyright 1965.

*World Book Encyclopedia.* C to Ch-Vol. 3, Field Enterprises Educational Corp., Copyright 1965.

*World Book Encyclopedia,* E-Vol. 6, Field Enterprises Corp., Copyright 1965.

*World Book Encyclopedia,* H-Vol. 9, Field Enterprises Educational Corp., Copyright 1965.

*World Book Encyclopedia,* I-Vol. 10, Field Enterprises Educational Corp., Copyright 1965.

*World Book Encyclopedia,* J-K-Vol. 11, Field Enterprises Educational Corp., Copyright 1965.

World Book Encyclopedia, M-Vol. 13, Field Enterprises Educational Corp., Copyright 1965.

*World Book Encyclopedia,* N-O-Vol. 15; Field Enterprises Educational Corp., Copyright 1965.

*World Book Encyclopedia,* P-Vol. 15, Field Enterprises Educational Corp., Copyright 1965.

*World Book Encyclopedia,* QR-Vol. 16, Field Enterprises Educational Corp., Copyright 1965.

*World Book Encyclopedia,* U-V-Vol. 19, Field Enterprises, Educational Corp., Copyright 1965.

*World Book Encyclopedia,* W-X-Y-Z-Vol. 20, Field Enterprises Educational Corp., Copyright 1965.